Using the Operating System

D1738862

OS/2

Version 2.1

> **Note**
>
> Before using this information and the product it supports, be sure to read the general information under Appendix J, "Notices" on page 489.

First Edition (May 1993)

Contributors

Authors

Marion Lindsey
Karla Stagray

Contributing Authors

Cynthia Didio
Val Enright
Mary Nolterieke
Anita Soto
Vince Spadea

Editor

Marilyn Dichtenberg

Graphics and Design Consultant

Brian Black

Graphics Support

Ronald Abbott

National Language Support

Mike Bresnahan
Al Sanchez-Cifuentes

New Product Administrator

Linda Chilton

OS/2 Publications Manager

John D. Lloyd

OS/2 Publications Planner

Elizabeth Tripi

Production Assistant

Monique Bias

Production Coordination

Lila Kenney

Tools Support

Rick Goldsmith
Gene Ignatowski
Sherry Reardon

Usability Testing

Lynn Lathrop

Summary of Contents

Contents

OS/2 2.1
Desktop

Startup

Drives

Command
Prompts

Productivity

Games

Information

Master Help
Index

Drive A

Minimized Window Viewer

Shredder

Templates

Printer

Migrate
Applications

WIN-OS/2
Groups

ATM Control
Panel

Network

Multimedia
Features

System
Performance

Video
Support

Printer
Support

Hardware
Support

Moving to
OS/2 2.1

Moving from
Windows

Appendices

About This Book

The purpose of this book is to help you use OS/2 2.1. It contains information to acquaint you with the operating system and instructions for completing some of the most common tasks using the Workplace Shell. It also provides information on installing and using programs and printers, and describes the software and hardware support provided by OS/2 2.1.

Who Should Read This Book

Anyone who will be using OS/2 2.1 should read this book. It explains how to get started using the operating system and how to use the *online* information provided with it. Online information is information you can display on your screen.

This book also describes the parts of the operating system and how to install and use your programs. Tips and techniques for using the operating system are also provided.

Keep this book as a reference.

Conventions Used in This Book

In this book the following conventions are used to help distinguish elements of the text:

Text Element	Use
bold	Indicates the name of an item you need to select.
italics	Indicates the first time a new term is used. A definition of the term immediately follows the italicized terms and usually the term is defined in the glossary. Italics are also used to indicate a book title or variable information that must be replaced by an actual value.
monospace	Indicates an example such as a fictitious path and file name or text that is displayed on your screen, such as an error.
UPPERCASE	Indicates a file name, command name, or acronym.
*	Indicates trademarks of the IBM Corporation.
**	Indicates trademarks of other companies.

How This Book Is Organized

This book is organized into the following parts:

- Part 1 describes how to use objects and windows and shows you how to shut down your system.
- Part 2 describes the objects that you see after you have installed the operating system. You will learn how to use the functions associated with each object.
- Part 3 provides information for installing new programs. It also describes how to use Microsoft Windows programs and the Adobe Type Manager for WIN-OS/2.
- Part 4 describes how to install a printer, manage print jobs, and solve printing problems.
- Part 5 describes the software and hardware support provided by OS/2 2.1 and suggests solutions for problems you might encounter.
- Part 6 is for users of OS/2 Version 1.3 or Microsoft Windows. It describes how common tasks done in OS/2 Version 1.3 and Microsoft Windows are done in OS/2 2.1.
- Appendix A describes the keys and mouse actions used in tasks.
- Appendix B contains some of the most common error messages.
- Appendix J contains the Trademarks and Service Marks.

Note: Telephone numbers in this book are only for the United States.

Related Information

The following list describes the books and online information that comes with OS/2 2.1.

Quick Reference
> This card provides you with a brief set of instructions on how to start the installation of the OS/2 operating system.

Installation Guide
> This book describes how to prepare for and install the operating system. It also provides information about installing more than one operating system on your computer.

Book Catalog
> This catalog describes other books and products related to the OS/2 operating system that you can purchase. A CD-ROM, the *OS/2 Online Book Collection*, contains over 100 related books about OS/2. A video, *Moving to the OS/2 Workplace Shell*, helps make your transition to the Workplace Shell easier. Ordering information and prices are included.

Tutorial   This online, interactive program shows you the basics of the operating system. The tutorial starts automatically after you install the operating system.

Start Here   This online, alphabetic list contains an overview of common tasks. It provides a quick path to information about some common tasks you might do on a daily basis.

Master Help Index
This online, alphabetic list contains all of the information you need to use OS/2 2.1.

Glossary   This online, alphabetic list contains computer and operating system terms and definitions.

Command Reference
This online information describes how to use OS/2 commands.

REXX Information
This online information describes how to use the Restructured Extended Executor (REXX) procedures language.

Using the Information

As described in "Related Information" on page xxvi, there is a variety of information provided to assist you when installing, learning, and using OS/2 2.1. The following list shows you how to use this information:

Installing   Both a card and a book are provided to help you install OS/2 2.1.

- Use the *Quick Reference* card if you want to accept the preselected installation choices. The preselected choices are what most users will find suit them best.

- Use the *Installation Guide* if you want to make specific choices about how the OS/2 operating system is installed. For example, if you need to partition your hard disk, or install more than one operating system, you will prefer to use the Installation Guide.

Learning   Both online information and this book are provided to help you learn OS/2 2.1. The tutorial and this book were designed to help you learn about the operating system quickly:

- Use the online *OS/2 Tutorial* as your primary means of learning how to use a mouse, and to gain an understanding of the basic concepts. You will be able to practice common tasks before you actually use OS/2 2.1.

All OS/2 2.1 users should complete the online tutorial. This small investment of time will prove to be very valuable as you use the operating system.

- Use this book to review the basics, and as a reference when you are learning about common tasks, or how to use the online information, or when you are using a keyboard or a mouse and need some quick assistance.

Using   Both online information and this book are provided to help you when you are using OS/2 2.1.

- Use the online *Start Here* to help you start using the operating system quickly. For example, initially, you might only be interested in installing programs or printing letters. This online information gets you going in these daily tasks.

- Use the online *Master Help Index* as the central place to find all of the information about OS/2 2.1. Once you have learned the system and are comfortable using it, you can rely on the *Master Help Index* to provide immediate online assistance for any topic you are interested in.

- Use this book as a reference. It expands upon some of the topics in the tutorial; for example, copying and moving. It also has other information you will find interesting as you become proficient using OS/2 2.1; for example, customizing the operating system, or adding printers.

New Features in OS/2 2.1

The following is an overview of the new features of OS/2 2.1. For more information about some of the features in this list, refer to the online Start Here object.

- The object-oriented approach implemented in OS/2 2.0, which has been fine-tuned in OS/2 2.1, allows users to manage many types of objects such as programs, data files, printers, network servers, and drives from a single, graphical user interface called the Workplace Shell.

- Users now can run Windows standard-mode programs and certain enhanced-mode programs (except those requiring a specific type of Windows enhanced mode virtual device drivers called VxD's) side-by-side in windows on the desktop. Users also can start a DOS or an OS/2 program from WIN-OS/2.

  WIN-OS/2 has been enhanced to include the WIN-OS/2 File Manager, Microsoft Windows Version 3.1 printer drivers, and selected WIN-OS/2 accessories, including the following:

  - Calculator
  - Calendar
  - Character Map
  - Media Player
  - Notepad
  - Object Packager
  - Paintbrush
  - Sound Recorder
  - Write
  - Clock
  - Cardfile

  Users with limited disk space are given the option of installing the WIN-OS/2 accessories. In addition, users can elect to install the WIN-OS/2 feature on a separate partition on their hard disk.

- New, 32-bit SVGA display device drivers supporting the chipsets found on most popular display adapters are included in OS/2 2.1. These SVGA device drivers allow users to display programs in 256-color modes, at resolutions of up to 1024x768, running side-by-side in windows in either the background or foreground sessions.

  Comparable support is also provided for the 8514 and XGA displays.

- New printers supported in OS/2 2.1 include the following:

  - HP Laserjet 4

- HP Deskjet 500 Series
- Epson and compatibles
- Laserjet compatibles
- Postscript printers

- OS/2 2.1 now can be installed from a CD-ROM drive, which saves time and improves the ease of installing the system. IBM has tested a variety of SCSI-based CD-ROM drives (Sony, Toshiba, Hitachi, IBM, Pioneer, Texel, and NEC) in combination with the most popular SCSI-based adapter drivers (Adaptec, Future Domain, IBM, and DPT). Additionally, OS/2 2.1 includes support for Kodak's multi-session photo CD technology (on selected CD-ROM drives).

  OS/2 2.1 has also been tested with and supports a broad range of other hardware devices including hard disk drives, diskette drives, tape drives, optical disk drives, display adapters, and pointing devices.

- Multimedia Presentation Manager/2 (MMPM/2) Version 1.1 has been added to this version. MMPM/2 enhances the functionality of the OS/2 operating system by adding audio, image, and motion video playback capabilities (without hardware assistance), which can be combined with traditional text and graphics.

  MMPM/2 includes support for the following:

  - The Sound Blaster family of audio adapters
  - The ProAudio Spectrum 16 audio adapter
  - The Ultimotion software motion video formats

- OS/2 2.1 supports the Personal Computer Memory Card International Association (Level 2.0) specification. Inclusion of this set of standard interfaces allows the manufacturers of credit-card-sized memory and adapter cards to write OS/2 device drivers. OS/2 2.1 complies with the Advanced Power Management specification, providing extended battery life for mobile computers. The implementation of a larger cursor in OS/2 2.1 than in OS/2 2.0 improves visibility of the cursor on the screen for users of LCD displays.

Welcome to OS/2*, the operating system that puts the power of your computer to work for you. Because your computer can process information much faster than you can enter it, the computer is inactive the majority of the time. OS/2 2.1 remedies this situation by supporting the running of more than one program at a time. This is called *multitasking* and means that while you are working on something, the computer can be working on something else.

In addition to its power, OS/2 2.1 is very versatile. It can run programs written for OS/2, DOS, and Microsoft** Windows**. This helps reduce the need to replace existing programs or learn new ones.

Because of the power and versatility of this operating system you might expect it to be difficult to use. This is not so. IBM* developed the Workplace Shell* to let you manage your work without having to learn the complexities of the operating system. The Workplace Shell is a graphical interface that represents your office or workplace.

1

Chapter 1. Using the Workplace Shell

This chapter will familiarize you with the Workplace Shell and explain how to complete some common tasks. The explanations in this chapter assume that you have a mouse attached to your computer. If you do not, see Appendix A, "Keyboard and Mouse Use" on page 405 for a list of keys to use.

If you have a mouse, but do not know how to use it, refer to the OS/2 Tutorial for instructions. See "Tutorial" on page 123 for information about starting the tutorial. When you complete the mouse topic in the tutorial, return here to learn more about the Workplace Shell.

The following terms are used throughout this book to describe mouse actions:

Point	Move the mouse pointer.
Click	Press and release a mouse button. Instructions explain whether you should click mouse button 1 or 2.
Double-click	Press and release mouse button 1 twice in quick succession.
Drag	Move an object across the computer screen with a mouse.
Select	Point to an item and click mouse button 1. Instructions explain which item to point to.
Open	Point to an item and double-click. Instructions explain which item to point to.

Becoming Familiar with the Workplace Shell

The Workplace Shell is your view of the OS/2 operating system. It has two main components:

- The desktop, which is the screen that represents your work area.
- Objects, displayed as *icons*, which are small graphical representations. These objects represent items in your work environment and appear on the desktop. There are four different kinds of objects supplied with the Workplace shell:

A *data file* object contains information. Text files, memos, letters, spreadsheets, video, and sound are examples of data-file objects.

A *program* object represents a reference to an executable application program. Text editors, database programs, games, and tools are examples of program objects. *Program-file objects* are the actual executable files, such as files with the extension EXE or COM.

A *device* object represents a physical device. Printers, plotters, modems, and facsimile machines are examples of device objects.

A *folder* object contains other objects, which can be other folders. A folder is similar to a directory.

When you *open* an object, the contents of the object appear on the screen in an area called a *window*. When you completed the installation of the OS/2 operating system, the OS/2 Tutorial was displayed on the screen. The contents of the tutorial were displayed in a window.

OS/2 System Editor

To open an object:

1. Point to the object.
2. Double-click.

Parts of a Window

This section will help you understand the parts of a window and the Window List. To learn about the parts of a window and their purpose, open the System Editor object by pointing to the object and clicking mouse button 1. The following screen appears.

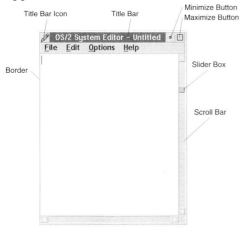

The *border* surrounds the window and is used to identify which window is *active* (can accept input from the user). The border is also used to change the size of the window.

When a window is active, its border is highlighted. An active window always appears in the *foreground* (on top of other windows on the desktop). To make a window active:

Select the window by clicking in the window.

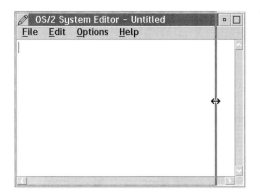

To size a window:

1. Point to the border (the mouse pointer will turn into a bi-directional arrow).
2. Press and hold mouse button 1.
3. Drag the border to size the window.
4. Release mouse button 1.

In addition to being able to make a temporary change to the size of a window, you also can change the *default size* of a window. The default size is the size that the window will appear each time it is opened.

To change the default size of a window:

1. Press and hold the Shift key.
2. Point to the border (the mouse pointer will turn into a bi-directional arrow).
3. Press and hold mouse button 1.
4. Drag the border to size the window.
5. Release mouse button 1.
6. Release the Shift key.

The *title bar* contains the name of the window and is used to move the window.

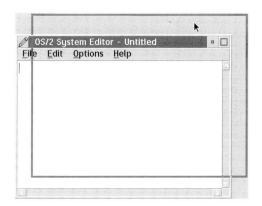

To move the window:

1. Point to the title bar.
2. Press and hold mouse button 1.
3. Drag the window to the new location.
4. Release mouse button 1.

The *title-bar icon* is a picture of the object that represents the window. The title-bar icon is in the upper-left corner of the window. The icon can be used to close the window or display a *pop-up menu* that contains the available operations for the window.

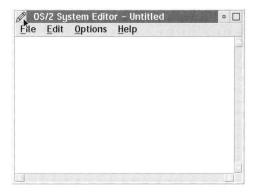

To close the window:

1. Point to the title-bar icon.
2. Double-click.

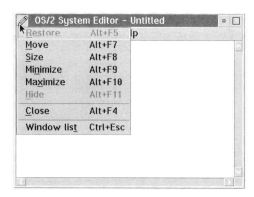

To display a pop-up menu:

1. Point to the title-bar icon.
2. Click button 2.

The *minimize button* is used to shrink the window to an icon. The minimize button is in the upper-right corner of the window. Minimized windows are still open and continue to run. The titles of minimized windows are placed in the *Window List* which contains the titles of windows that are currently open. The icons for the minimized windows are placed in either the Minimized Window Viewer or on the desktop (depending on the window settings).

Some windows have a *hide button*, instead of a minimize button. Hiding a window works just like minimizing a window with one exception: the objects for the hidden window are not placed on the desktop or in the Minimized Window Viewer. However, the titles of hidden windows are placed in the Window List. For more information about the Window List, see "Using the Window List" on page 11.

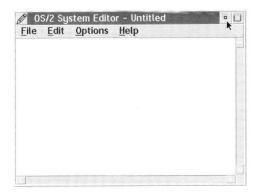

To minimize a window:

Select (minimize button).

To hide a window:

Select (hide button).

To display a minimized or hidden window:

1. Point to an empty area on the desktop.
2. Click mouse buttons 1 and 2 at the same time to display the Window List.
3. Point to the title of a minimized or hidden window.
4. Double-click.

To display a minimized window in the Minimized Window Viewer:

1. Open **Minimized Window Viewer**.
2. Open a minimized window.

To display a minimized window on the desktop:

Open a minimized window.

The *maximize button* is used to make the window its largest possible size. Generally, when maximized, a window fills the entire screen.

When a window is maximized the maximize button changes to a *restore button*. This button is used to return the window to the size it was before it was maximized.

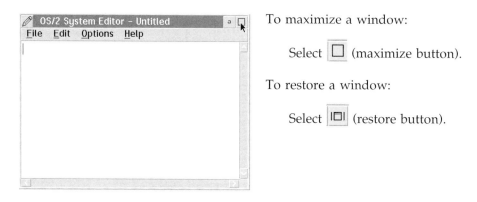

To maximize a window:

Select ☐ (maximize button).

To restore a window:

Select ◧ (restore button).

The *scroll bar* is used to scroll through the information in the window. A scroll bar is displayed whenever more information exists than can be shown in the window.

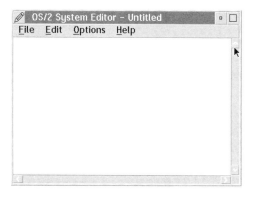

To scroll a window:

1. Point to the up, down, right, or left arrow in the scroll bar.
2. Press and hold mouse button 1.
3. Release mouse button 1 to stop scrolling.

The *slider box* is used to scroll one page of information at a time in the window. It is also used to indicate the relative position of the information in the window. For example, if the slider box is at the midpoint of the scroll bar, you are approximately halfway through the information.

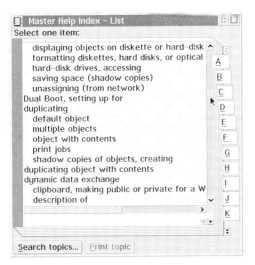

To scroll a page:

> Select above, below, to the right of, or to the left of the slider box in the scroll bar.

Using the Window List

The Window List shows the titles of the objects you are using and programs that are running. This list also can include objects or programs that are hidden or minimized.

Tip

The titles are added to the Window List in the order that the objects are opened. Frequently used objects should be opened first to lessen the need for scrolling the Window List.

To display the Window List:

1. Point to an empty area on the desktop.
2. Click mouse buttons 1 and 2 at the same time.

To display a window whose title appears on the Window List:

1. Point to the title of the window you want to display.
2. Double-click.

Using Pop-Up Menus

Every object has its own menu called a *pop-up menu*. The pop-up menu contains choices that are the available operations for that specific object. As a result, each pop-up menu might be different. However, the following choices are common to most pop-up menus:

Open
Help
Create another
Copy
Move
Delete
Create shadow
Find

Tip

Although you can use pop-up menus to select these choices, you might find it easier to do most of these tasks using the *direct-manipulation* method. With direct manipulation, you use a mouse or other pointing device to work with objects instead of using menus.

An arrow to the right of a choice on a pop-up menu indicates that additional choices are available. There are two types of arrows:

- A button-like arrow, (▣) which indicates that one of the subsequent choices has a check mark next to it and is the default action when you select your original choice
- A flat arrow, (➔) which indicates that selecting the main choice opens another menu, from which you must make a choice

To see the additional choices, click on the arrow next to the choice. An additional menu appears.

A pop-up menu is available for:

- Objects
- Windows
- The desktop

Note: The pop-up menu for the desktop contains choices that apply to all the objects on the desktop and to the operating system.

Displaying the Pop-Up Menu for an Object

OS/2 System

To display the pop-up menu for an object, such as the OS/2 System folder:

1. Point to the object.
2. Click mouse button 2.

   Note: Make sure the mouse pointer is *on* the object when you click mouse button 2; otherwise, the pop-up menu for the desktop appears.

To display a pop-up menu for multiple objects:

1. Press and hold Ctrl.
2. Select the objects.
3. Release Ctrl.
4. Point to one of the objects.
5. Click mouse button 2.

Displaying a Window Pop-Up Menu

To display the pop-up menu for a window:

1. Point to an empty area in the window.
2. Click mouse button 2.

Or:

1. Point to the title-bar icon.
2. Click mouse button 2.

Displaying the Desktop Pop Up Menu

To display the pop-up menu for the desktop:

1. Point to an empty area on the desktop.
2. Click mouse button 2.

Working with Objects and Windows

You can work with objects in a way that is similar to the way you already work. For example, during your work day, you might select letters or file folders you need to work with, or you might copy letters at a copier. With objects, you can do the same kinds of tasks. You can open an object and work with it, or you can copy, move, discard, or print it.

Selecting an Object

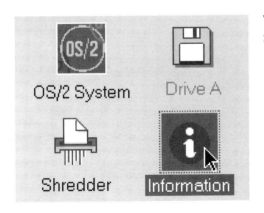

To *select* (highlight) an object using direct manipulation:

1. Point to the object.
2. Click mouse button 1. (When you click on an object it is selected, and all other objects are deselected.)

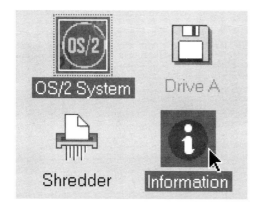

To select multiple (more than one) objects using direct manipulation:

1. Press and hold Ctrl.
2. Select the objects.
3. Release Ctrl.

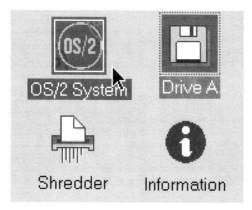

Or:

To select multiple objects that are next to one another using direct-manipulation:

1. Point to an object.
2. Press and hold mouse button 1.
3. Point to the other objects you want to select.
4. Release the mouse button.

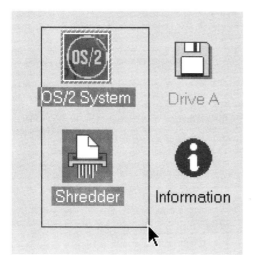

Or:

1. Point to just outside one of the objects you want to select.
2. Press and hold mouse button 1.
3. Drag the box until all the objects you want to select are inside the box.
4. Release the mouse button.

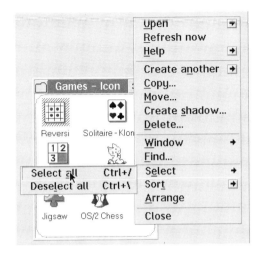

To select all the objects in an *open folder* (one in which you can see the objects it contains) using a pop-up menu:

1. Point to an empty area in the folder.
2. Click mouse button 2.
3. Select **Select**.
4. Select **Select all**.

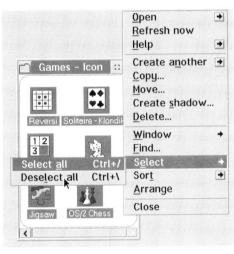

To deselect all the objects in an open folder using the pop-up menu:

1. Point to an empty area in the folder.
2. Click mouse button 2.
3. Select **Select**.
4. Select **Deselect all**.

To deselect all the highlighted items using direct manipulation:

1. Point to an empty area in the folder.
2. Click mouse button 1.

Opening an Object

You can open an object to display its contents. The contents are displayed on the screen in a window.

To open an object using direct manipulation:

1. Point to the object.
2. Double-click.

To open an object using a pop-up menu:

1. Point to the object.
2. Click mouse button 2.
3. Select **Open**.

Copying an Object

You can duplicate an object so that more than one copy of the object exists. The copied object can be placed on the desktop or in an open or closed folder. If you copy an object to the same folder as the original object, the duplicate object is given a slightly different name than the original.

To copy an object using direct manipulation:

1. Point to the object.
2. Press and hold Ctrl.
3. Press and hold mouse button 2.
4. Drag the object to the place where you want the copy.
5. Release mouse button 2.
6. Release Ctrl.

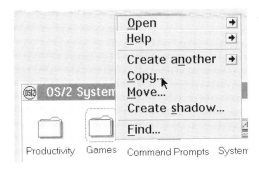

To copy an object using a pop-up menu:

1. Point to the object.
2. Click mouse button 2.
3. Select the **Copy** choice. The Copy notebook is displayed.
4. Optional: Type a new name in the **New name** field.
5. Select the folder object that represents the location where you want the object to be copied.
6. Select the **Copy** push button.

Note: Certain objects cannot be copied. Instead, a *shadow* of the object is placed in the target location. A shadow differs from a copy of the object in that the shadow changes whenever the original changes. A shadow object has lighter title text than original objects.

Creating a Shadow Object

You can create a shadow object that represents the original object and its contents. Creating a shadow differs from copying because the original and a copy do not automatically exchange data, but a shadow does. In effect, a shadow works with its original, while a copy works independently. An action performed on either the original or the shadow (for example, a name change) occurs in both objects. The exceptions are Move and Delete.

Creating a shadow is useful because you can access data-file objects (objects that contain data, like a spreadsheet) or folder objects that are on other physical devices (for example, a second hard disk) without physically moving the data-file object or folder object to your desktop.

Notes:

1. Although you can create a shadow of a program-file object, it is better to use a program object. When you use a program object, any changes you make to the shadow or the program object do not affect the executable file.

2. The **Original** menu choice on a shadow object lets you locate the original object and perform actions such as Delete.

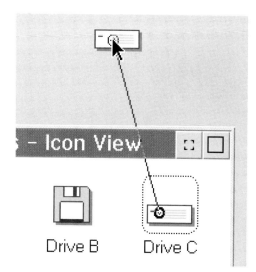

To create a shadow of an object using direct manipulation:

1. Point to the object.
2. Press and hold Ctrl+Shift.
3. Press and hold mouse button 2.
4. Drag the object to where you want the shadow to appear.
5. Release mouse button 2.
6. Release Ctrl+Shift.

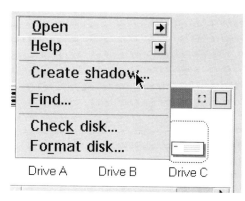

To create a shadow of an object using a pop-up menu:

1. Point to the object.
2. Click mouse button 2.
3. Select the **Create shadow** choice. The Create Shadow notebook is displayed.
4. Select the folder object that represents the location where you want the shadow to appear.
5. Select **Create**.

You can move an object so that it appears in a place that is more convenient. Objects can be moved to a different folder or to the desktop. If you move an object to a folder that already contains an object with the same name, the duplicate object is given a slightly different name.

To move an object using direct manipulation:

1. Point to the object.
2. Press and hold mouse button 2.
3. Drag the object to the new location.
4. Release mouse button 2.

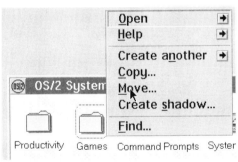

To move an object using a pop-up menu:

1. Point to the object.
2. Click mouse button 2.
3. Select the **Move** choice. The Move notebook is displayed.
4. Optional: Type a new name in the **New name** field.
5. Select the folder object that represents the location where you want the object to be moved.
6. Select the **Move** push button.

Note: Certain objects cannot be moved. Instead, a shadow of the object is placed in the target location.

Deleting an Object

You can delete an object from the desktop or from a folder. Before you delete an object consider that you might not be able to recover it.

- If you delete a folder object, the folder and its contents are deleted.
- If you delete a shadow of an object, only the shadow is deleted; the original is not affected.
- If you delete a program object, only the program object is deleted; the actual program files are unaffected.

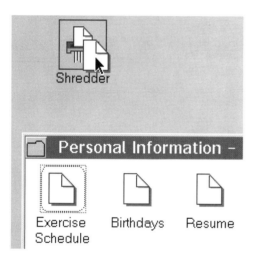

To delete an object using direct manipulation:

1. Point to the object.
2. Press and hold mouse button 2.
3. Drag the object to the **Shredder**.
4. Respond to all messages to confirm the deletion. (To avoid getting confirmation messages with future deletions, see "Confirming Delete Actions" on page 81.)

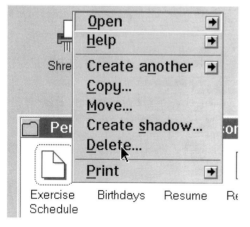

To delete an object using a pop-up menu:

1. Point to the object.
2. Click mouse button 2.
3. Select **Delete**.
4. Respond to all messages to confirm the deletion. (To avoid getting confirmation messages with future deletions, see "Confirming Delete Actions" on page 81.)

You can change the name of an object to anything you like.

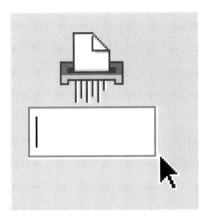

To rename an object using direct manipulation:

1. Point to the text (title) under the object that you want to change.
2. Press and hold Alt.
3. Click mouse button 1.
4. Type your changes. Press Backspace or Del to erase any unwanted characters or lines. Press Enter to add another line.
5. Point to an empty area on the desktop.
6. Click mouse button 1 to accept the new name.

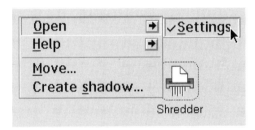

To rename an object using a pop-up menu:

1. Point to the object whose name you want to change.
2. Click mouse button 2.
3. Select the arrow to the right of **Open**.
4. Select **Settings**.
5. Select the **General** tab.
6. Type the new name in the **Title** field.
7. Point to the title-bar icon.
8. Double-click.

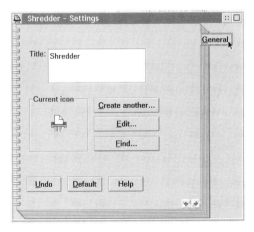

Printing an Object

You can print or plot the contents of a data-file object.

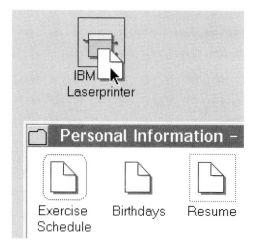

To print a data-file object on the default printer using direct manipulation:

1. Point to the data-file object you want to print (for example, a memo).
2. Press and hold mouse button 2.
3. Drag the data-file object to a printer object. The contents of the object are printed.

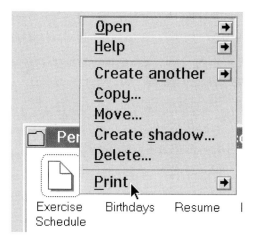

To print the contents of an object on the default printer using a pop-up menu:

1. Point to the data-file object.
2. Click mouse button 2.
3. Select **Print**.

To print the contents of an object on a printer other than the default:

1. Point to the data-file object.
2. Click mouse button 2.
3. Select the arrow to the right of **Print**.
4. Select the name of the printer you want to use.

For more information on printing, see Chapter 16, "Printers and Plotters."

Changing Object Settings

You can customize the settings for an object to match your preferences. Every object has *settings*. Settings are properties or characteristics of an object. For example, a program object has settings that tell the operating system how the program should start each time you open the program object.

If you change a setting, the change takes place immediately. You do *not* have to make a selection to save the change.   If you change your mind, select **Undo**. The settings are set back to what they were before you opened the notebook. Some notebooks also have a **Default** push button. Use it to change the settings back to what they were when the operating system was installed.

For more detailed information about any of the pages in the Settings notebooks, see "Program Object Settings" on page 185.

Important

Changes to settings that are specific to DOS and WIN-OS/2* programs are *not* saved automatically. Use the **Save** push button to save your changes.

For more information about changing program-object settings, refer to "Program Object Settings" on page 185.

To change the settings for an object using a pop-up menu:

1. Point to an object.
2. Click mouse button 2.
3. Select the arrow to the right of **Open**.
4. Select **Settings**. (The settings notebook for the object appears.)
5. Select a *tab* (used to indicate another page exists in the notebook).
6. Change the settings to meet your needs.
7. Point to the title-bar icon.
8. Double-click.

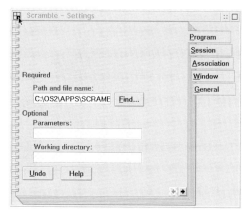

Displaying Object Information

You can view and change certain file information about an object. Some of the information is provided by the system; other information is added or changed by the owner or user of the object. For example, you can view information about an object's creation date or its size in bytes.

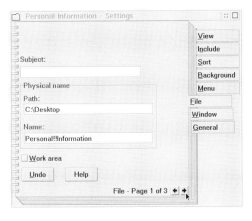

To view or change the file settings for an object using a pop-up menu:

1. Point to the object.
2. Click mouse button 2.
3. Select the arrow to the right of **Open**.
4. Select **Settings**.
5. Select the **File** tab.
6. Select the left or right arrow at the bottom of the Settings notebook to scroll through the 3 pages of the File tab.
7. Change the information to meet your needs.
8. Point to the title-bar icon.
9. Double-click. For more information about using Settings notebooks, refer to "Program Object Settings" on page 185.

You also can view the size and date information for the contents of a folder by selecting the **Details view** from the **Open** menu choices.

Finding Objects

You can search for an object located anywhere on the system.

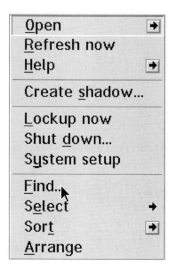

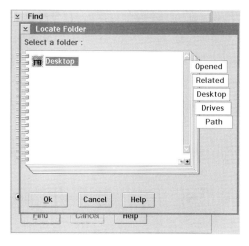

To find an object:

1. Point to a folder object or an empty area on the desktop.
2. Click mouse button 2.
3. Select **Find**.
4. Type the name of the object you want to find in the **Name** field. Type an * if you do not know the name.
5. Select the type of object you are looking for. You can select more than one type of object from the list. If you do not know what type of object you are looking for, select **Object**. (To deselect an object in the list, click on it again.)
6. Select **Locate** to specify where you want to search for the object.

   The Locate push button lets you expand or limit the scope of the search. The tabs on the Locate page are:
   - *Opened* lists all folders that are currently open.
   - *Related* lists all the folders on the drive that contains the OS/2 operating system.
   - *Desktop* lists all the folders found on the desktop.
   - *Drives* lists all the drives on the system.
   - *Path* allows you to specify a path to search.

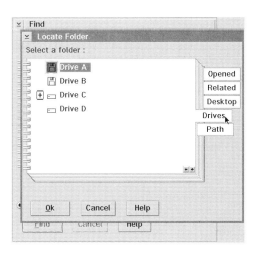

7. Select a tab on the Locate Folder page.
8. Select the folder that you want to search. (For example, if you want to search Drive C, you can select Drive C on the Drives page.)
9. Select **OK**.
10. Select either **Search just this folder** or **Search all subfolders**.
11. Select **Find**.

A Find Results folder is displayed and contains shadows of the objects found. If no objects are found, a message is displayed.

Tip

You can use the objects in the Find Results folder, or you can select **Original** from the object pop-up menu and locate the original object.

If you rename an object in the Find Results folder, the name of the original object is also changed.

Sorting Objects

You can specify how you want the contents of a folder (including the desktop) sorted. You can sort by name, type, or specific attributes such as size.

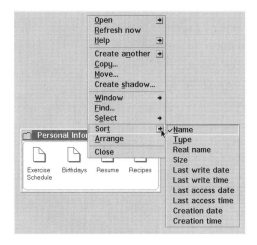

To sort the contents of a folder or desktop using a pop-up menu:

1. Point to a folder object or to an empty area in the open folder or the desktop.
2. Click mouse button 2.
3. Select the arrow to the right of **Sort**.
4. Select the choice that best describes how you want the folder sorted.

Arranging Objects

You can automatically rearrange the objects on the desktop and within open folders into rows. The rows start at the upper-left corner of the folder or desktop and continue until each object is placed in a row.

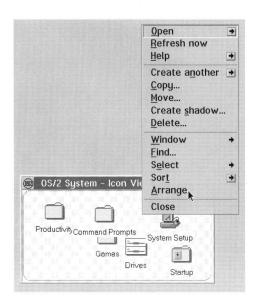

To arrange *all* the objects in an open folder or on the desktop using a pop-up menu:

1. Point to an empty area in an open folder or on the desktop.
2. Click mouse button 2.
3. Select **Arrange**.

Arranging Windows

In addition to arranging objects in open folders, you also can arrange open windows. You can *cascade* (place the windows in an overlapped sequence with the active program on top), *tile* (place the windows side by side with the active program in the upper-left corner of the screen), or arrange each window individually.

To cascade or tile all the windows whose titles appear in the Window List using a pop-up menu:

1. Point to an empty area on the desktop.
2. Click mouse buttons 1 and 2 at the same time.
3. Point to the title-bar icon in the Window List.
4. Click mouse button 2.
5. Select the arrow to the right of **Select**.
6. Select the **Select all** choice.
7. Point to one of the titles in the Window List.
8. Click mouse button 2.
9. Select either **Tile** or **Cascade**.

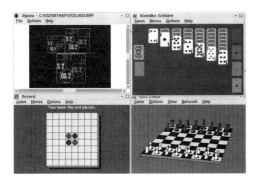

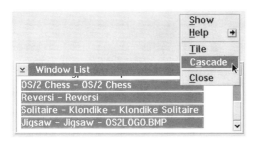

To cascade or tile multiple windows whose titles appear in the Window List using a pop-up menu:

1. Click mouse buttons 1 and 2 at the same time.
2. Press and hold Ctrl.
3. Select the titles of the windows you want to cascade or tile.
4. Release Ctrl.
5. Point to one of the selected titles.
6. Click mouse button 2.
7. Select either **Cascade** or **Tile**.

To cascade or tile multiple windows using direct manipulation:

1. Point to an empty area on the desktop.
2. Click mouse buttons 1 and 2 at the same time.
3. Press and hold Ctrl.
4. Select the titles of the windows you want to arrange.
5. Release Ctrl.
6. Point to one of the selected titles in the Window List.
7. Click mouse button 2.
8. Select either **Tile** or **Cascade**.

Switching between Running Programs

You can switch between running programs using the following:

- Window List
- Minimized Window Viewer
- Keyboard

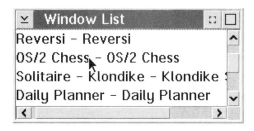

To switch between running programs using the Window List:

1. Point to an empty area on the desktop.
2. Click mouse buttons 1 and 2 at the same time.
3. Point to the title of the object you want to display.
4. Double-click.

Minimized
Window Viewer

To switch to a running program using the Minimized Window Viewer:

Note: By default, most running program objects appear in the Minimized Window Viewer folder on the desktop.

1. Open **Minimized Window Viewer**.
2. Open the program object you want.

To switch between running programs using the keyboard:

Press Alt+Esc.

Each time you press Alt+Esc you bring up the next running program.

Closing Objects or Windows

You can close objects or windows that you will not be using for a while. You can close each window or object individually or you can use the Window List to close a window or object plus all of its associated windows.

Note: You cannot close the desktop from the Window List. To close the desktop, you need to follow the OS/2 operating system shut-down procedure (see "Shutting Down Your System" on page 41).

Tip

To improve system performance:

- Close opened programs when you are not going to use them again.
- Close folders that you do not need.
- Move commonly used functions out of folders and onto your desktop; then close the folders that contained the objects.

To close an object using a pop-up menu:

1. Point to the object.
2. Click mouse button 2.
3. Select **Close**.

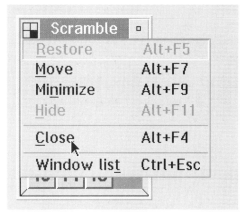

To close a window using a pop-up menu:

1. Point to the title-bar icon.
2. Click mouse button 2.
3. Select **Close**.

To close a window using direct manipulation:

1. Point to the title-bar icon.
2. Double-click.

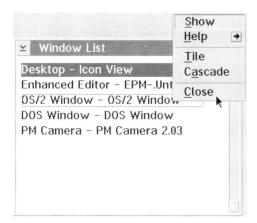

To close a window and its associated windows using the Window List:

1. Point to an empty area on the desktop.
2. Click mouse buttons 1 and 2 at the same time.
3. Point to the title of the window in the Window List.
4. Click mouse button 2.
5. Select **Close**.

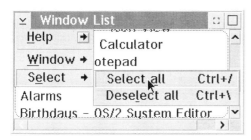

To close all the open windows using the Window List:

1. Point to an empty area on the desktop.
2. Click mouse buttons 1 and 2 at the same time.
3. Point to the title-bar icon in the Window List.
4. Click mouse button 2.
5. Select the arrow to the right of **Select**.
6. Select **Select all**.
7. Point to one of the selected titles in the Window List.
8. Click mouse button 2.
9. Select **Close**.

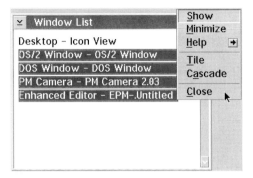

To close multiple windows and their associated windows using direct manipulation:

1. Point to an empty area on the desktop.
2. Click mouse buttons 1 and 2 at the same time.
3. Press and hold Ctrl.
4. Select the titles of the windows you want to close.
5. Point to one of the selected titles in the Window List.
6. Click mouse button 2.
7. Select **Close**.

Tip

To close all open objects within a folder whenever you close the folder using the Window List, create a work-area folder (see "Creating Work-Area Folders" on page 39).

Organizing the Desktop Folder

The Desktop folder is a special folder. It fills the entire screen and contains objects, some of which are folders. Every folder corresponds to a directory in the file system. The following is an example of the Desktop folder.

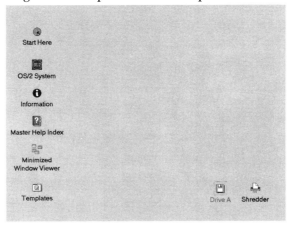

You can minimize windows for objects to avoid desktop clutter and then easily access them from the Minimized Window Viewer. For more information, see Chapter 13, "Minimized Window Viewer" on page 145.

You can organize your desktop to suit your needs by arranging your objects into folders that make sense to you. You also can create work-area folders to organize objects in folders that relate to a specific task.

Using Folders to Organize Your Work

This typical office scenario shows you how you might use folders to organize your work.

For example, assume you work with the following items on a daily basis:

- A printer (device object)
- An editing program (program object)
- Corporate policy letters (data-file objects)
- Personnel memos (data-file objects)
- A company newsletter (data-file object)

Here is how you might organize your work:

- You create a folder by dragging a folder object from the Templates folder to the desktop and then name it "Daily Work" (for more information, see Chapter 15, "Templates" on page 151).
- You want to put the corporate policy letters, personnel memos, and the company newsletter in the "Daily Work" folder, but you also want to keep them separate; therefore, you drag three folders from the Templates folder to the "Daily Work" folder.

  The following shows the three folders in the Daily Work folder, which is displayed in an icon view. For more information about displaying objects in different views, see "Opening an Object" on page 18.

- If there are one or more printers you want to use with your letters (data-file objects) in these folders, you can place printer objects in the "Daily Work" folder as well. If each type of letter requires a different printer, or the same printer with different settings (for example, landscape or portrait layout), you can create a different printer object for each, give it a unique name, and place it in the individual subfolders: Corporate, Newsletter, or Personnel.

  Tip

  You can drag printer objects already set up to these folders, or you can create and customize new printer objects. For more information, see "Creating a Printer Object" on page 165.

- Place your data-file objects and any data-file templates you created (for example, the "Company letterhead" template) in the folders you want. The settings of the template data-file object might already be customized (for example, associated to more than one editing program). For more information about data-file templates, see "Creating a Template of an Object" on page 153.
- Customize the "Daily Work" folder to be a work-area folder (see "Creating Work-Area Folders" on page 39 next).

Creating Work-Area Folders

Create a work-area folder when you want to gather objects that are related to a specific task. For example, you might have one work-area folder with a current report, previous reports, and a printer with customized settings, and another work-area folder with charts, documents, and a plotter.

The work-area folder has two special features:

- When you close the folder, all windows belonging to the objects within the folder are closed automatically, and the view of each object is saved. When you open the folder the next time, each object is displayed with its previous view.

- When you hide a folder window, all open windows belonging to the objects within the folder are hidden automatically. When you show the folder window (using the **Show** choice in the Window List), each object is displayed with its previous view.

To create a work-area folder:

1. Point to folder object.
2. Click mouse button 2.
3. Select the arrow to the right of **Open**.
4. Select **Settings**.
5. Select the **File** tab.
6. Select the **Work area** check box.
7. Point to the title-bar icon.
8. Double-click.

For additional information about using Settings notebooks, see "Changing Object Settings" on page 25.

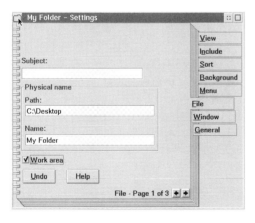

You can lock the keyboard and mouse on your computer. The lockup program helps protect important information and also provides a screen saver. The lockup program can be activated manually or automatically after a period of keyboard and mouse inactivity.

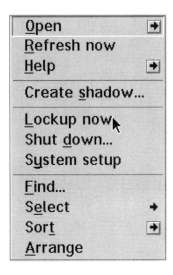

To lock your system manually:

1. Point to an empty area on the desktop.
2. Click mouse button 2.
3. Select **Lockup now**.

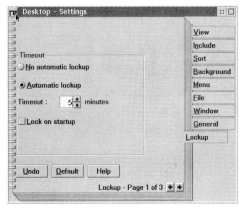

To set the Lockup program so it activates automatically after a period of inactivity:

1. Point to an empty area on the desktop.
2. Click mouse button 2.
3. Select the arrow to the right of **Open**.
4. Select **Settings**.
5. Select the **Lockup** tab.
6. Select **Automatic lockup**.
7. Select the up or down arrow in the **Timeout** field to set an amount of time.
8. Point to the title-bar icon.
9. Double-click.

You can preserve your desktop and the integrity of the operating system by doing a shut down on your system before turning it off. The shut-down process stores information about which windows are open, their placement on the desktop, and with some programs even their current state, in addition to writing the information that is in the *cache* (storage buffer) to the hard disk.

Note: Be sure to check all programs for unsaved information (such as documents you are editing) *before* you start the shut-down procedure.

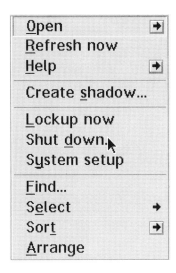

To shut down your system using a mouse:

1. Point to an empty area on the desktop.
2. Click mouse button 2.
3. Select **Shut down**.
4. Select **Yes**.
5. Wait for a message that states that the shut down is complete.
6. Turn off the computer.

To shut down your system using the keyboard:

1. Press Alt+Shift+Tab. (If you are in a full-screen session, press Alt+Esc before you press Alt+Shift+Tab.)
2. Press Ctrl+\ to deselect the icons on the desktop.
3. Press Shift+F10 to display the pop-up menu for the desktop.
4. Use an arrow key to highlight **Shut down**.
5. Press Enter.
6. Press Enter again to select **Yes**.
7. Wait for a message that states that the shut down is complete.
8. Turn off the computer.

As a general rule, you should shut down your system before turning off your computer; otherwise, you might lose information.

However, there are situations where you might want to restart your system without using the shutdown procedure. Following are two examples of such situations:

- If you opened several folders containing many icons, and you want to avoid waiting for the system to save the positions of the icons, or

- If you changed the positions of the icons on the desktop during the session, and you want them to revert back to their previous positions.

Note: Be sure that you will not lose anything of importance before you consider this action.

To shut down your system without using the **Shut down** choice:

1. Press Ctrl+Alt+Del.
2. Wait until the screen is cleared.
3. Turn off your computer.

Note: If you decide not to use the Shut down procedure, you should always press Ctrl+Alt+Del and wait until the screen clears before you turn off your system.

Online Information

Most of the information needed to master OS/2 is online. Whether you need help, want to learn about the operating system, need a term defined, or want to explore topics related to concepts, procedures, and commands, the information is online.

The online information has four major advantages over books:

- It can be displayed on your screen while you work.
- It is part of the operating system, so you cannot misplace it.
- It can provide *context-sensitive* help. (Help specific to the task you are doing).
- It can search for a particular word or phrase quicker.

OS/2 offers the following online information to help you use the operating system.

OS/2 Tutorial

The OS/2 Tutorial provides information about how to use a mouse, work with objects and folders, use windows, get help, and more.

To open the OS/2 Tutorial:

1. Open **Information**.
2. Open **Tutorial**.

For more information about the OS/2 Tutorial, see "Tutorial" on page 123.

Start Here

The Start Here object provides an overview and a quick path to information about some common tasks you might do on a daily basis.

To open the Start Here object:

1. Point to the Start Here object.
2. Double-click.

For more information about the Start Here object, see Chapter 2, "Start Here" on page 53.

Glossary

The Glossary provides an alphabetic list of terms with definitions.

To open the Glossary:

1. Open **Information**.
2. Open **Glossary**.

For more information about the Glossary, see "Glossary" on page 130.

OS/2 Command Reference

The *OS/2 Command Reference* provides information about commands, such as their purpose, parameters, and syntax. It also has information about batch files, command operators, redirection symbols, and substitution variables.

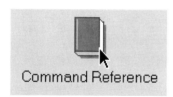

To open the Command Reference:

1. Open **Information**.
2. Open **Command Reference**.

For more information about the OS/2 Command Reference, see "Command Reference" on page 124.

REXX Information

The *REXX Information* provides information about the commands you can use to write powerful REXX programs.

To open REXX Information:

1. Open **Information**.
2. Open **REXX Information**.

For more information, see "REXX Information" on page 131.

Master Help Index

The Master Help Index provides an alphabetic list of topics related to understanding and using the OS/2 operating system. The list contains the following kinds of topics:

- Things to consider before performing a task
- The steps you need to take to complete a task
- Operating system concepts

To open the Master Help Index:

1. Open **Master Help Index**

For information about using this index, see Chapter 11, "Master Help Index" on page 135.

Help

Online help is always available. You can get help by:

- Pressing F1.
- Clicking on a **Help** push button.
- Clicking on the **Help** choice in a pop-up menu.

 and

To get help for an object using F1:

1. Select an object.
2. Press F1.

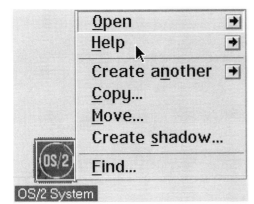

To get help for an object using the pop-up menu:

1. Point to an object.
2. Click mouse button 2.
3. Select **Help**.

and

To get help for a pop-up menu choice using F1:

1. Point to an object (or the desktop).
2. Click mouse button 2.
3. Point to a pop-up menu choice.
4. Press and hold mouse button 1.
5. Press F1.
6. Release mouse button 1.

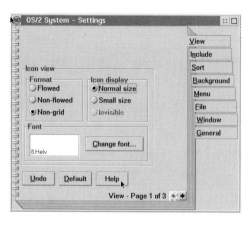

To get help for a window that contains a **Help** push button:

1. Select the **Help** pushbutton.

After you display help, you can search for other helps, print a help, review the help index, or display help for a word or phrase that is highlighted in a help window.

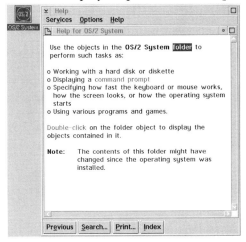

The following describes how to search, print, review the help index, and display help for a highlighted word or phrase. For more detailed information, review the OS/2 Tutorial or request help from within a help window.

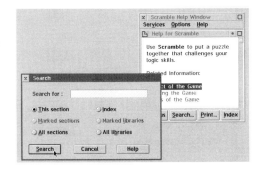

To search for help information from within a help window:

1. Select **Search**.
2. Type the word or words that describe what you want to find into the **Search for**.
3. Select **Search**.
4. When the list of available help information appears, move the mouse pointer to an item in the list.
5. Double-click.

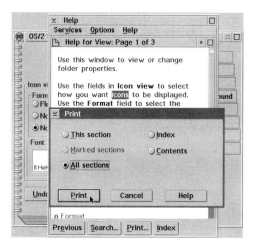

To print help information from within a help window:

1. Select **Print**.
2. If you want to print only the help that is currently displayed, the default choice shown in this window is **This section**. You can change this if you want to print more than one help window, the help index, or the table of contents.

   Note: The help index and table of contents choices only print their entries, they do not print the text of the entries.

3. Select **Print**.

Sometimes a word or a phrase in a help window is *highlighted*. The highlighting means that additional help information is available. The additional help information might be a definition, help for a field, related information, or trademark information.

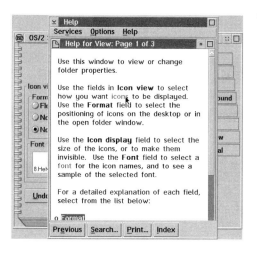

To display the additional help:

1. Point to the highlighted word or phrase.
2. Double-click or press Esc. (The additional help information appears in the help window.)
3. Select **Previous** to return to the previous help window.

Displaying Help for OS/2 Messages

You can get information to help you understand, correct, and respond to OS/2 messages. The way you request help depends upon how and where the message is displayed.

To get help for a message that appears in a window with a **Help** push button:

1. Select the **Help** push button.

To get help for a message that appears on a full screen and is enclosed in a box:

1. Use the up or down arrow key to highlight **Display Help**.
2. Press Enter.

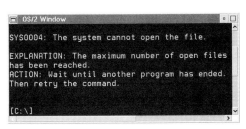

To get help for an error message that has a message number, preceded by the letters SYS:

1. At the OS/2 command prompt, type HELP followed by a space and the message number. (It is not necessary to type the letters SYS or the leading zeros.)
2. Press Enter.

For example, if you received this message:

SYS0002: The system cannot find the file specified.

To request help, you type: HELP 2

Press Enter. The following help appears:

SYS0002: The system cannot find the file specified.

EXPLANATION: The file named in the command does
not exist in the current directory or search path
specified. Or, the file name was entered
incorrectly.
ACTION: Retry the command using the correct
file name.

The Desktop is a folder that contains other objects, some of which are folders. If you selected **Install all features** at system installation time, your screen shows the Desktop folder with the following objects:

Start Here

The Start Here object helps get you started using the Workplace Shell interface by providing a list of basic tasks.

OS/2 System

The OS/2 System object contains the objects that allow you to tailor certain properties of the operating system, such as mouse characteristics and screen colors. For more information, see Chapter 3, "OS/2 System."

Information

The Information object contains online information, including the *Tutorial*, *Command Reference*, *Glossary*, and *REXX Information*. For more information, see Chapter 10, "Information" on page 123.

Master Help Index

The Master Help Index object provides an alphabetic list which contains most of the information you need to use OS/2 2.1. For more information, see Chapter 11, "Master Help Index" on page 135.

Templates

The Templates object contains forms (templates) that help you create new files, folders, programs, and other objects. For more information, see Chapter 15, "Templates."

Drive A

The Drive A object works the same as Drive A located in the Drives folder (see Chapter 6, "Drives"). This object displays a directory listing of the files on a diskette in drive A. For more information, see Chapter 12, "Drive A" on page 139.

51

Minimized
Window
Viewer

The Minimized Window Viewer object provides quick access to windows that you have minimized. When you open the Minimized Window Viewer, the minimized window object is in the folder. For more information, see Chapter 13, "Minimized Window Viewer" on page 145.

Shredder

The Shredder object is used to permanently delete an object. If you drop an object on the Shredder, you receive a warning message that the object is about to be discarded. For more information, see Chapter 14, "Shredder" on page 147.

If multimedia support is installed (see Chapter 6 in the *OS/2 2.1 Installation Guide*) the desktop also contains the following :

Volume
Control

The Volume Control object is used to globally adjust the volume of all applications being controlled by Multimedia Presentation Manager/2* (MMPM/2).

Multimedia

The Multimedia object contains the multimedia applications selected during the installation of MMPM/2.

Start Here

The Start Here object contains information to help get you started using the Workplace Shell interface. Some of the topics in Start Here are:

- About OS/2 2.1
- Customizing Your Desktop
- Doing Everyday Tasks
- Finding Information
- Installing Printers
- Multimedia Added to OS/2
- New OS/2 2.1 Features
- Printing
- Sharing Data
- Shutting Down Your System
- Understanding Multitasking

To open the Start Here object:

1. Point to **Start Here**.
2. Double-click.

To select a topic in the Contents:

1. Open **Start Here**.
2. Point to a topic.
3. Double-click.

Sometimes a word or a phrase in the Start Here window is *highlighted*. The highlighting means that additional information is hidden "beneath" the word or phrase. The additional information might be a definition, an explanation, or instructions.

To view the text "beneath" the highlighted phrase:

1. Point to the highlighted word or phrase.
2. Double-click. (The additional information appears in the Start Here window.)
3. Select **Previous** to return to the previous window.

You can print one or all of the topics in Start Here.

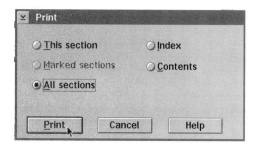

To print one topic:

1. Open the topic you want to print.
2. Select **Print**.
3. Select **This section**.
4. Select **Print**.

To print all the topics:

1. Select **Print**.
2. Select **All sections**.
3. Select **Print**.

You can search the Start Here information to help you find what you are looking for.

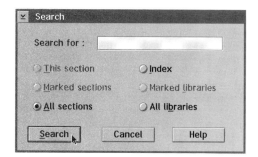

To search for information within the Start Here window:

1. Select **Search**.
2. Type a word or phrase you want to find.
3. Select **This section**, **All sections**, or **Index**.
4. Select **Search**.
5. Select a topic from the resulting list.

   Note: If you chose **This section** in your search criteria, a list is not displayed.

To search all the online information on the system, including the Start Here information:

1. Select **Search**.
2. Type a word or phrase you want to find.
3. Select **All libraries**.
4. Select **Search**.
5. Select a topic from the resulting list.

Chapter 3. OS/2 System

OS/2 System

The OS/2 System object contains folders that let you personalize your desktop and tailor certain properties of the operating system.

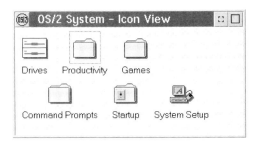

When you open OS/2 System, the following objects appear:

System Setup

System Setup

The System Setup folder contains many objects used to change settings for system options such as colors, fonts, mouse and keyboard controls, country support, and system time.

For more information, see Chapter 4, "System Setup."

Startup

Startup

The Startup folder is intended to contain application programs that start automatically at system startup time.

For more information, see Chapter 5, "Startup."

Drives

Drives

The Drives folder contains objects that let you access diskette drives and hard disk drives installed on your system. Use these objects to display directory structures and copy files.

For more information, see Chapter 6, "Drives."

Command Prompts

Command Prompts

The Command Prompts folder contains objects that let you access the OS/2 and DOS full-screen and OS/2 and DOS window command prompts, and WIN-OS/2 full-screen sessions.

For more information, see Chapter 7, "Command Prompts."

Productivity

Productivity

The Productivity folder contains tools that assist you in operating system and business tasks.

For more information, see Chapter 8, "Productivity."

Games

Games

The Games folder contains programs that you can use for entertainment or educational purposes.

For more information, see Chapter 9, "Games."

Chapter 4. System Setup

System
Setup

The System Setup object contains objects that help you customize your system.

To open System Setup:

1. Open **OS/2 System**
2. Open **System Setup**.

or

1. Point to an empty area on the desktop.
2. Click mouse buttons 1 and 2 at the same time.
3. Select **System Setup**.

Color Palette

Color
Palette

The Color Palette is used to customize the colors on your screen. You can change the color of the following parts of the Workplace Shell:

- Desktop
- Titles of the objects on the desktop and in folders
- Different parts of the windows, such as push buttons, scroll bars, and the background.

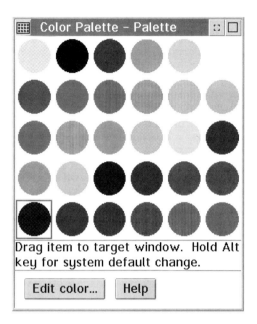

When you open the Color Palette object, the following window appears. It contains 30 primary and secondary color samples.

Changing Screen Colors

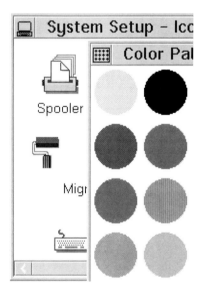

To globally change the color of an item (for example, change the color of the background in every window):

1. Open **OS/2 System**.
2. Open **System Setup**.
3. Open **Color Palette**.
4. Make sure that the item you want to change is visible.
5. Point to a color on the color palette.
6. Press and hold Alt.
7. Press and hold mouse button 2.
8. Drag the color to the item you want to change. The mouse pointer changes to a ⊤ (paint roller).
9. Release mouse button 2.
10. Release Alt. The color of all instances of the item changes to the new color.
11. Point to the title-bar icon.
12. Double-click.

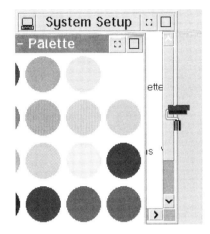

To change the color of a specific item (for example, change the color of the vertical scroll bar in this window only):

1. Open **OS/2 System**.
2. Open **System Setup**.
3. Open **Color Palette**.
4. Make sure that the item you want to change is visible.
5. Point to a color on the color palette.
6. Press and hold mouse button 2.
7. Drag the color to the item you want to change.
8. Release mouse button 2. The color of the item changes to the new color.
9. Point to the title-bar icon.
10. Double-click.

Changing the Color of Object Titles

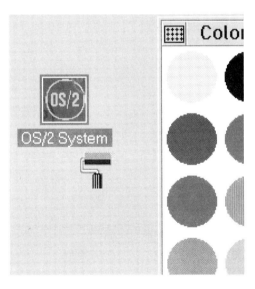

To change the color of the titles of objects:

1. Open **OS/2 System**.
2. Open **System Setup**.
3. Open **Color Palette**.
4. Make sure an object title is visible in the folder. (You cannot change an individual title color. Changing one title color changes every title color in the folder.)
5. Point to a color on the Color Palette.
6. Press and hold Ctrl.
7. Press and hold mouse button 2.
8. Drag the color to a title in the folder.
9. Release mouse button 2.
10. Release Ctrl. The color of every title in the folder changes to the new color.

Changing the Colors on the Color Palette

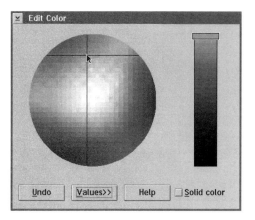

You can change the colors available on the Color Palette:

1. Open **OS/2 System**.
2. Open **System Setup**.
3. Open **Color Palette**.
4. Select the color on the Color Palette that you want to change.
5. Select **Edit color**.

   A window appears in which you can make adjustments to or change the color. For more information about the choices available in this window, select the **Help** push button.
6. When the correct color appears in the box on the color bar in the window, point to the title-bar icon.
7. Double-click. The Color Palette window is displayed with the new color.

Country

Country

When you installed OS/2 2.1, you determined settings like date, time, numbers, and currency of a specific country. The Country settings notebook lets you change these settings.

You can select a specific country and have all the formats changed automatically, or you can make individual format selections.

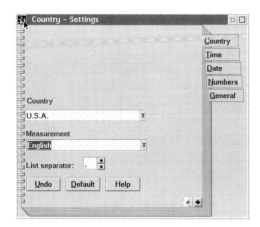

To change country formats:

1. Open **OS/2 System**.
2. Open **System Setup**.
3. Select **Country**.

Tip

Using the Selective Install object in the System Setup folder, you can reconfigure the operating system to support another national language without having to reinstall the entire operating system (see "Selective Install" on page 76).

For country-dependent information, refer to the COUNTRY statement in the online *Command Reference*.

Device Driver Install

Device Driver Install

Many devices that you attach to a computer, such as a CD-ROM drive, mouse, display, and printer come with a *device driver diskette*. The device driver diskette (sometimes called a device support diskette) contains the code needed by the computer to recognize and operate the device.

The Device Driver Install object is used to install any device driver except those for printers and plotters. To install a device driver for a printer or plotter, see "Installing a Printer" on page 164.

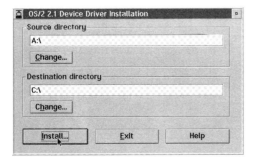

To install a device driver (other than one for a printer or plotter):

1. Open **OS/2 System**.
2. Open **System Setup**.
3. Open **Device Driver Install**.
4. Insert the device driver diskette.
5. Select **Install**.
6. Select the device driver to install from the list.
7. Select **OK**.

For additional information, refer to the documentation that came with the device.

Note: Do not use the Device Driver Install object to install device drivers found on the OS/2 Installation diskettes.

Font Palette

Font Palette

The Font Palette allows you to:

- Change the typeface of any text in the Workplace Shell interface
- Change the sample typefaces currently available on the Font Palette
- Add new fonts to your system
- Delete existing fonts from your system

A *font* is a collection of characters and symbols of a particular size and style used to produce text on displays and printers. When you install the OS/2 2.1 operating system, the IBM Core Fonts are automatically installed, unless you specify otherwise. The IBM Core Fonts can be used by your display and IBM LaserPrinter, HP** LaserJet**, and PostScript** printers.

The IBM Core Fonts consist of a set of 13 Adobe** Type 1 fonts that work with the Adobe Type Manager** (ATM). The following table lists the IBM Core Fonts.

Table 1. IBM Core Fonts	
Family Name	**Typeface**
Times New Roman**	Times New Roman
	Times New Roman Bold
	Times New Roman Bold Italic
	Times New Roman Italic
Helvetica**	Helvetica
	Helvetica Bold
	Helvetica Bold Italic
	Helvetica Italic
Courier	Courier
	Courier Bold
	Courier Bold Italic
	Courier Italic
Symbol Set	Symbol Set

The Adobe Type Manager is an integral part of the OS/2 2.1 operating system and works with existing OS/2 and WIN-OS/2 application programs to produce the sharpest possible fonts on the screen and on the printed page. Because it incorporates PostScript outline font technology, the ATM program eliminates jagged fonts so that your screen can display high-quality typefaces of any size or style. The ATM program also enables even inexpensive printers to print PostScript language fonts that are crisp and smooth.

Note: If you want to use the fonts for both OS/2 and WIN-OS/2 applications, you must install the font files using both the Font Palette and the ATM Control Panel.

Changing Fonts

The Font Palette window displays sample typefaces of eight of the fonts installed on your system. You can use these samples to change any text in the Workplace Shell interface.

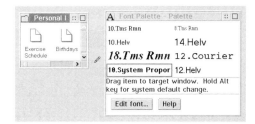

To change the typeface of text:

1. Open **OS/2 System**.
2. Open **System Setup**.
3. Open **Font Palette**.
4. Point to the sample typeface you want to use.
5. Press and hold mouse button 2. The mouse pointer changes to a 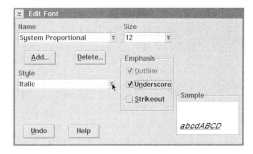 (pencil).
6. Drag the sample typeface to the object whose text font you want to change.

   If you drag a sample typeface to an object on the desktop, the text of all the objects on the desktop changes to that typeface. If you drag a sample typeface to an open object, such as a folder, the typeface will change only for the objects within the folder.
7. Release mouse button 2.

Selecting Sample Typefaces for the Font Palette

To change which sample typefaces appear on the Font Palette:

1. Open **OS/2 System**.
2. Open **System Setup**.
3. Open **Font Palette**.
4. Select the sample typeface you want to change.
5. Select **Edit font**. The Edit Font window appears.
6. Select the down arrow for the **Name** field.
7. Select a new typeface from the list.
8. Select the **Style** and **Size** if desired.
9. Select the appropriate **Emphasis** if desired.
10. Point to the title-bar icon.
11. Double-click.

Adding Fonts to Your System

There are thousands of additional font styles in the Adobe Type 1 font-file format that are available for use with the OS/2 operating system. These fonts require two files for each typeface. These files have an AFM and PFB file-name extension. The Font Palette converts the AFM file to an OFM file when it installs the new font.

Note: If the set of fonts you want to install is supplied on multiple diskettes, you might need to copy the files into a temporary directory, because the font installation process requires that both files for a given typeface be available at the same time.

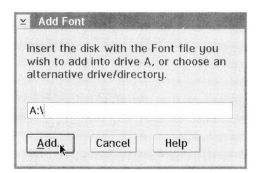

To add more fonts to your system:

1. Open **OS/2 System**.
2. Open **System Setup**.
3. Open **Font Palette**.
4. Select **Edit font**. The Edit Font window appears.
5. Select **Add**.
6. Follow the instructions on the Add Font window; then select **Add**.
7. Select the names of the font files that you want to install on your system.
8. Select **Add**.
9. Point to the title-bar icon.
10. Double-click.

See "Selecting Sample Typefaces for the Font Palette" on page 66 if you want to add one of the new typefaces to the Font Palette samples.

Removing Fonts from Your System

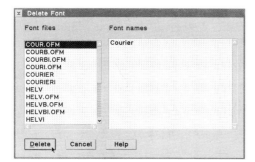

To remove a font from your system:

1. Open **OS/2 System**.
2. Open **System Setup**.
3. Open **Font Palette**.
4. Select **Edit font**. The Edit Font window appears.
5. Select **Delete**.
6. Select the names of the font files that you want to delete from your system.
7. Select **Delete**.
8. When the files have been deleted, point to the title-bar icon.
9. Double-click.

Note: Removing a font deletes the corresponding files from your hard disk unless they are needed by the WIN-OS/2 Adobe Type Manager. For more information about the WIN-OS/2 Adobe Type Manager, see Chapter 19, "Adobe Type Manager for WIN-OS/2" on page 211.

Keyboard

Keyboard

The Keyboard object is used to adjust the blink rate of the cursor, change the speed at which a key repeats when held down, and customize the keyboard to make it easier to use for those with special needs.

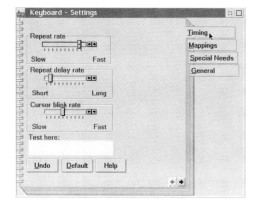

To customize the keyboard:

1. Open **OS/2 System**.
2. Open **System Setup**.
3. Open **Keyboard**.
4. Select the tab for the setting you want to change.
5. Point to the title-bar icon.
6. Double-click.

Select the **Special Needs** tab to change the settings to meet your special requirements. For example, you can make keys "sticky" so that you can press and release a series of keys (for example, Ctrl+Alt+Del) sequentially but have the keys operate as if the keys were pressed and released at the same time.

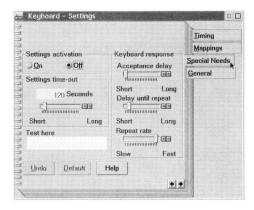

To enable sticky keys:

1. Open **OS/2 System**.
2. Open **System Setup**.
3. Open **Keyboard**.
4. Select **Special Needs**.
5. Select the Settings activation **On** radio button.
6. For each key you want to act as a sticky key, press Shift three times; then press the key you want to stay stuck down.
7. Repeat the previous step for each key that you want to operate as a sticky key.
8. Point to the title-bar icon.
9. Double-click.

To deactivate sticky keys, press and release each sticky key once.

Migrate Applications

Migrate
Applications

Some programs do not place a program object in a folder or on the desktop during their installation. Without the object, you cannot use the Workplace shell to start the program. To correct this situation, you can run the Migrate Applications program. The Migrate Applications program uses a database to identify possible programs, set the correct DOS settings, and select an appropriate program object for the migrated OS/2, DOS, and Windows programs.

You can create your own migration database to be used with the Migrate Applications program. For more information, see the *OS/2 Installation Guide*.

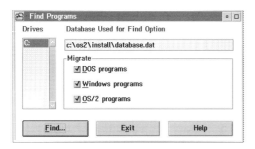

To migrate applications:

1. Open **OS/2 System**.
2. Open **System Setup**.
3. Open **Migrate Applications**.

   The Find Programs window appears.
4. From the **Drives** field, deselect (click on again) the drives you do not want to search.
5. Deselect the types of programs you do not want to migrate in the **Migrate** field. The default is to migrate all the listed programs.
6. Select **Find**. The Migrate Programs window appears. Programs are listed in the Applications list.

If your programs are not listed, see the note below.

7. Select **Migrate** to migrate all the selected programs. When migration is complete, the Find Programs window appears.
8. Select **Exit**.

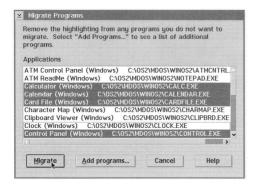

Note: If your programs are not in the list:

1. Select **Add Programs**. The Add Programs window appears and programs are listed in the **Available Programs** field.
2. Select a program. The **Working directory** and **Program title** fields are filled in. You can type a new title if you want.
3. Type the appropriate parameters in the **Parameters** field. (Refer to the instructions that came with your program.)
4. Select **Add**. The program moves to the Selected Programs field.
5. Select **OK**. The Migrate Programs window appears.

The Migrate Applications program creates a DOS Programs folder, a Windows Programs folder, and a WIN-OS/2 Groups folder. The programs in these folders have preselected settings that work best for the performance of your programs.

If you use the **Add Programs** push button, the Migrate Applications program creates the Additional DOS Programs folder and the Additional Windows Programs folder. It also creates the Additional OS/2 Programs folder, if you select **OS/2 programs**. The programs in these folders have default settings. If these programs do not run correctly, you can specify other settings. Refer to "DOS and WIN-OS/2 settings" in the Master Help Index.

Some Windows groups contain DOS programs. After migration, these DOS program objects are placed in the WIN-OS/2 Groups folder and also in a DOS folder if you migrated DOS programs.

Instead of using the default database, DATABASE.DAT, you can create your own database. See the *OS/2 Installation Guide* for more information.

Tip

If your computer had a previous version of the OS/2 operating system, you might see a folder on your desktop with the same name as one of your old *groups*. This folder contains program objects that represent your old programs; however, the Migrate Applications program also puts these programs and program objects in new folders (DOS Programs or Windows Programs folders).

Use the program objects in these new folders rather than the old *group name* folders because the preselected settings will work best for the performance of your program.

Mouse

Mouse

The Mouse object is used to change the behavior of your mouse. You can:

- Control the speed of the mouse pointer
- Change the mouse for left-hand use
- Customize the Alt, Shift, and Ctrl key combinations

Note: You can change the speed of your mouse for your WIN-OS/2 sessions using the WIN-OS/2 Control Panel.

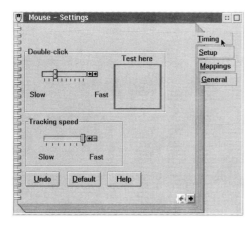

To change the mouse settings:

1. Open **OS/2 System**.
2. Open **System Setup**.
3. Open **Mouse**.

Use the Timings page to change the speed at which actions occur when you use the mouse. Use the Setup page to customize the mouse for left-hand use or right-hand use. If you change the setting, the button settings on the Mappings page are automatically updated; however, you also can use the Mappings page to customize them individually.

Tip

Using the Selective Install object in the System Setup folder, you can reconfigure the operating system to support another pointing device without having to reinstall the entire operating system (see "Selective Install" on page 76).

Scheme Palette

Scheme
Palette

The Scheme Palette contains ten predefined color schemes. Each scheme has a preset color for the following:

- Desktop
- Titles of the objects on the desktop and in folders
- Different parts of the windows such as push buttons, scroll bars, and the background.

You can use these schemes as they are, or you can change their colors. In addition, you can also use the Scheme Palette to change the width of the borders around the windows, and the font used.

Changing Color Schemes

To use a predefined scheme to change the colors of one folder or window:

1. Open **OS/2 System**.
2. Open **System Setup**.
3. Open **Scheme Palette**.
4. Make sure that the folder or window you want to change is visible.
5. Point to a scheme on the palette.
6. Press and hold mouse button 2.
7. Drag the color scheme to the window.
8. Release mouse button 2. The window colors change to the new scheme.

Globally Changing Color Schemes

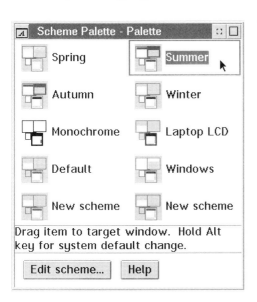

To use one of the predefined schemes to change the colors of all the folders and objects:

1. Open **OS/2 System**.
2. Open **System Setup**.
3. Open **Scheme Palette**.
4. Point to a scheme on the palette.
5. Press and hold Alt.
6. Press and hold mouse button 2.
7. Drag the color scheme to the desktop.
8. Release mouse button 2.
9. Release Alt. The colors change to the new scheme.

Changing the Colors on the Scheme Palette

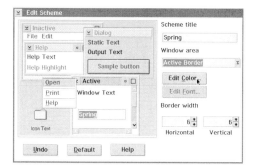

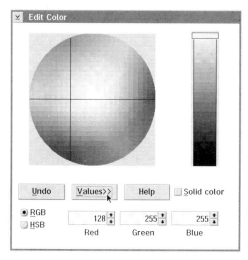

To change the colors within a scheme on the Scheme Palette:

1. Open **OS/2 System**.
2. Open **System Setup**.
3. Open **Scheme Palette**.
4. Select the scheme on the Scheme Palette that you want to change.
5. Select **Edit Scheme**.
6. Select the part of the window (in the **Window area** field) whose color you want to change.
7. Select **Edit Color**. A window appears in which you can make adjustments to or change the color. (For more information about the choices available in this window, select the **Help** push button.)
8. Adjust the color until the correct color appears in the box on the color bar in the window.
9. Point to the title-bar icon.
10. Double-click. The selected window part changes to the new color on the Scheme Palette.
11. When all the color changes have been made, point to the title-bar icon.
12. Double-click.

Tip

You can point to an area on the sample palette and click mouse button 2 to select the part of the window to be changed, instead of using the **Window area** field to select it. This reduces the amount of scrolling needed to find the correct window part.

Changing the Fonts in a Scheme

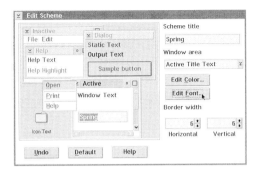

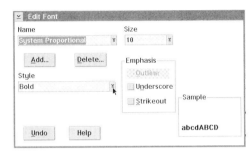

To change the font of text within the scheme:

1. Open **OS/2 System**.
2. Open **System Setup**.
3. Open **Scheme Palette**.
4. Select the scheme on the Scheme Palette that you want to change.
5. Select **Edit Scheme**.
6. Select the part of the window (in the **Window area** field) whose font you want to change.
7. Select **Edit Font**.
8. Select the name, style, size, and emphasis that you want to use.
9. Point to the title-bar icon.
10. Double-click. The font of the selected window part changes on the Scheme Palette.

For more information about fonts, see "Font Palette" on page 64.

Tip

To display a colorful picture (bit map) on the background of your folder windows or the Desktop folder:

1. Display the pop-up menu for a folder.
2. Select the arrow to the right of **Open**.
3. Select **Settings**.
4. Select the **Background** tab.
5. Select the **Image** radio button in the **Background type** field.
6. Select the arrow to the right of the **Image File** field.
7. Select a file with a .BMP file-name extension.

The image appears in the background of your folder.

Selective Install

Selective
Install

The Selective Install object is used to add features that you did not include when you originally installed the operating system. You also can use the Selective Install object to change the mouse, display adapter, or country information for your system.

Note: You will need the OS/2 2.1 installation diskettes for each of the following procedures.

Adding Options after Installation

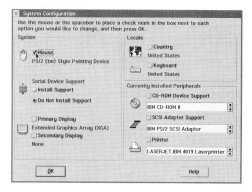

To add options after installation:

1. Open **OS/2 System**.
2. Open **System Setup**.
3. Open **Selective Install**.
4. Select from the System Configuration window any of the choices that you want to change or add.
5. Select **OK**.
6. Place a check mark to the left of any feature you want to add. (For more information about a feature, press F1.) If a **More** push button is displayed to the right of a feature, select it to see additional choices.

Adding Online Documentation after Installation

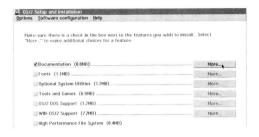

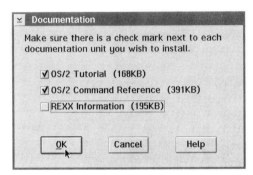

To add online documentation after installation:

1. Open **OS/2 System**.
2. Open **System Setup**.
3. Open **Selective Install**.
4. Select **OK** when the System Configuration window is displayed.
5. Select the check box to the left of **Documentation**.
6. Select **More** to the right of **Documentation**.
7. Select the check box to the left of any documentation units to deselect the ones you do not want to add.
8. Select **OK**.
9. Select **Install**.
10. Follow the instructions on the screen.

Changing Display Adapter Support

Adding or changing display adapter support is done automatically by the OS/2 Installation program.

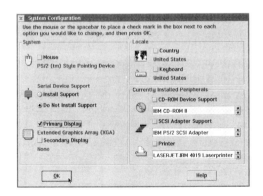

To change the display adapter support after installation:

1. Open **OS/2 System**.
2. Open **System Setup**.
3. Open **Selective Install**.
4. Select **Primary Display** or **Secondary Display** from the System Configuration window.
5. Select **OK**.
6. Select the display adapter that you want from the list provided.
7. Select **OK**.
8. Follow the instructions on the screen.

Sound

Sound

The Sound object is used by an application to generate a Warning Beep. The beep can be turned off.

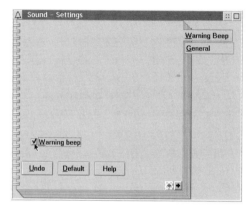

You can indicate whether a beep should be heard when a warning message is displayed or an invalid key is pressed. To customize the sound settings:

1. Open **OS/2 System**.
2. Open **System Setup**.
3. Open **Sound**.

Note: If you install Multimedia Presentation Manager/2 (MMPM/2), additional sound options are available. For more information, see Chapter 22, "Multimedia Applications" on page 231.

Spooler

Spooler

The Spooler stores jobs that are waiting for an available printer or port. OS/2 2.1 includes a spooler for printouts you request in OS/2, DOS, and WIN-OS/2 *sessions* (an instance of a command prompt or started program). When you print, the system creates a spool file which is held in place in the SPOOL directory. The SPOOL directory is created by the system during installation. You can use the Spooler object to change the location of the spooler path and to disable or enable the spooler.

Enabling and Disabling the Spooler

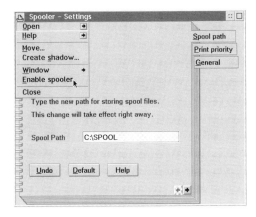

To enable the spooler:

1. Open **OS/2 System**.
2. Open **System Setup**.
3. Open **Spooler**.
4. Point to the title-bar icon.
5. Click mouse button 2.
6. Select **Enable spooler** If the
   . (If **Disable spooler** choice is
   indicated, it means that the spooler is
   already enabled.)
7. Point to the title-bar icon.
8. Double-click.

Spooling takes effect immediately. You
do not need to restart your system.

Changing the Spooler Path

Use this procedure if you print often, or if you print large jobs and need a separate
storage area, such as a large disk, for spool files. Be sure to wait until all your jobs
finish printing, or delete any pending jobs.

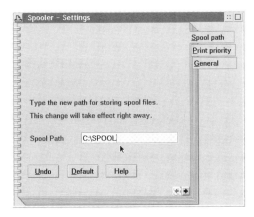

To change the spooler path:

1. Select all the printer objects.
2. Select **Hold** from the pop-up menu of
   each printer object.
3. Open **OS/2 System**.
4. Open **System Setup**.
5. Open **Spooler**. By default, the
   Spooler Settings notebook appears.
6. Select **Spool path**.
7. In the **Spool path** field, type the new
   path.
8. Point to the title-bar icon.
9. Double-click.

Changing the Print Priority

You can set the print priority higher or lower to adjust the speed at which spooled print jobs are printed.

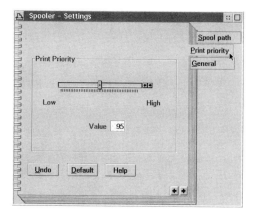

To set the print priority:

1. Open **OS/2 System**.
2. Open **System Setup**.
3. Open **Spooler**. By default, the Spooler Settings notebook appears.
4. Select the **Print priority** page.
5. Move the **slider arm** to select priority.
6. Point to the title-bar icon.
7. Double-click.

Disabling the Spooler

You might want to disable the spooler to print jobs that have a high-security risk. Disabling the spooler prevents others from viewing your print jobs in a printer-object window. However, you cannot disable spooling to a network printer on a network server.

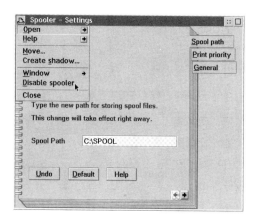

To disable the spooler:

1. Open **OS/2 System**.
2. Open **System Setup**.
3. Open **Spooler**.
4. Point to the title-bar icon.
5. Click mouse button 2.
6. Select **Disable spooler**. (If the **Enable spooler** choice is indicated, it means that the spooler is already disabled.)
7. Restart your system.

When the Spooler is disabled, your print jobs go directly to a printer. However, a printout might contain material from different jobs mixed together.

System

System

The System object is used to change system defaults. You can select how you want a window that is already open to be displayed and where you want windows that you have minimized to be displayed. This notebook is also used to specify that a confirmation message should display and to turn off the product information window.

Confirming Delete Actions

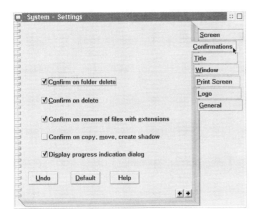

To specify if you want a confirmation message displayed each time you delete an object or a folder:

1. Open **OS/2 System**.
2. Open **System Setup**.
3. Open **System**.
4. Select the **Confirmations** tab.
5. Place a check mark next to each item you want a confirmation message for.
6. Point to the title-bar icon.
7. Double-click.

Resolving Title Conflicts

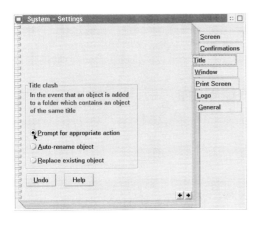

To specify how the system is to respond to title conflicts if you create, copy, or move an object into a folder that already has an object with the same name:

1. Open **OS/2 System**.
2. Open **System Setup**.
3. Open **System**.
4. Select the **Title** tab.
5. Select the choice that best describe how you want the system to respond when a title conflict appears.
6. Point to the title-bar icon.
7. Double-click.

Changing System Defaults

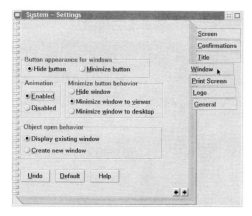

To change the system defaults for a window:

1. Open **OS/2 System**.
2. Open **System Setup**.
3. Open **System**.
4. Select the **Window** tab.
5. Select the choices that best describe how you want the windows to behave.
6. Point to the title-bar icon.
7. Double-click.

Printing a Screen

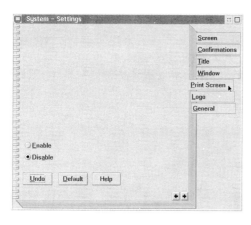

To be able to print the information in an open window:

1. Open **OS/2 System**.
2. Open **System Setup**.
3. Open **System**.
4. Select the **Print Screen** tab.
5. Select **Enable**.
6. Point to the title-bar icon.
7. Double-click.

To print the open window:

1. Select the open window.
2. Press **Print Screen**.

Displaying Logos

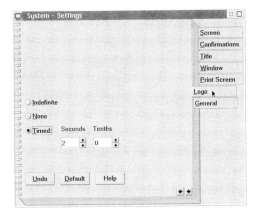

To specify if you want a logo to be displayed and how long to display it:

1. Open **OS/2 System**.
2. Open **System Setup**.
3. Open **System**.
4. Select the **Logo** tab.
5. Select the choices that best describes how you want the system to handle product information and logos.
6. Point to the title-bar icon.
7. Double-click.

Changing Screen Resolution

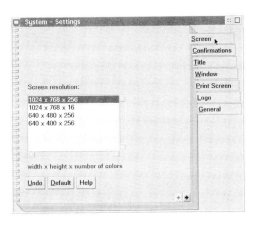

To change the screen resolution for an XGA* display adapter.

1. Open **OS/2 System**.
2. Open **System Setup**.
3. Open **System**.
4. Select the **Screen** tab.
5. Select the resolution you want to use.
6. Point to the title-bar icon.
7. Double-click.

Note: The **Screen** tab appears on the System Settings notebook only if you have an XGA display adapter.

For more information on XGA display adapters, see "XGA Systems" on page 340.

Tip

After changing screen resolutions from a higher resolution to a lower resolution, some applications might open windows that are partially off the screen. If this occurs:

1. Press Alt+Spacebar.
2. Select **Move**.
3. Use the mouse or the arrow keys to move the window.
4. Click mouse button 1 or press Enter.

Or

1. Point to an empty area on the desktop.
2. Click mouse buttons 1 and 2 at the same time.
3. Point to the name of the program.
4. Click mouse button 2.
5. Select **Tile** or **Cascade**. The window will now appear on the screen.

System Clock

System
Clock

The System Clock object is used to set the system date and time or to set an alarm. You can display the clock in either analog or digital mode.

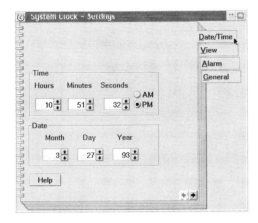

To set the system clock:

1. Open **OS/2 System**.
2. Open **System Setup**.
3. Select **System Clock**.
4. Display the pop-up menu for System Clock.
5. Select the arrow to the right of **Open**.
6. Select **Settings**.
7. Select the tab for the setting you want to change.
8. Select **View**; change to the View page if necessary. (To view a different View page, use an arrow at the lower-right corner of the window.)
9. Point to the title-bar icon.
10. Double-click.

WIN-OS/2 Setup

WIN-OS/2
Setup

The WIN-OS/2 Setup object is used to select a public or private *clipboard* or *dynamic data exchange* (DDE). The clipboard and DDE are features that allow data exchange between programs. You also can use this object to preselect WIN-OS/2 settings for *all* Windows programs before you start them. If you change a setting, the change affects only subsequent Windows programs that are started. Programs that are currently running are not affected.

If you are using Windows programs that can share information using the clipboard or Dynamic Data Exchange (DDE) feature, then you can change the way these features work in all WIN-OS/2 sessions.

Note: Be sure you check with the instructions that came with your program to determine if these features are supported.

The clipboard is an area that temporarily holds data. Data is placed in the clipboard by selecting **cut** or **copy** from a menu. You can *cut* (move) or *copy* data from one document and *paste* it into another document, even if the other document is in a different program. For example, you can place a spreadsheet from one program into a document from another program.

The DDE feature enables the exchange of data between programs. Any change made to information in one file is applied to the same information in an associated file. In the example above, if changes are made to the original spreadsheet, corresponding changes are made to the spreadsheet in the document. If changes are made to the spreadsheet in the document, corresponding changes are made to the original spreadsheet.

The clipboard and DDE can be set to *Public* or *Private*. When DDE is set to Public, information can be shared with OS/2 and WIN-OS/2 sessions. Information cannot be shared with DOS sessions. When the clipboard or DDE is set to Private, sharing data between sessions is restricted. This means that only information for those programs running in that single session can be shared. When OS/2 is installed, the clipboard and DDE are set to Public.

Windows programs that have the clipboard or DDE feature are set up during installation of the OS/2 operating system to use a Public setting for all WIN-OS/2 sessions. You can use the WIN-OS/2 Setup object to set these features to private. You can further customize the way you use these features by using the Settings notebook of the program object (see "Program Object Settings" on page 185).

Note: Changing the clipboard and DDE features to Private will not affect the performance of your Windows programs.

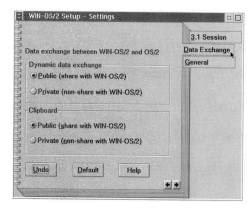

To change the clipboard or DDE feature to Private:

1. Open **OS/2 System**.
2. Open **System Setup**.
3. Open **WIN-OS/2 Setup**.
4. Select **Data Exchange**.
5. Select **Private** for **Dynamic Data Exchange** or **Clipboard**.
6. Point to the title-bar icon.
7. Double-click.

Note: If you change the settings for the clipboard or DDE while a program is running in a WIN-OS/2 session, the settings for the program will take effect immediately.

For related information about the clipboard, DDE, WIN-OS/2, and Windows Programs, see Chapter 18, "Using Windows Programs" on page 193.

Power

The Power object manages and tracks power consumption in battery-powered computers that support the APM standard. The APM standard defines the way the hardware and software work together to reduce power consumption and help extend battery life.

If your computer supports the APM standard, the Power object might be automatically installed during the OS/2 2.1 installation process. If it was not installed, you can install it by using Selective Install and selecting **Advanced Power Management**. For information about Selective Install, see "Selective Install" on page 76.

To open the Power object:

1. Open **OS/2 System**.
2. Open **System Setup**.
3. Open **Power**.

Chapter 5. Startup

Startup

The Startup folder contains objects that you want to automatically start every time the system starts.

This chapter describes how to use the Startup folder to start objects. It also describes how to customize your system startup by placing variables in your CONFIG.SYS file.

Starting Programs Automatically

You can start programs automatically at system startup using a Startup folder, a STARTUP.CMD file, or both.

Startup Folder

You can place objects of frequently used programs and batch files in a Startup folder so that every time you start your computer, the programs and batch files will start. The objects in the Startup folder are started when the Desktop folder is opened at system startup. You cannot specify the order in which the objects in the folder are started.

You should place a shadow of the program objects in the Startup folder instead of the original object. This ensures that any changes made to the original object are applied to the object in the Startup folder.

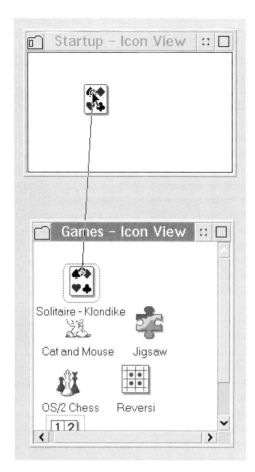

To create a shadow of an object and place it in the Startup folder:

1. Point to the object.
2. Press and hold Ctrl+Shift.
3. Press and hold mouse button 2.
4. Drag the object to the Startup folder.
5. Release mouse button 2.
6. Release the Ctrl and Shift keys.

STARTUP.CMD File

A STARTUP.CMD file is similar to the Startup folder in that it is used to automatically start programs and batch files at system startup. If a STARTUP.CMD file is present, it will be run prior to the starting of the desktop. For more information about creating and running a STARTUP.CMD file, refer to the online *Command Reference*.

Preventing Automatic Startup

Programs located in the Startup folder or programs running at the time the computer was shut down will automatically start when the computer is restarted. To prevent these programs from starting:

1. Press Ctrl+Alt+Del to restart the computer.
2. When you see the desktop animation (similar to an exploding box), press and hold Ctrl+Shift+F1.
3. Hold the keys for approximately 15 seconds, or until the desktop appears. (If the hard disk light stops flashing during this time, your computer might be suspended. Release the keys quickly, and then resume holding the keys until the desktop objects appear.)

Customizing Your CONFIG.SYS for Startup

You can customize the way your Workplace Shell starts by changing the system variables at either a command prompt or in the CONFIG.SYS file. Precede each of the variables with the SET command.

The system variables for the Workplace Shell are:

AUTOSTART   Determines the parts of the Workplace Shell that are automatically started. Eliminating any of the options from the statement restricts the user from accessing portions of the shell.

Example:

`SET AUTOSTART=FOLDERS, PROGRAMS, TASKLIST, CONNECTIONS`

FOLDERS Allows a user to open additional folders after startup.

PROGRAMS Allows a user to open additional programs after startup.

TASKLIST Allows a user to open the Window List.

CONNECTIONS Recreates the network connections established during the last log on.

OS2_SHELL   Sets the command processor for OS/2 sessions.

Example:

`SET OS2_SHELL=C:\OS2\CMD.EXE`

RESTARTOBJECTS   Sets the objects that will be automatically started by the Workplace Shell.

Example:

```
SET RESTARTOBJECTS=STARTUPFOLDERSONLY
```

YES   Starts all the objects that were running at the time of shutdown and all objects in the Startup folder. This is the default.

NO   Does not start any of the applications that were running at the time of shutdown and does not start the objects in the Startup folder.

STARTUPFOLDERSONLY   Starts only those objects in the Startup folder.

REBOOTONLY   Starts objects only when the Workplace Shell is started by pressing Ctrl+Alt+Del or turning on the computer.

RUNWORKPLACE   Sets the interface that is started by the OS/2 operating system. PMSHELL.EXE is the program for the Workplace Shell interface.

Example:

```
SET RUNWORKPLACE=C:\OS2\PMSHELL.EXE
```

SYSTEM_INI   Determines the INI file to be used by the Workplace Shell for system information about such items as default colors and printer drivers.

Example:

```
SET SYSTEM_INI=C:\OS2\OS2SYS.INI
```

USER_INI   Determines the INI file to be used by the Workplace Shell for system information about such items as program defaults, display options, and file options.

Example:

```
SET USER_INI=C:\OS2\OS2.INI
```

For more information about customizing the user interface, refer to the online *Command Reference.*

The DISKCACHE statement in the CONFIG.SYS file is set up so that it automatically runs the CHKDSK program upon startup if the system shuts down improperly. The CHKDSK program analyzes and fixes disk problems caused by the improper shutdown.

If you add hard disk drives or partitions after the installation of the OS/2 operating system, you should edit the CONFIG.SYS file and update the x parameter to reflect the new additions.

DISKCACHE

> **AC:** Starts the auto-check feature on the specified drives when the system shuts down improperly.
>
> x Represents the letters of the disks or partitions on the system that you want to check. Substitute the correct drive letters for this parameter.

Example:

If you want to check disks C and D, and your existing DISKCACHE statement is:

```
DISKCACHE=64,LW
```

change it to read

```
DISKCACHE=64,LW,AC:CD
```

For more information about the DISKCACHE statement, refer to the online *Command Reference*.

Chapter 6. Drives

Drives

This chapter describes how to use the Drives folder to access and use the different types of storage media installed in your computer.

When opened, the Drives folder provides a view of all drive objects in the system. For example, the following drive types could be accessed from the Drives folder:

- Diskette
- Hard disk
- CD-ROM
- Tape backup
- Optical disc

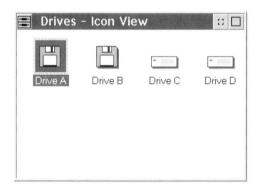

To view the Drive objects:

1. Open **OS/2 System**.
2. Open **Drives**.

About Hard Disks and Diskettes

There are two kinds of disks:

Hard disk A non-removable disk that is built into a hard-disk drive. Hard disks come in a variety of *capacities*, and can hold large amounts of information. Capacity is the maximum amount of information that a diskette or disk can hold. Information can be stored on and erased from the disk over and over again. The computer can write to and read information from the hard disk much faster than it can from a diskette.

Diskette A removable disk that can be inserted in and removed from a diskette drive. Diskettes come in a variety of capacities. Diskettes cannot hold as much information as a hard disk. Information can be stored on and erased from the diskette over and over again. The computer cannot write to or read information from a diskette as fast as it can from a hard disk. There are two sizes of diskettes:

- 5.25-inch diskettes are thin, flexible, and somewhat fragile. A 5.25-inch diskette has a write-protect notch located on the right side. You can place a write-protect tab over the notch to protect the information stored on the diskette.

  To store information on or erase information from the diskette, you must remove the write-protect tab from the diskette.
- 3.5-inch diskettes are protected by a hard plastic cover that makes them more durable. A 3.5-inch diskette can be write protected by sliding a built-in tab to reveal the write-protect opening.

  To store information on or erase information from the diskette, you must slide the tab over the write-protect opening on the diskette.

Note: If a diskette does not have a write-protect notch or tab, the diskette is permanently write protected. Many software manufacturers use permanently write-protected diskettes to prevent the information on the diskettes from being accidentally changed or deleted.

The capacity of a diskette and a hard disk is measured in bytes. A diskette must be formatted at a capacity less than or equal to the capacity of the diskette drive in order for the diskette and the drive to be compatible. So even though a diskette is the correct size physically, its capacity might not be compatible with the diskette drive in the computer.

For example, a 3.5-inch diskette drive designed to work with 2.88MB diskettes can use 1.44MB diskettes, but a 1.44MB diskette drive cannot use a 2.88MB diskette. The following terms are used to describe the capacity of disks and the size of files:

Byte   Amount of space it takes to store a character.

Kilobyte   1024 bytes and is abbreviated as KB.

Megabyte   1024KB (approximately a million bytes) and is abbreviated as MB.

Gigabyte   1024MB (approximately a billion bytes) and is abbreviated as GB.

The following terms are equivalent:

```
1MB = 1024KB = 1048576 bytes
```

Each diskette drive and hard disk drive in a computer has a letter assigned to it. This letter is the name that both you and the computer use to identify the drive. For example, on many computers the diskette drive is called drive A and the hard disk drive is called drive C.

Accessing Hard Disks and Diskettes

You can use the Drives folder to access the information on your hard disk and diskette drives. This allows you to view disk information, display the files on the disks, and copy and move files. The files can be viewed as objects so they can easily be copied and moved with the mouse.

> **Tip**
>
> For specific instructions on using the Drive A object, see Chapter 12, "Drive A" on page 139.

Viewing Disk Information

To view the size of a disk:

1. Open **OS/2 System**.
2. Open **Drives**.
3. Open the drive object you want information about.

Displaying Objects

The drive objects are used to display the contents of the drives on your computer. The contents of the drive can be displayed in three different views:

Icon view   Displays the contents of the disk as icons. This is the default if the disk does not have folders (directories).

Tree view   Displays the contents of the disk in a tree. This is the default if the disk has folders (directories). A plus (+) sign to the left of a folder indicates that additional folders exist inside the folder. By selecting the plus (+) sign, you can see the other folders in the folder. Pointing to a folder and double-clicking displays the contents of the folder in an icon view.

Details view   Displays the contents of the disk in a table with the following additional information:

- Icon
- Title
- Real name
- Size
- Last write date and time
- Last access date and time
- Creation date and time
- Flags

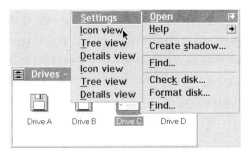

To display the contents of a drive as icons:

1. Open **OS/2 System**.
2. Open **Drives**.
3. Point to the object that you want to display.
4. Click mouse button 2.
5. Select the arrow to the right of **Open**.
6. Select **Icon view**.

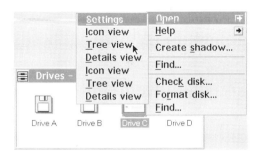

To display the contents of a drive in a tree view:

1. Open **OS/2 System**.
2. Open **Drives**.
3. Point to the object that you want to display.
4. Click mouse button 2.
5. Select the arrow to the right of **Open**.
6. Select **Tree view**.
7. If a plus (+) sign appears to the left of a folder, select it to expand the contents.
8. To display the contents of a folder, point to the folder; then double-click.

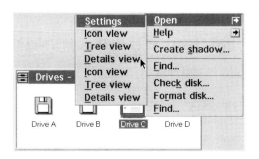

To display details about the contents of a drive:

1. Open **OS/2 System**.
2. Open **Drives**.
3. Point to the object that you want to display.
4. Click mouse button 2.
5. Select the arrow to the right of **Open**.
6. Select **Details view**.
7. Select the scroll bars at the bottom and side of the window to scroll the information.

Copying Objects

Note: If you want to copy the object to a folder object or another drive object, the target object must be visible before you start the copy.

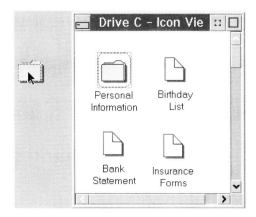

To copy an object from a drive to another location:

1. Open the drive containing the object you want to copy.
2. Press and hold Ctrl.
3. Point to the object you want to copy.
4. Press and hold mouse button 2.
5. Drag the object to a folder, the desktop, or another drive object.
6. Release mouse button 2.
7. Release Ctrl.

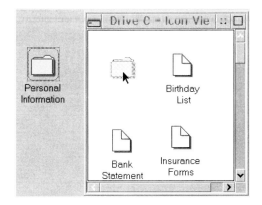

To copy an object from another location to a drive:

1. Point to the object you want to copy.
2. Press and hold Ctrl.
3. Press and hold mouse button 2.
4. Drag the object to the drive object.
5. Release mouse button 2.
6. Release Ctrl.

Moving Objects

There are times when you need to *move* an object (copy the object to a different location and delete it from the original location).

Note: If you want to move the object to a folder object or another drive object, the target object must be visible before you start the move.

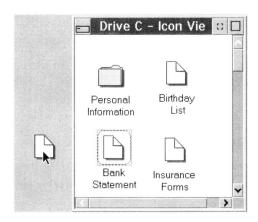

To move an object from a drive to another location:

1. Open the drive containing the object you want to move.
2. Press and hold Shift.
3. Point to the object you want to move.
4. Press and hold mouse button 2.
5. Drag the object to a folder, the desktop, or another drive object.
6. Release mouse button 2.
7. Release Shift.

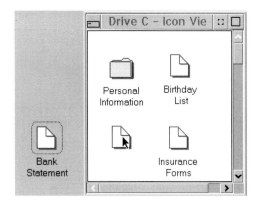

To move an object from another location to a drive:

1. Point to the object you want to move.
2. Press and hold Shift.
3. Press and hold mouse button 2.
4. Drag the mouse to the drive object.
5. Release mouse button 2.
6. Release Shift.

Deleting Objects from a Drive

You can *delete* (erase) unwanted objects from a drive.

To delete an object from a drive:

1. Open the drive.
2. Point to the object you want to delete.
3. Press and hold mouse button 2.
4. Drag the object to the **Shredder**.
5. Release mouse button 2.

Formatting a Disk

You can *format* a disk. When a disk is formatted, it is checked for defects and prepared to accept data. During this process, all existing data is erased from the disk.

Note: Before you format a disk, make sure that it does not contain any information that is important.

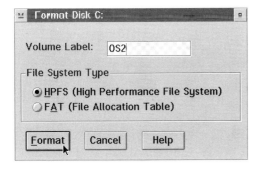

To format a disk:

1. Point to the disk you want to format.
2. Click mouse button 2.
3. Select **Format disk**.
4. When the Format Disk window appears, type a Volume Label (name for the disk).
5. Select the type of file system (FAT or HPFS) you want to use on the disk. (For more information about these file systems, see Appendix D, "The OS/2 File Systems" on page 437).
6. Select **Format**.
7. When the format is complete, select **OK**.

Checking a Disk

You can check a disk for:

Defects
Errors in the file allocation table or directory on the disk. If you select **Write corrections to disk**, any problems found will be fixed.

Current Usage
The amount of the disk being used for directories, user files, and extended attributes. It also shows the amount of space that is reserved on the disk.

File system type
Type of file system on the disk. (All diskettes are formatted for the FAT file system.)

Total disk space
The capacity of the disk in bytes.

Total amount of disk space available
The amount of free space left on the disk.

Note: You cannot check a disk that is currently being used or is locked by another process (for example, the disk that OS/2 2.1 is running on).

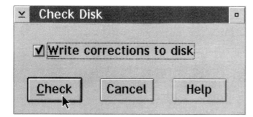

To check a disk:

1. Point to the drive that you want to check.
2. Click mouse button 2.
3. Select **Check disk**.
4. Select **Write corrections to disk**.
5. Select **Check**.
6. When the check is done, the Check Disk - Results window is displayed. Select **Cancel** to remove the window.

Chapter 7. Command Prompts

Command
Prompts

The Command Prompts folder contains objects that open DOS, OS/2, and WIN-OS/2 *sessions*. A session is one instance of a command prompt or started program. Each session is separate from all other sessions that might be running on the computer.

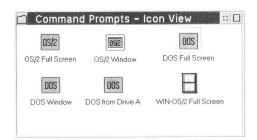

To open the Command Prompts object:

1. Open **OS/2 System**.
2. Open **Command Prompts**.

OS/2 Command Prompts

OS/2 Full
Screen

OS/2
Window

The OS/2 Full-Screen and OS/2 Window objects are used to access an OS/2 command prompt. At these command prompts, you can start programs and enter OS/2 commands. For a description of OS/2 commands that can be used at these prompts, see the OS/2 *Command Reference* in the Information folder.

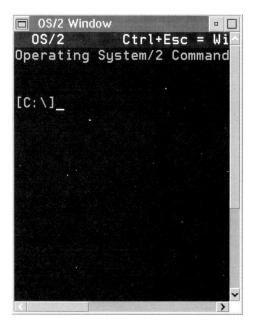

To start an OS/2 command prompt session:

1. Open **OS/2 System**.
2. Open **Command Prompts**.
3. Open **OS/2 Full Screen**, **OS/2 Window**, or both.

When you close a session, the session and its related windows are automatically closed. Make sure that you save all important data in the session before you close it.

To close an OS/2 command prompt session:

1. Type **Exit**.
2. Press Enter.

You can *switch* (temporarily leave without closing) from an OS/2 command prompt session to another running program. When you switch sessions, your command prompt session is saved and then restored when you switch back.

To temporarily leave an OS/2 command prompt session:

1. Press Ctrl+Esc.
2. Point to a title on the Window List.
3. Double-click.

Or:

1. Press Alt+Esc to switch to another open object.

DOS Full
Screen

DOS
Window

The DOS Full-Screen and DOS Window objects are used to access a DOS command prompt. At these command prompts, you can start programs and enter DOS commands. For a description of DOS commands that can be used at these prompts, see the OS/2 *Command Reference* in the Information folder.

To start a DOS command prompt session:

1. Open **OS/2 System**.
2. Open **Command Prompts**.
3. Open **DOS Full Screen**, **DOS Window**, or both.

When you close a session, the session and its related windows are automatically closed. Make sure that you save all important data in the session before you close it.

To close a DOS command prompt session:

1. Type **Exit**.
2. Press Enter.

You can switch from a DOS command prompt session to another running program. When you switch sessions, your command prompt session is saved and then restored when you switch back.

To temporarily leave a DOS command prompt session:

1. Press Ctrl+Esc.

2. Point to a title on the Window List.
3. Double-click.

Or:

1. Press Alt+Esc to display the desktop.

DOS from Drive A

DOS from
Drive A:

The DOS from Drive A object is used to start a specific version (3.0 or later) of DOS from a diskette. By using a specific version of DOS, you can use programs that will not run under the DOS provided with OS/2 2.1.

Before you can start a specific DOS version from a diskette, you must create the diskette used to start the DOS version. This diskette is commonly known as a DOS Startup diskette or DOS Bootable diskette.

Creating a DOS Startup Diskette

Note: If you already have a DOS Startup diskette go to step 6 to make sure the diskette is set up to work correctly with the DOS from Drive A object.

To create a DOS Startup diskette:

1. Boot your system with a version of DOS. You can use a:
   • DOS installation diskette
   • Hard disk that DOS has been installed on
   • Diskette that DOS has been installed on
2. Type **FORMAT A: /S**
3. Place a blank diskette into drive A.
4. Press Enter. This transfers the system files to the diskette.
5. When the format is complete, remove the diskette.
6. Start OS/2 by pressing Ctrl+Alt+Del.
7. Select **OS/2 System**.
8. Select **Drives**.
9. Select **Drive C**.
10. Open the OS/2 folder; then open the MDOS folder.
11. Place the formatted diskette containing the system files into drive A.
12. Copy the following data-file objects from **Drive C** to the **Drive A** object:
    FSFILTER.SYS
    FSACCESS.EXE

You can copy as many additional DOS files to the diskette as you want.

13. Open the **Templates** folder.
14. Copy a **Data File** object to the desktop.
15. Point to the data-file object and double-click. The OS/2 System Editor starts.
16. Type the following information into the data file:

```
DEVICE=FSFILTER.SYS
DOS=HIGH,UMB
DEVICE=C:\OS2\MDOS\ANSI.SYS
FILES=20
BUFFERS=20
```

17. Point to the title-bar icon of the OS/2 System Editor; then double-click.
18. Select **Save as**; then type A:\CONFIG.SYS and press Enter.
19. Point to the data-file object again and double-click.
20. Type the following information into the data file.

```
ECHO OFF
PROMPT $P$G
SET COMSPEC=A:\COMMAND.COM
C:\OS2\MDOS\MOUSE.COM
PATH A:\
```

21. Point to the title-bar icon of the OS/2 System Editor; then double-click.
22. Select **Save as**; then type A:\AUTOEXEC.BAT and press Enter.

Starting DOS from Drive A

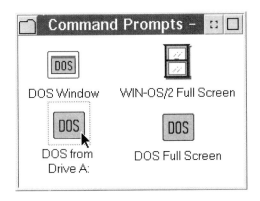

To start a DOS from Drive A session:

1. Insert the DOS Startup diskette in drive A.
2. Open **OS/2 System**.
3. Open **Command Prompts**.
4. Open **DOS from Drive A**.

To close a DOS from Drive A session:

1. Press Ctrl+Esc.
2. Point to **DOS from Drive A** in the Window List.
3. Click mouse button 2.
4. Click on **Close**.

You can switch from a DOS from Drive A session to another running program. When you switch sessions, your command prompt session is saved and then restored when you switch back.

To temporarily leave a DOS from Drive A session:

1. Press Ctrl+Esc.
2. Point to a title on the Window List.
3. Double-click.

Or

1. Press Alt+Esc to display the desktop.

WIN-OS/2 Full Screen

WIN-OS/2
Full Screen

The WIN-OS/2 Full-Screen object is used to run multiple Windows programs in a full-screen session. For more information about WIN-OS/2, see Chapter 18, "Using Windows Programs" on page 193.

To start a WIN-OS/2 Full-Screen session, open the object.

To close a WIN-OS/2 Full-Screen session:

1. Point to the title-bar icon.
2. Double-click.

To switch to the OS/2 desktop:

1. Point to the OS/2 object in the lower left corner of the screen.
2. Double-click.

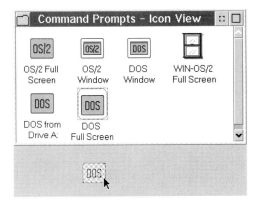

You can have multiple sessions of any object open.

To open more than one session of an object:

1. Open **OS/2 System**.
2. Open **Command Prompts**.
3. Copy one of the objects (for example, DOS Window) by holding down the Ctrl key and mouse button 2 and dragging the object to the same or another folder. Then release the mouse button and the Ctrl key.
4. Open the object to start the session.
5. Repeat the steps to create and open another session.

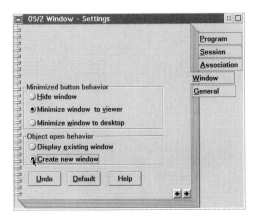

Or, if you need multiple copies of objects often, you can alter the settings of the object so that it creates another session every time you open it. Do the following:

1. Open **OS/2 System**.
2. Open **Command Prompts**.
3. Point to the object.
4. Click mouse button 2.
5. Select the arrow to the right of **Open**.
6. Select **Settings**.
7. Select the **Window** tab.
8. Select the **Create new window** radio button.
9. Close the notebook by double-clicking mouse button 1 on the title-bar icon. Now, each time you select the object a new session starts.

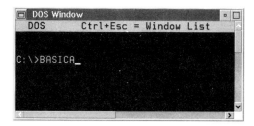

To start the BASICA or QBASIC programs:

Note: BASICA will only run on IBM computers.

1. Open **OS/2 System**.
2. Open **Command Prompts**.
3. Open **OS/2 Full Screen**, **OS/2 Window**, **DOS Full Screen**, or **DOS Window**.
4. Type **BASICA** or **QBASIC** at the command prompt; then press Enter.

To exit the BASICA program:

1. Type **SYSTEM**.
2. Press Enter.

To exit the QBASIC program:

1. Select **File**.
2. Select **Exit**.
3. Select **Enter**.

Chapter 8. Productivity

Productivity

The Productivity folder provides programs that assist you in editing text and icons, keeping a diary, creating charts and drawings, searching for files or text, displaying system utilization, and using a terminal emulator.   Each productivity program has a set of help menus to assist you with using the program.

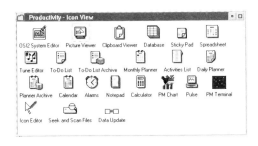

To open a Productivity program:

1. Open **OS/2 System**.
2. Open **Productivity**.
3. Open the program you want to use.

For information about using a program in the Productivity folder, press F1 after the program is opened.

Activities List

Activities
List

Before you use the Activities List, you must create a list of events in the Daily Planner (see "Daily Planner" on page 115). The Activities List displays the list entries from the Daily Planner. You can customize the list by changing its colors and font size.

Alarms

Alarms

Alarms is a program that enables you to set alarms to go off during the day. This program is related to the Activities List (see "Activities List") and the Daily Planner (see "Daily Planner" on page 115). Also use the Tune Editor to create and edit tunes for this program (see "Tune Editor" on page 119).

Calculator

Calculator

The Calculator program is an electronic calculator that you can use to perform mathematical calculations. You enter calculations with a mouse or the keyboard. The tally is displayed in a window and can also be printed. The calculator has memory recall and a menu that you can use to customize decimal placement, colors, and font sizes.

Calendar

Calendar

Calendar is a program that enables you to look at a day, month, and year of your choice. You can view statistics for the current year; however, you must have used related programs such as Daily Planner (see "Daily Planner" on page 115), Monthly Planner (see "Monthly Planner" on page 116), or Activities List (see "Activities List" on page 113).

Clipboard Viewer

Clipboard Viewer

Clipboard Viewer is a program that enables you to view the contents of the OS/2 clipboard. The system clipboard is used to share information between programs in the same session or in different sessions (for information about sessions, see Chapter 7, "Command Prompts" on page 105). It temporarily holds data being passed from one program to another. You can copy or cut information to the clipboard from a program in one session and then paste the information from the clipboard to a program in a different session. For more information about the clipboard, refer to "Using the Clipboard and Dynamic Data Exchange Features" on page 205.

Daily Planner

Daily Planner

Daily Planner is a program that enables you to keep track of your past and future activities. With the planner you can set an alarm for a future activity, mark an activity as completed, and archive the activity for future reference. You also can customize the planner by changing its colors and font size.

The Daily Planner is related to the Alarms (see "Alarms" on page 113), Activities List (see "Activities List" on page 113), and To-Do List Archive (see "To-Do List Archive" on page 119) programs.

Database

Database

Database is a program that enables you to keep a miniature database. The data base consists of a group of one or more records with each record containing eight lines (fields). An example of a data base is a telephone list of people you know.

Enhanced Editor

Enhanced Editor

Enhanced Editor is an editor you can use to create and edit text files. It also enables you to work on multiple files at the same time. You can start the Enhanced Editor by opening its object or by typing **EPM** at the OS/2 command prompt and pressing Enter.

The Enhanced Editor has a number of features and functions. These features and functions are thoroughly explained in the Quick Reference help file located under the **Help** menu bar choice of the Enhanced Editor.

Icon Editor

Icon Editor

Icon Editor is a tool that enables you to create, edit, and convert image files. These files include icons, bit maps, and pointers. An icon is a graphical representation of an object or a minimized program. A bit map is a special type of image made up of a series of dots. (The OS/2 logo is an example of a bit map.) A pointer is a small symbol on the screen that reflects the movement of the mouse.

Monthly Planner

Monthly Planner

Monthly Planner is a tool for recording and viewing activities of the current month. The window shows alarms that are set for the specific days. The planner works in conjunction with the Alarm (see "Alarms" on page 113) and Daily Planner (see "Daily Planner" on page 115) programs.

Notepad

Notepad

Notepad is a convenient place to keep personal notes. The Notepad contains 5 pages that are stacked on top of each other. You type directly on the top page and then file the page to save your notes. The menu choices provide access to several features for customizing a page. One particularly nice feature lets you select a picture. The picture is automatically placed on the top page of the Notepad.

OS/2 System Editor

OS/2 System Editor

The OS/2 System Editor is used to create and edit text files. You can use the System Editor to edit your CONFIG.SYS and AUTOEXEC.BAT system files. The System Editor runs in a window. You can start several sessions of the System Editor so that you can edit several files at once.

You can start the System Editor two ways:

- By selecting its object
- Opening a data file associated with the System Editor. (All data files area associated with the System Editor by default.)
- By typing **E** (and pressing Enter) at an OS/2 command line

  If you want to edit a particular file, you follow the E with a space and then type the path and file name of the file.

Picture Viewer

Picture
Viewer

Picture Viewer displays and prints metafile (files with a .MET file name extension) and picture interchange format (files with a .PIF file name extension) files. You also can view spooler files (files with a .SPL file name extension); however, the file must contain a picture in a standard OS/2 format. Picture Viewer lets you zoom in or zoom out of a picture after it is displayed. Move the mouse pointer to the portion of the picture you want to zoom in and then double-click mouse button 1.

Planner Archive

Planner
Archive

Planner Archive is a list of entries that were archived with the Daily Planner. You can view specific archived entries, create a statistics panel, and print the archive file.

PM Terminal

PM
Terminal

PM Terminal is a communications program. It emulates terminals and allows for data transfer between two computers. A modem is required.

PM Chart

PM Chart

PM Chart is a chart-making program. You can easily create business presentations, charts, and drawings. The program has a menu that provides editing functions, a color palette for text and screen, and more. The tool bar (along the left side of the window) contains selections that include a work sheet, aids for drawing, windows for text alignment, and font selection.

Pulse

Pulse

Pulse is a system monitor. Use Pulse to see a graphic representation of how different activities affect the system and how much processor power is still available for other programs. You can change the colors of the graphic, adjust the graph line, and freeze the screen image.

Seek and Scan Files

Seek and
Scan Files

Seek and Scan Files is a program that quickly searches one or more disks for files or text. When a file match is found, it is displayed in a selection list. Then you can open (or run) the selected file.

Spreadsheet

Spread
sheet

Spreadsheet is a *spreadsheet program*. A spreadsheet program displays a worksheet in which a table of cells is arranged in rows and columns. Changing the contents of numeric cells causes a recalculation of the worksheet based on how the relations among the cells are defined. The Spreadsheet program has 26 columns and 80 rows. Use this spreadsheet to keep track of monthly expenditures, sales figures, or any other information.

Sticky Pad

Sticky Pad

Sticky Pad is a place to keep small reminder notes that can "stick" anywhere on your computer screen. You can have up to ten Sticky Pad notes on your screen at one time.

To-Do List

To-Do List

To Do List is a program that tracks your daily activities. Each day you can type what has to be completed, assign it a priority, and then sort the list by priority. After each task is completed, you can mark each line. You can customize the list by changing its colors and font size.

To-Do List Archive

To-Do List
Archive

To-Do List Archive is a list of entries that were archived with the To-Do List. You can print the archive file, sort it, or view specific entries.

Tune Editor

Tune Editor

Tune Editor is a program that enables you to create and edit tunes to be used with the Alarms (see "Alarms" on page 113) program. Each file can contain up to 36 individual tunes. Using the menu bar, you can play the tunes, or if you know how to read and write music, you can edit the tunes.

Chapter 9. Games

Games

The **Games** folder provides you with entertainment.

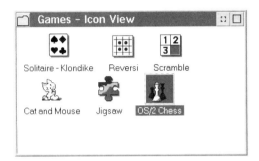

To start a game:

1. Open **OS/2 System**.
2. Open **Games**.
3. Open the game you want to play.

For information about playing a game in the Games folder, press F1 after the game is opened.

Cat and Mouse

Cat and Mouse

Cat and Mouse is a game to help you learn how to use the mouse. It also teaches you how to use a window control called a slider bar. After you enable the cat with the Cat and Mouse window settings, when you move the mouse pointer, the cat follows it until you stop. When the mouse pointer is stopped, the cat goes to sleep. You can change the play time, speed, and step of the cat.

Jigsaw

Jigsaw

Jigsaw is a puzzle you can solve. It allows you to solve a puzzle by dragging the pieces of the puzzle in any direction with a mouse. You can select from the available bit map or use your own bit maps.

Klondike Solitaire

Solitaire
Klondike

Klondike Solitaire is a popular card game for one person. The object of this game is to find the aces and build on them in suit and in ascending order. You use the mouse to move the cards to their new location.

OS/2 Chess

OS/2
Chess

With OS/2 Chess, you can play a game of chess against another person playing on the same computer or on a network workstation. You also can play against the computer. The object of the game is to checkmate your opponent's king.

Reversi

Reversi

Reversi is a board game that requires skill and strategy. The object of the game is to have more red color pieces on the board at the end of the game than the computer has blue.

Scramble

Scramble

Scramble is a small puzzle that is solved when you arrange the puzzle pieces in the correct order. You must move the pieces of the puzzle in one direction at a time. The mouse cursor turns into an arrow when you select a piece.

Chapter 10. Information

Information

The **Information** folder contains information to aid you in using OS/2 2.1.

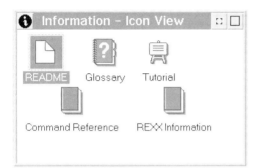

To open the Information folder:

1. Point to **Information**
2. Double-click.

The Information folder contains all the online documents described in this chapter.

Tutorial

Tutorial

The OS/2 Tutorial is an interactive and animated look at the OS/2 Workplace Shell interface. It explains how to use a mouse, work with objects and folders, use windows, and get help.

If you are new to OS/2, you should spend the 40 minutes (approximate) it takes to go through the tutorial. You will find that it is time well spent.

To start the OS/2 Tutorial:

1. Open **Information**
2. Open **Tutorial**

Command Reference

**Command
Reference**

Before there were friendly operating system interfaces like the Workplace Shell, computer users communicated with a computer using a predefined set of instructions called *commands*. Users would type a command at a prompt, and the computer would perform the requested task.

Some people still like to communicate with the computer in this way. For that reason, OS/2 supplies both DOS and OS/2 command prompts and the OS/2 Command Reference.

The *Command Reference* explains each OS/2 and DOS command, graphically shows the correct syntax of the command, and gives examples of when and how to use the command.

In addition, it explains the commands that can be used to create a *batch file* (a series of commands that are processed sequentially). Batch files are useful for automating the entering of commands that are used over and over again.

To open the OS/2 *Command Reference*:

1. Open **Information**.
2. Open **Command Reference**.

To open the OS/2 *Command Reference* and get information about a specific command:

1. At an OS/2 command prompt, type **HELP** followed by the name of the command. For example:

   HELP COPY

2. Press Enter. The *Command Reference* is opened to the COPY command page.

Using the Contents Window

The Contents window is the first window that appears when the *Command Reference* is opened. Notice that some of the topics in this window have a plus (+) sign beside them. The plus sign indicates that additional topics are available.

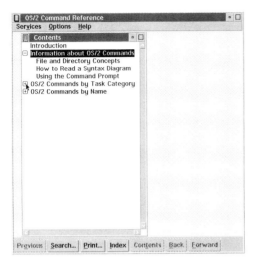

To expand the Contents and view the additional topics:

> Select the + sign.

To collapse the topics in the Contents:

> Select the − sign.

To open a topic:

1. Point to the title of the topic.
2. Double-click.

Obtaining Additional Information

When a topic is opened, the information for the topic is displayed in a window. Highlighted words and phrases in the window indicate that additional information is hidden "beneath" the word or phrase.

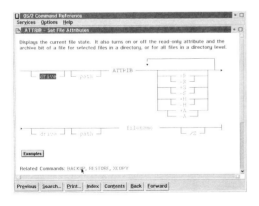

To view the additional information::

1. Point to the highlighted word or phrase.
2. Double-click.

To return to the previous window of information:

> Select **Previous**.

Searching for Information

There might be times when you are using the *Command Reference* when you have an idea of what you want, but you cannot remember where it is. The search function can help you find the information you need.

To search for a word or phrase in all the topics in the Command Reference:

1. Select **Search**.
2. Type the word or words you want to find. You can also use the ? and * wildcard characters in the search field.
3. Make sure that **All sections** is selected; then select **Search**.

A Search Results window appears containing a list of topics that have the word or phrase that you were trying to find. To open a topic, point to a topic and double-click.

Sometimes, you have a general idea where the information is. You can limit the search to those topics by marking the topics.

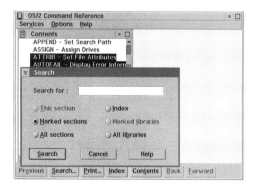

To mark a topic:

1. Press and hold Ctrl.
2. Select the topics that you want to search.
3. Release Ctrl.

To unmark a topic:

1. Press and hold Ctrl.
2. Select the topic.
3. Release Ctrl.

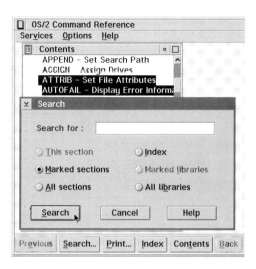

To search for a word or phrase in marked topics:

1. Select the + signs in the Contents window.
2. Mark the topics you want to search.
3. Select **Search**.
4. Type the word or words you want to find.
5. Make sure that **Marked sections** is selected; then select **Search**.

When the Search Results window appears, open the topics and read them.

Using a Bookmark

Information that you refer to frequently can be flagged using a bookmark. Setting a bookmark duplicates the topic in a bookmark window.

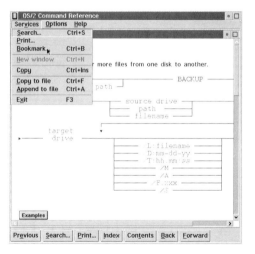

To set a bookmark:

1. Open the topic that you want to mark with a bookmark.
2. Select **Services**.
3. Select **Bookmark**.
4. Change the name used for the bookmark (optional).
5. Make sure **Place** is selected; then select **OK**.

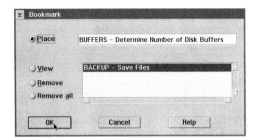

To view bookmarked information:

1. Select **Services**.
2. Select **Bookmark**.
3. Select **View**.
4. Select the topic you want to open.
5. Select **OK**.

To remove a bookmark:

1. Select **Services**.
2. Select **Bookmark**.
3. Select **Remove**.
4. Select the topic you want to remove.
5. Select **OK**.

Printing a Topic

Some people prefer to read information in a hardcopy format. You can print a topic, some topics, all topics, the table of contents, and the index of the *Command Reference*.

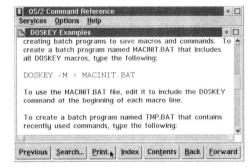

To print a topic:

1. Open the topic you want to print.
2. Select **Print**.
3. Make sure that **This section** is selected; then select **Print**.

To print more than one topic:

1. Press and hold Ctrl.
2. Select the topics that you want to print.
3. Release Ctrl.
4. Select **Print**.
5. Make sure that **Marked sections** is selected; then select **Print**.

To print the table of contents, index, or all the topics:

1. Select **Print**.
2. Select the item you want to print.
3. Select **Print**.

Note: The **Contents** and **Index** choices only print the entries; they do not print the text associated with the entries. The **All sections** choice prints the entire *Command Reference*. Before electing to do this, be aware that the document is large and will take a long time to print.

Glossary

Glossary

The Glossary is an alphabetic listing of terms used in the Workplace Shell interface and the online help system.

To open the Glossary:

1. Open **Information**.
2. Open **Glossary**.

There are three ways to find a term in the glossary. You can type the first letter of the word you are looking for, scroll through the list or use the search function.

To scroll through the list to find a term in the glossary:

1. Select the letter that the word begins with. If the letter is not visible, select the tab arrow until the letter is visible; then select the letter.
2. Select the up or down arrow in the scroll bar until the term is visible.
3. Point to the term.
4. Double-click.

To use the search function to find a term in the glossary:

1. Select **Search topics**.

2. Type the term that you want to find.

3. Select **Search**.

4. When the list of matching entries appears, point to the term; then double-click.

REXX Information

REXX
Information

REXX is a procedures language designed to make basic OS/2 programs easier to write and debug. Both beginning and experienced programmers will find REXX easy to use because it uses common English words, arithmetic and string functions, and OS/2 commands within a simple framework.

To view the REXX Information:

1. Open **Information**.
2. Open **REXX Information**.

For information about using the Contents window, searching, printing and getting additional information, see "Command Reference" on page 124.

README

README

README is a file that contains late-breaking news about compatibility, tips, and techniques that might be of use to you in certain situations.

Note: Before calling for service, scan the information in this file for an answer to your question.

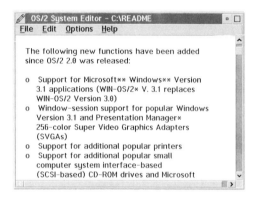

To view **README**:

1. Open **Information**
2. Open **README**

Finding Information in README

If you need information about a certain topic, you can search for the topic, rather than read the entire file.

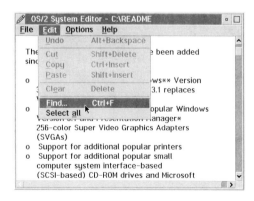

To find a word or phrase:

1. Select **Edit**.
2. Select **Find**.
3. Type the word or phrase.
4. Select **Find**. The word or phrase is highlighted in the README file.
5. To find the next instance of the word or phrase, select **Find** again.

Printing the README

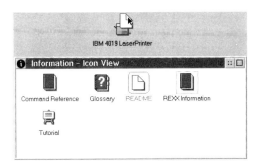

To print the information in README:

1. Point to the **README** object.
2. Press and hold mouse button 2.
3. Drag the **README** object to the **Printer**.
4. Release mouse button 2.

Chapter 11. Master Help Index

Master
Help
Index

The **Master Help Index** is an online, alphabetic list of topics available to help you while using OS/2 2.1. This index contains information about:

- Things to consider before performing a task
- The steps to take to complete a task
- OS/2 concepts
- DOS error messages

To open the Master Help Index:

1. Point to **Master Help Index**.
2. Double-click.

Index Entries

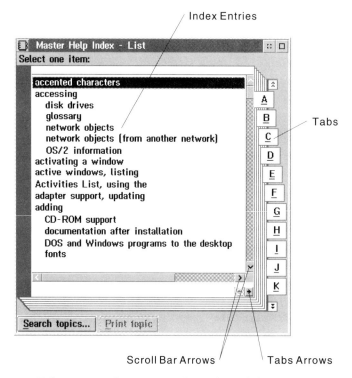

Tabs

Scroll Bar Arrows   Tabs Arrows

Tabs turn to the page in the index of the selected alphabet letter.

Tab arrows scroll the tabs but do not scroll the index entries.

Scroll bar arrows (vertical scroll bar) scroll the index entries one line at a time. Scroll bar arrows (horizontal scroll bar) scroll the index entries to the left or right so you can read information that does not fit into the window.

Index entries are the online help for the OS/2 operating system.

To open an index entry for viewing:

1. Point to the entry.
2. Double-click.

Accessing Additional Information

When an index entry is opened, the information for the topic is displayed in a window.

Some entries have highlighted words and phrases in the window, which indicate that additional information is hidden "beneath" the word or phrase.

To view the additional information::

1. Point to the highlighted word or phrase.
2. Double-click.

To return to the previous window of information:

1. Select **Previous**.

Searching for a Topic

You can search the Master Help Index for an entry using one or more words that describe the topic. For example, to search for information about how to duplicate an object, you might search using the word "duplicate," "duplicates," or even "duplicating." The result of a search (using duplicate, duplicates, or duplicating) is "copying an object."

To search for a topic:

1. Open the Master Help Index.
2. Select **Search topics**.
3. In the **Search string** field, type the word or words that describe the topic.
4. Select **Search**.
5. When the list of topics (matched items) appears, open the entry you want to read.

Printing a Master Help Index Entry

To print a Master Help Index entry:

1. Open the index entry you want to print.
2. Select **Print topic**.

For more information about using the Master Help Index, review the OS/2 Tutorial.

Chapter 12. Drive A

Drive A

The **Drive A** object provides quick access to the diskette drive in your computer referred to as A.

You can use the Drive A object to:

- Display the objects on a diskette
- Display information about the objects on the diskette
- Copy objects on a diskette to another location
- Copy objects from another location to a diskette
- Move objects on a diskette to another location
- Move objects from another location to a diskette
- Delete objects from a diskette
- Format a diskette
- Check a diskette for defects and fix it

This chapter discusses only the **Drive A** object. For information about other drive objects and a discussion about disks and diskettes, see Chapter 6, "Drives" on page 95.

Display the Objects on a Diskette

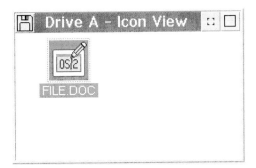

To display the objects on a diskette:

1. Place a diskette into diskette drive A.
2. Open **Drive A**.

The Drive A window appears showing the contents of the diskette. The actual layout of the window that appears depends upon the contents of the diskette.

Tree view   Displays the objects on the diskette in a directory (tree) structure with folders representing the directories. This view comes up when the objects on the diskette are placed in directories. To view the contents of a directory, point to a folder; then double-click.

139

Icon view   Displays the objects on the diskette as pictures (icons). This view comes up when all the objects on the diskette are in the root directory.

Displaying Information about the Objects on a Diskette

The tree and icon views give limited information about the objects on a diskette. However, the details view gives the following information about the objects on the diskette:

Title of the object   The name that appears below the icon that represents the object.

Real name of object   The actual name of the object.

Size   The amount of space in bytes that the object occupies.

Last write date   The date that the information in the object was last changed.

Last write time   The time of day that the information in the object was last changed.

Last access date   The date that the information in the object was last viewed.

Last access time   The time of day that the information in the object was last viewed.

Creation date   The date that the object was first created.

Creation time   The time that the object was first created.

Flags   Characteristics of the file that allow it to be used a certain way.

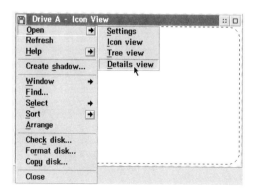

To display detailed information about the objects on a diskette:

1. Place a diskette into drive A.
2. Open **Drive A**.
3. Point to the title-bar icon.
4. Click mouse button 2.
5. Select the arrow to the right of **Open**.
6. Select **Details view**.

Copying Objects to or from a Diskette

There are times when you need to *copy* an object (duplicate the object and place it in a different location).

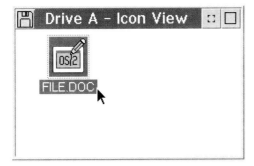

Note: If you want to copy the object to a folder object or another drive object, the target object must be visible before you start the copy.

To copy an object from a diskette in Drive A to another location:

1. Place a diskette into drive A.
2. Open **Drive A**.
3. Point to the object you want to copy.
4. Press and hold mouse button 2.
5. Drag the object to a folder, the desktop, or another drive object.
6. Release mouse button 2.

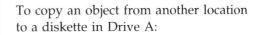

To copy an object from another location to a diskette in Drive A:

1. Place the diskette you want to copy the object to into drive A.
2. Point to the object you want to copy.
3. Press and hold mouse button 2.
4. Drag the mouse to the Drive A object.
5. Release mouse button 2.

Moving Objects to or from a Diskette

There are times when you need to *move* an object (copy the object to a different location and delete it from the original location).

Note: If you want to move the object to a folder object or another drive object, the target object must be visible before you start the move.

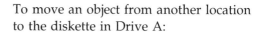

To move an object from the diskette in Drive A to another location:

1. Place a diskette into drive A.
2. Open **Drive A**.
3. Point to the object you want to move.
4. Press and hold Alt+Shift.
5. Press and hold mouse button 2.
6. Drag the object to a folder, the desktop, or another drive object.
7. Release mouse button 2.
8. Release Alt+Shift.

To move an object from another location to the diskette in Drive A:

1. Place the diskette you want to move the object to into drive A.
2. Point to the object you want to move.
3. Press and hold Alt+Shift.
4. Press and hold mouse button 2.
5. Drag the object to the Drive A object.
6. Release mouse button 2.
7. Release Alt+Shift.

Deleting Objects from a Diskette

You can *delete* (erase) unwanted objects from a diskette.

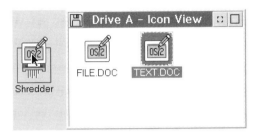

To delete an object from a diskette:

1. Place the diskette you want to delete the object from into drive A.
2. Open **Drive A**.
3. Point to the object you want to delete.
4. Press and hold mouse button 2.
5. Drag the object to the **Shredder**.
6. Release mouse button 2.

Formatting a Diskette

You can *format* a diskette using the Drive A object. When a diskette is formatted, it is checked for defects and prepared to accept data. During this process, all existing data is erased from the diskette.

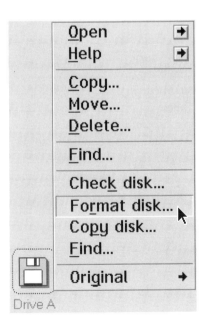

To format a diskette:

1. Place the diskette you want to format into drive A.
2. Point to **Drive A**.
3. Click mouse button 2.
4. Select **Format disk**.
5. When the Format Disk window appears, type a Volume Label (name for the disk or diskette).
6. Select **Format**.
7. When the format is complete, select **OK**.

Checking a Diskette

You can check a diskette for:

Defects   Errors in the file allocation table or directory on the diskette. If you select **Write corrections to disk**, any problems found will be fixed.

Current Usage   The amount of the diskette being used for directories, user files, and extended attributes. It also shows the amount of space that is reserved on the diskette.

File system type   Type of file system on the diskette. (All diskettes are formatted for the FAT file system.)

Total disk space   The capacity of the diskette in bytes.

Total amount of disk space available

                        The amount of free space left on the diskette.

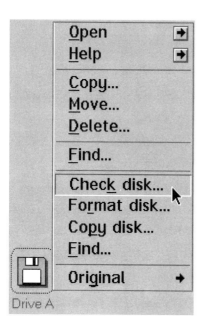

To check a diskette:

1. Place the diskette to be checked into drive A.
2. Point to **Drive A**.
3. Click mouse button 2.
4. Select **Check disk**.
5. Select **Write corrections to disk**.
6. Select **Check**.
7. After a few seconds, the Check Disk - Results window is displayed. Select **Cancel** to remove the window.

Chapter 13. Minimized Window Viewer

Minimized
Window
Viewer

The Minimized Window Viewer is where open objects are stored when they are minimized. This keeps your desktop organized but still allows you to have multiple objects open and running.

To open the Minimized Window Viewer:

1. Point to **Minimized Window Viewer**.
2. Double-click.

Displaying an Object in the Minimized Window Viewer

The objects in the Minimized Window Viewer are still open, but they are running in the *background* (cannot accept user input).

To display an object found in the Minimized Window Viewer:

1. Open the **Minimized Window Viewer**.
2. Point to the object.
3. Double-click.

Or

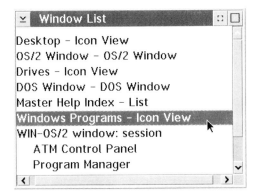

1. Point to an empty area on the desktop.
2. Click mouse buttons 1 and 2 at the same time.
3. Point to the title of the object you want to display.
4. Double-click.

Note: There may be more titles in the Window List than objects in the Minimized Window Viewer, because hidden windows are also displayed in the Window List.

Minimizing an Object to the Desktop

Some frequently used objects might be easier to re-access if they are minimized to the desktop instead of the Minimized Window Viewer.

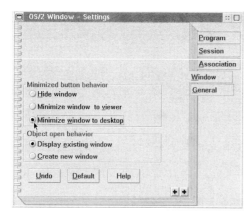

To make an object minimize to the desktop:

1. Point to the object you want to minimize to the desktop.
2. Click mouse button 2.
3. Select the arrow to the right of **Open**.
4. Select **Settings**.
5. Select the **Window** tab.
6. Select **Minimize button**. (If the choice is present.)
7. Select **Minimize window to desktop**.
8. Point to the title-bar icon.
9. Double-click.

Minimizing an Object to the Minimized Window Viewer

Most objects by default are set up to minimize to the Minimized Window Viewer. However, some objects are not.

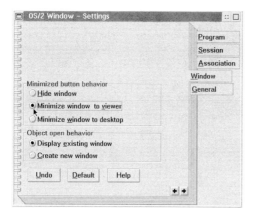

To make an object minimize to the Minimized Window Viewer:

1. Point to the object you want to minimize to the Minimized Window Viewer.
2. Click mouse button 2.
3. Select the arrow to the right of **Open**.
4. Select **Settings**.
5. Select the **Window** tab.
6. Select **Minimize button**. (If the choice is present.)
7. Select **Minimize window to viewer**.
8. Point to the title-bar icon.
9. Double-click.

Shredder

The **Shredder** object provides a quick and easy way to delete objects.

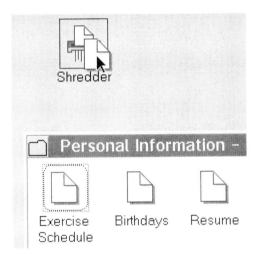

Shredder

To delete an object:

1. Point to the object.
2. Press and hold mouse button 2.
3. Drag the object to the **Shredder**.
4. Release mouse button 2.
5. Respond to confirmation messages (if applicable).

Customizing the Delete Confirmations

You can change the settings of your desktop to specify when confirmation messages appear, if any, when you delete an object. The following confirmation choices are available:

Confirm on folder delete   Displays a confirmation message whenever a folder object is deleted using either the Shredder object or a pop-up menu.

Confirm on delete   Displays a confirmation message whenever an object is deleted using either the Shredder object or a pop-up menu.

Important

Disabling the confirmation messages increases your chances of accidentally deleting an object.

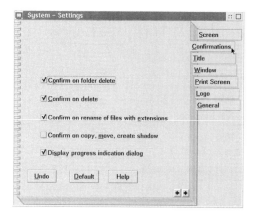

To change the settings:

1. Open **OS/2 System**.
2. Open **System Setup**.
3. Open **System**.
4. Select the **Confirmations** tab.
5. Make sure a check mark appears in each choice that you want to enable. To add or remove a check mark, select the choice.
6. Point to the title-bar icon.
7. Double-click.

Preparing Your System to Recover Deleted Objects

Chances are that at some point you will accidentally delete an object that you need. You can recover a deleted object if the DELDIR environment variable is enabled in your CONFIG.SYS file prior to deleting the object.

To enable DELDIR:

1. Edit your C:\CONFIG.SYS file and remove the REM statement from the beginning of the DELDIR statement.
   a. Open **OS/2 System**.
   b. Open **Drives**.
   c. Open **Drive C**. (If the OS/2 operating system is installed on a different drive, open that drive instead.)
   d. After the Drive C object opens, a tree view of its contents is displayed. Open the Drive C entry in the tree.
   e. Open the C:\CONFIG.SYS file.
   f. Select **Edit**.
   g. Select **Find**.
   h. Type DELDIR (all caps) in the **Find** field.
   i. Select **Find**.

   Note: If the DELDIR statement is not found, see the online *Command Reference* for instructions on how to add it.

j. Select the beginning of the DELDIR line.

k. Delete REM from the beginning of the line using the Del key.

l. Point to the title-bar icon.

m. Double-click.

n. Select **Save**.

o. Select **Type**.

p. Select **Set**.

2. Shut down your system; then restart it. Changes made to the CONFIG.SYS object are not initiated until the system is restarted.

The DELDIR statement specifies the size of the directory used to hold deleted objects. When the directory is full, the oldest files in the directory are removed in order to make room for the new objects.

If you delete an object, recover it as soon as possible afterwards, or it might be too late. For more information about DELDIR, see the online Command Reference.

Note: To be able to recover objects deleted in a DOS session, repeat the preceding procedure on the AUTOEXEC.BAT file.

Recovering Deleted Objects

You can recover a deleted or erased object using the UNDELETE command.

Note: The DELDIR environment variable must be enabled prior to the deletion of the object. For more information about DELDIR, see "Preparing Your System to Recover Deleted Objects" on page 148.

To recover a deleted object:

1. Open **OS/2 System**.
2. Open **Command Prompts**.
3. Open a DOS or OS/2 window.
4. Type UNDELETE /L and press Enter to see a list of file names associated with the recently deleted objects.
5. Write down the complete path and file name. Include the drive letter, directory names, and the file name. For example: C:\OS2\SAMPLE.TXT

6. Type UNDELETE followed by the complete path and file name. For example:

   `UNDELETE C:\OS2\SAMPLE.TXT`

   Press Enter.

The file associated with the deleted object has now been successfully recovered. For more information about UNDELETE, see the online *Command Reference*.

To place the object back on the desktop:

1. Open **Drives**.
2. Open the drive that contains the recovered file (object).
3. Find the object on the drive.
4. Point to the object.
5. Press and hold mouse button 2.
6. Drag the object to the desktop.
7. Release mouse button 2.

Chapter 15. Templates

Templates

A template is an object that you can use as a model to create additional objects. When you drag a template, you create another of the original object, as though you were peeling one of the objects off a stack. The new object has the same settings and contents as the templates in the stack.

Creating an Object from the Templates Folder

You can create new objects by using the objects in the Templates folder. To open the Templates folder:

1. Point to the Templates object on the desktop.
2. Double-click.

Creating a Folder Object

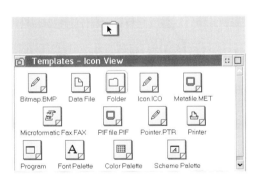

To use the Folder template to create a new folder:

1. Open **Templates**.
2. Point to the Folder template.
3. Press and hold mouse button 2.
4. Drag a copy of the Folder template to the desktop or to another folder.
5. Release mouse button 2. An empty folder is created.
6. Rename the folder (for example, "My new folder"). For information about renaming, see "Renaming an Object" on page 23.

Drag any objects you want (for example, program objects and data-file objects) to the new folder.

Creating a Data-File Object

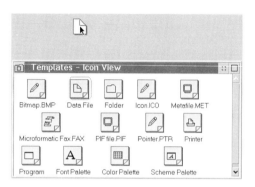

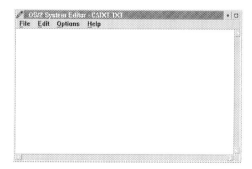

To use the Data File template to create a data-file object:

1. Open **Templates**.
2. Move the mouse pointer to the Data-File template.
3. Press and hold mouse button 2.
4. Drag the Data-File template to any folder (including the Desktop folder). A new data-file object is created.
5. Open the data-file object to begin editing the file with the System Editor.
6. When you are ready to save the file, select **File**; then select **Save**. Respond to the system prompts (for example, in the Save notification window, indicate if you want a file type such as plain text).
7. Double-click mouse button 1 on the title-bar icon to close the window.
8. Rename the object currently titled "Data File". Refer to "Renaming an Object" on page 23.

Note: If you use **Save as** on the File menu instead of **Save**, another object is created with the new name. "Data File" remains an empty file.

If you open a data-file object that is not associated with any other program, it automatically opens in the OS/2 System Editor. If you prefer, you can associate the data-file object with one or more program objects (for more information, see "Associating Data-File Objects with Program Objects" on page 188). For more information about using the OS/2 System Editor, select **Help** on the menu.

Creating a Program Object

A program object starts a program or a session. If you install a new OS/2, DOS, or Windows program, you might need to run the Migrate Applications program in the System Setup folder to create a program object. This is the recommended method of creating a program object.

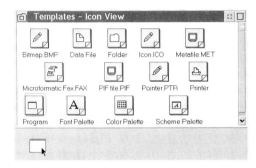

You also can create a program object using the Templates folder.

1. Open **Templates**.
2. Move the mouse pointer to the Program template.
3. Press and hold mouse button 2.
4. Drag the Program template to a folder or to the desktop.
5. Customize the program object using the Settings notebook. For example, select the session type, name the program object, or set up the associations.

Creating a Template of an Object

You can create a template of an object when you have an existing object (such as a form letter with a company letterhead) and you need another one. For example, you could make the form letter a template and then customize it for different customers. The new object will have the same settings (such as associations) and contents as the original.

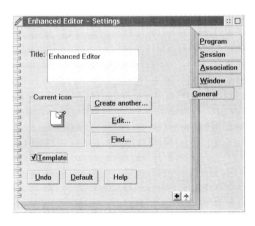

To create a template of an object:

1. Display the pop-up menu for the object by pointing at the object and then clicking mouse button 2.
2. Select the arrow to the right of **Open**.
3. Select **Settings**.
4. Select the **General** tab.
5. Select the **Template** check box.
6. Close the Settings notebook.

The object is now displayed as a template.

Drag a copy of the object from the template whenever you need a new copy. Customize the new object to your preference. For example, you can change the name of the object and add a new icon (see "Renaming an Object" on page 23).

If you want to move a stack of templates, rather than create an object from the top template, press the Shift key while dragging the stack.

Creating Another Object

All objects that have a **Create another** choice in their pop-up menu have a cascaded menu that lists their templates. When you create a template of your own, it is added to the cascaded menu.

The result of **Create another** is identical to creating an object from a template. If you select **Create another** from the pop-up menu of an object, a new object with the same default settings and data is created. If you select the arrow to the right of **Create another**, a cascaded menu is displayed. This menu contains a listing of all the template objects you created. You can select one of the choices to create another object from that template.

For example, suppose you created a template and named it "Company letterhead." This template is listed as a choice on the cascaded menu. Whenever you need to create a similar letter, select **Company letterhead**. The new data-file object contains whatever was in the original "Company letterhead" and the same settings (such as associations).

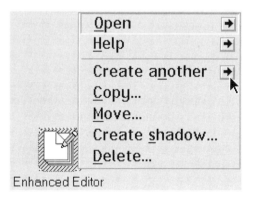

Enhanced Editor

To create another object using a pop-up menu:

1. Display the pop-up menu for the object by pointing at the object and then clicking mouse button 2.
2. Select **Create another** if you want to use one of your templates, or select the arrow to the right of **Create another** and select a template choice.

Note: The new object appears in the active folder; for example, if the object is on the desktop, the duplicate appears on the desktop.

Chapter 16. Printers and Plotters

Printer

If you installed a printer when you installed OS/2 2.1, a printer object is on your desktop. The printer object is used to print *jobs* (data files) and check their progress. If you want to add a printer object, see "Installing a Printer" on page 164.

Note: The explanations and instructions in this chapter apply to both printers and plotters.

Each printer object represents a certain arrangement of hardware, software, and configurations, which simplifies the printing process.

Printer objects can represent *local printers* and *network* printers. Local printers are connected to individual computers, or individual workstations on a network. Network printers are connected to local area network (LAN) servers and can be used by workstations connected to the network.

Printing

Printing a job is as simple as dragging and dropping a data-file object on a printer object.

Printing Data-File Objects

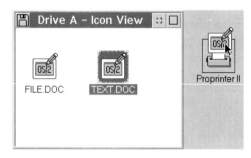

To print a data-file object using direct manipulation:

1. Make sure that you can see the printer object on the screen.
2. Point to the data-file object that you want to print.
3. Press and hold mouse button 2.
4. Drag the data-file object to the printer object.
5. Release mouse button 2. Sometimes the operating system cannot determine how to print the data in the job and prompts you to choose whether the job contains plain text or printer-specific data.

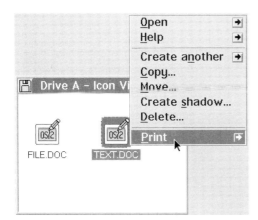

To print a data-file object using the pop-up menu:

1. Select one or more data-file objects.
2. Point to one of the selected objects.
3. Click mouse button 2.
4. Select **Print**.

Note: If you are using a program (for example, Lotus** 1-2-3**) and you want to print the data that you are preparing, follow the instructions that came with the program.

Tip

For easier access, move your printer object to either the desktop or into the folder that contains your data files.

Printing Screens

Screens printed from the Workplace Shell will go to the default printer. Screens printed from a full-screen session will go to LPT1 by default if a printer is assigned to that port.

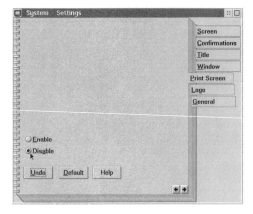

To print an open window, folder, or the desktop:

1. Point to the item you want to print.
2. Press **Print Screen**.

To disable or enable Print Screen:

1. Point to an empty area on the desktop.
2. Click mouse button 2.
3. Select **System Setup**.
4. Open **System**.
5. Select the **Print Screen** tab.
6. Select **Disable** or **Enable**.
7. Point to the title-bar icon.
8. Double-click.

Printing to a COM Port

To print from an application running in a DOS or OS/2 full-screen or window session to a communication port (for example, COM1), you must redirect the print job to the printer object that is connected to the COM port. There are two ways that you can do this. You can set up the printer object to automatically redirect the print job, or you can redirect using a command prompt.

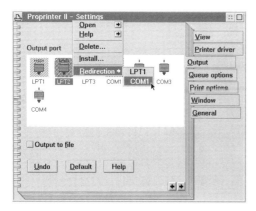

To set up a printer object to redirect to a COM port:

1. Point to the printer object connected to your communications port.
2. Click mouse button 2.
3. Select the arrow to the right of **Open**.
4. Select **Settings**.
5. Select the **Output** tab.
6. Point to the LPT port whose print jobs you want to send to your COM port. (For example, you might select LPT2 if you do not have a printer physically connected to the second parallel port.)
7. Click mouse button 2.
8. Select the arrow to the right of **Redirection**.
9. Select the COM port your printer object is connected to from the list that is displayed. Your jobs will now print on the printer attached to this communication port.

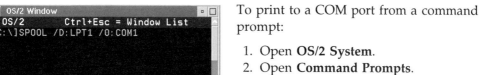

To print to a COM port from a command prompt:

1. Open **OS/2 System**.
2. Open **Command Prompts**.
3. Open **OS/2 Window** or **OS/2 Full Screen**.
4. Type:

```
SPOOL /D:port1  /O:port2
PRINT file-name /D:port1
```

For example, if you wanted to print MYFILE.TXT to communications port COM1, you might type:

```
SPOOL /D:LPT1 /O:COM1
PRINT MYFILE.TXT /D:LPT1
```

Note: Printer port redirection is used to redirect DOS and OS/2 full-screen and window print jobs from an LPT port to the printer object connected to another port. Only one printer object is required, and it must be connected to the port to which the printer is physically attached.

Printing on a Network

The OS/2 operating system supports printing on a network printer for OS/2, DOS, and Windows programs. The first time you use a network printer, the system might prompt you to install a printer driver. You must install the printer driver before you can use the network printer.

In addition, before you can print to a network printer, you might need to assign a port destination to the network printer so you can print from DOS or Windows programs and use operating system commands such as COPY and PRINT with the printer. See "Assigning a Port Name to a Network Printer" on page 160 for instructions.

Assigning a Port Name to a Network Printer: Some programs and operating system commands cannot recognize a network printer by its network name. If you are using such an application, you need to assign a port name to the network printer.

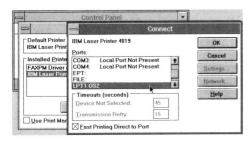

To assign a port name so you can use a network printer with DOS and Windows programs:

1. Point to the network printer object.
2. Click mouse button 2.
3. Select **Assign port**.
4. Select a parallel port (LPT*x*) from the **Assign port** field. If you want to use the network printer with DOS only, the port is now assigned a port name. If you want to use the network printer with Windows programs, continue with the next step.
5. Open **OS/2 System**.
6. Open **Command Prompts**.
7. Open **WIN-OS/2 Full Screen**.
8. Open **Control Panel**.
9. Open **Printers**.
10. Select the Windows printer driver.
11. Select **Connect**.
12. Select **LPT*x*.OS2** to enable printing to a network from a Windows program.
13. Select **OK**.
14. Point to the title-bar icon.
15. Double-click.

PSVANGO QMS PS 2000

To assign a port name so you can use a network printer with operating system commands:

1. Point to the network printer object.
2. Click mouse button 2.
3. Select **Assign port**.
4. Select a port in the **Assign port** field.
5. Select **OK**. You can now redirect the output of a PRINT or COPY command to your network printer using an OS/2 or DOS command-prompt session. For example, type:

```
COPY MYFILE.TXT LPT3
```

Managing Your Print Jobs

The printer object contains a list of the jobs waiting to be printed. The actual files that contain the information are stored temporarily on your hard disk in a spooler directory until the job finishes printing. The spooler manages the jobs for all your printer objects. No matter how many printer objects you have, your system has only one spooler. You change where the files are temporarily stored by changing the settings for the Spooler object. For more information about the Spooler, see "Spooler" on page 78.

Viewing Job Information in the Printer Object

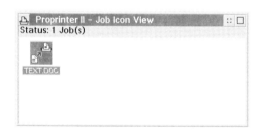

To view information about the jobs in the printer object:

1. Point to the printer object.
2. Double-click.

The default setting for the printer object is **Icon view**. The icon view shows the names and the order of the jobs in the printer object. If you change the setting to **Details view** the job ID, document name, date, time, status, and owner information about the jobs in the printer object are displayed.

To change the default setting:

1. Point to the printer object.
2. Click mouse button 2.
3. Select the arrow to the right of **Open**.
4. Select **Settings**.
5. Select either **Icon view** or **Details view**.
6. Point to the title-bar icon.
7. Double-click.

Holding and Releasing Print Jobs

You can *hold* (keep it from printing) or *release* (allow it to print) any job in the printer object. This is useful if you are not sure whether you really need to print the job or you just want to wait until another time to print it.

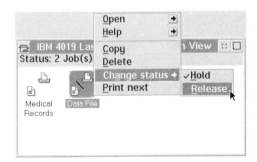

To hold or release a job in the printer object:

1. Open the printer object.
2. Select the job you want to hold or release.
3. Click mouse button 2.
4. Select **Change status**.
5. Select either **Hold** or **Release**.
6. Point to the title-bar icon.
7. Double-click.

Changing the Order in Which Jobs Print

The order that the jobs appear in the printer object is the order in which they will print.

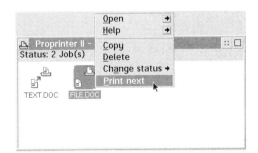

To change the order in which jobs print:

1. Open the printer object.
2. Select the job you want to print next.
3. Click mouse button 2.
4. Select **Print next**.
5. Point to the title-bar icon.
6. Double-click.

Setting Up Job Properties

Your print jobs have properties that describe how you want the data file printed. You can view the properties for a print job and, in some cases, make changes before the job prints.

There are several ways that you can view and change the properties for a print job:

- You can specify that you want the system to prompt you for job properties each time you print a job.
- You can set default job properties for a printer object.
- You can set the job properties through a program.

Prompting for Job Properties at Print Time

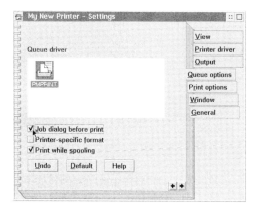

To set up a printer object so that the system prompts you for print-job properties each time you print from the Workplace Shell:

1. Point to the printer object.
2. Click mouse button 2.
3. Select the arrow to the right of **Open**.
4. Select **Settings**.
5. Select the **Queue options** tab.
6. Select **Job dialog before print**.
7. Point to the title-bar icon.
8. Double-click.

Now, each time you drag and drop a job on a printer object, a window appears in which you can select the job properties.

Setting Default Print-Job Properties: You can set up your printer so that it uses the same job properties for each job you print without prompting you for input.

To set default properties for your print jobs:

1. Point to the printer object.
2. Click mouse button 2.
3. Select the arrow to the right of **Open**.
4. Select **Settings**.
5. Select the **Printer driver** tab.
6. Select **Job properties**.
7. Select the appropriate settings.
8. Point to the title-bar icon.
9. Double-click.

Setting Job Properties from within a Program: Some programs allow you to select the job properties from within the program. Most of these programs have a menu that contains a printer setup choice.

Installing a Printer

Even if you did not select a printer during the OS/2 2.1 installation, you still can add a printer to the system. There are several different procedures to choose from. From the following list, choose the procedure that best describes your situation, then follow the instructions to add the printer.

- Create a printer object but use a printer driver that is currently installed on the system. See "Creating a Printer Object" on page 165.
- Create a printer object and install a new printer driver to use with it. See "Creating a Printer Object and Installing a Printer Driver" on page 166.
- Install a new printer driver but use an existing printer object. See "Installing a Printer Driver Only" on page 168.
- Change the printer driver being used with an existing printer object. See "Changing Printer Drivers" on page 170.
- Install an OS/2 printer driver for use with WIN-OS/2. See "Installing a Printer Driver for WIN-OS/2" on page 171.
- Install an OEM (Other Equipment Manufacturer) printer driver for use with WIN-OS/2. See "Installing a Printer Driver from Another Manufacturer for WIN-OS/2" on page 172.

Note: When you create an OS/2 printer object, you might be prompted to create an equivalent WIN-OS/2 printer object. If you choose to create the

WIN-OS/2 printer object, you also are prompted to install a WIN-OS/2 printer driver. If the printer drivers supplied with OS/2 2.1 support your printer model, you do not need to install the equivalent WIN-OS/2 printer driver as a separate operation.

Creating a Printer Object

This procedure involves adding a printer object and selecting a printer driver. Use this procedure if you have existing printer drivers installed on your system and you want this new printer object to use one of them.

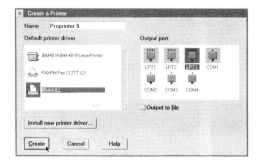

To create a printer object to use with an existing printer driver:

1. Open **Templates**.
2. Point to the Printer template.
3. Press and hold mouse button 2.
4. Drag the template to a folder or the desktop.
5. Release mouse button 2. The Create a Printer window is displayed.
6. Type a name for the printer in the **Name** field.
7. Select the port to which the printer is connected.
8. Select the printer driver that corresponds to your printer model.
9. Select **Create**.
10. Respond to the "Do you want to install an equivalent WIN-OS2 printer configuration" question; then follow the instructions on the screen to complete the installation.

A new printer object is on your desktop. If you want to customize the settings for this new printer object, see "Setting Printer Properties" on page 173.

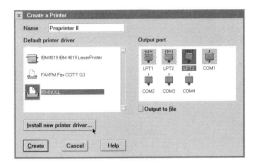

This procedure involves creating a printer object and installing a printer driver. Use this procedure if you want to create a printer object and install a new printer driver.

1. Open **Templates**.
2. Point to the Printer template.
3. Press and hold mouse button 2.
4. Drag the template to a folder or the desktop.
5. Release mouse button 2.
6. Type a name for the printer in the **Name** field.
7. Select the port to which the printer is connected.
8. Use the instructions in the following list to install your printer driver:

   • If your printer driver came with the OS/2 operating system, follow the instructions for **Printer Driver Shipped with OS/2**.
   • If your printer driver did not come with the OS/2 operating system, follow the instructions for **Other Printer Driver**.

Printer Driver Shipped with OS/2

1. Select one or more printer drivers in the list.
2. Select **Install**.
3. Ensure that the information in the **Directory** field is correct.
4. Select **OK**.

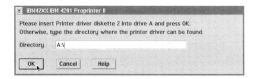

Other Printer Driver

1. Insert the diskette containing the printer drivers in drive A, or type the appropriate drive designation and path in the **Directory** field.
2. Select **Refresh**. Wait until the window fills with printer drivers.
3. Select one or more drivers. If the driver you need is not listed, insert another diskette or change the information in the **Directory field** and select **Refresh** again.
4. Select **Install**.

A new printer object is on your desktop. If you want to customize the settings for this new printer object, see "Setting Printer Properties" on page 173.

Tip

Many printers have multiple printer drivers available. For example, Hewlett Packard has several drivers for their LaserJet IIID printer. To ensure that you get the correct driver with the printer model you select, scroll the **Printer Driver** field to the right until you can see the name of the printer driver.

Installing a Printer Driver Only

Sometimes you have an existing printer object, but you do not have the correct printer driver on your system. This might happen if you add a different printer to your system.

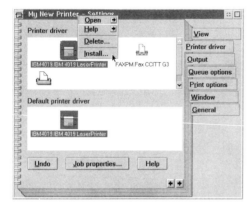

To install a new driver for an existing printer object:

1. Point to the printer object.
2. Click mouse button 2.
3. Select the arrow to the right of **Open**.
4. Select **Settings**.
5. Select the **Printer driver** tab.
6. Point to one of the printer driver objects.
7. Click mouse button 2.
8. Select **Install**.
9. Use the instructions in the following list to install your printer driver:

   - If your printer driver came with the OS/2 operating system, follow the instructions for **Printer Driver Shipped with OS/2**.
   - If your printer driver did not come with the OS/2 operating system, follow the instructions for **Other Printer Driver**.

Printer driver shipped with OS/2

1. Select one or more printer drivers in the list.
2. Select **Install**.
3. Ensure that the information in the **Directory** field is correct.
4. Select **OK**.

Other Printer Driver

1. Insert the diskette containing the printer drivers in drive A, or type the appropriate drive designation and path in the **Directory** field.
2. Select **Refresh**.
3. Select one or more drivers. If the driver you need is not listed, insert another diskette or change the information in the **Directory field** and select **Refresh** again.
4. Select **Install**.

A new printer driver is installed. If you want to customize the settings for this new printer driver, see "Setting Printer Properties" on page 173.

Tip

Many printers have multiple printer drivers available. For example, Hewlett Packard has several drivers for their LaserJet IIID printer. To ensure that you get the correct driver with the printer model you select, scroll the **Printer Driver** field to the right until you can seethe printer driver name.

Changing Printer Drivers

You might already have both the printer object and the printer driver installed on your system, but you need to connect them. This might happen if you like to use different printer drivers with a printer object.

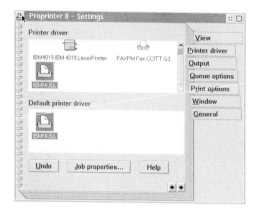

To change to a different printer driver:

1. Point to the printer object.
2. Click mouse button 2.
3. Select the arrow to the right of **Open**.
4. Select **Settings**.
5. Select the **Printer driver** tab.
6. Select the printer driver.
7. Point to the title-bar icon.
8. Double-click.

The printer object is now set up to use a different printer driver. See "Setting Printer Properties" on page 173 for information about setting the properties to match the capabilities of the new printer driver.

Installing a Printer Driver for WIN-OS/2

WIN-OS/2 programs print directly to the OS/2 spooler. Therefore, multiple print jobs can be spooled from one WIN-OS/2 session or multiple WIN-OS/2 sessions.

To install a printer driver in WIN-OS/2:

1. Open **WIN-OS/2 Main**.
2. Open **Control Panel**.
3. Open **Printers**.
4. Select **Add** and then select a printer driver in the list.
5. Select **Install.**
6. Insert the diskette containing the printer drivers in drive A, or type the appropriate drive designation and path in the Install Driver pop-up window.
7. Select **OK**.
8. Select **Connect**.
9. Select **LPT1.OS2**, **LPT2.OS2**, or **LPT3.OS2**.

   Note: You can select a **COM**x port, but no spooling to the OS/2 Print object will occur. However, you will still be able to use the Print Manager in WIN-OS/2.

10. Select **OK**.
11. Point to the title-bar icon.
12. Double-click.

Installing a Printer Driver from Another Manufacturer for WIN-OS/2

OS/2 2.1 has a wide variety of printer drivers available for use with WIN-OS/2. However, there might be times when you want to use a driver supplied by another printer manufacturer.

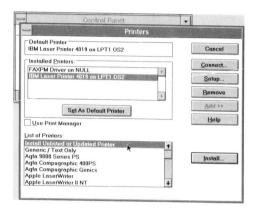

To add a WIN-OS/2 printer driver supplied by another printer manufacturer:

1. Open **OS/2 System**.
2. Open **Command Prompts**.
3. Open **OS/2 Window** or **OS/2 Full Screen**.
4. Open **Control Panel**.
5. Open **Printers**.
6. Select **Add**.
7. Select **Install Unlisted or Updated Printer** from the beginning of the list of printers.
8. Select **Install**.
9. Insert the diskette containing the printer drivers in drive A, or type the appropriate drive designation and path in the Install Driver pop-up window.
10. Select **OK**.
11. Select **Connect**.
12. Select **LPT1.OS2**, **LPT2.OS2**, or **LPT3.OS2**.
13. Select **OK**.
14. Point to the title-bar icon.
15. Double-click.

Tip

If you also want to create an OS/2 printer object for use with the same driver, follow the instructions for "Creating a Printer Object" on page 165 and make the following selections:

- Select the same port you selected for your printer, using the WIN-OS/2 Control Panel.
- Select the OS/2 printer driver, IBMNULL, as the default driver. (IBMNULL is installed during system installation.)

Setting Printer Properties

A printer driver has settings called printer *properties*. Printer properties describe the way your printer is physically set up. Examples of printer properties are:

- Type of paper feed (tractor or bin)
- Number and location of paper trays
- Forms defined for your printer
- Forms loaded in the paper feed or trays of your printer
- Font cartridges loaded on the printer
- Installed soft fonts
- Additional features installed, such as extended symbol sets and patterns
- Resolution
- Orientation
- Compression

Examples of plotter properties are:

- Number of carousels
- Active carousel
- Color type of each pen in a carousel

The number and kind of properties available depend upon the type of printer or plotter you have.

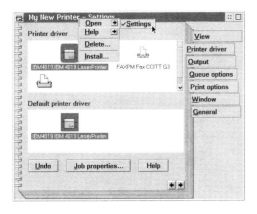

To set the printer properties:

1. Point to the printer object.
2. Click mouse button 2.
3. Select the arrow to the right of **Open**.
4. Select **Settings**.
5. Select the **Printer driver** tab.
6. Point to a printer driver.
7. Click mouse button 2.
8. Select the arrow to the right of **Open**.
9. Select **Settings**.
10. Change the properties to match your printer setup.
11. Point to the title-bar icon.
12. Double-click.

Your printer object is now set up to print a job. For information about how to print a job, see "Printing an Object" on page 24.

OS/2 2.1 has the ability to run multiple programs at the same time. You can run OS/2, DOS, and Windows programs side by side using objects on the desktop. During installation, if you had existing OS/2, DOS, or Windows programs and selected the **Migrate Applications** choice from the Advanced Options window, OS/2 2.1 migrated these programs to the OS/2 2.1 environment.

Making efficient use of your system's performance when running multiple programs is important. When running programs in the Workplace Shell, consider the following:

- If a program is always used, place the program in the Startup folder. The program will start at system startup.

- If several different programs are used, their objects can be placed on the desktop or in a folder. The folder can be set to open at system startup.

- To avoid reloading programs, minimize the program after use, and then maximize the session to use the program again. The program object appears in the Minimized Window Viewer or on the desktop.

- To further conserve system resources:

  - Close programs when they are not going to be used again.
  - Close folders if they are not needed.
  - Move commonly-used functions out of folders and to the desktop, and close the folder that contained the object.

- The program type directly affects the amount of system resource required. For example, a program creating a spreadsheet uses a large amount of memory while it is processing.

Chapter 17. Preparing Your Programs

During system installation, your existing programs are installed in folders on the desktop if you selected the **Migrate Applications** choice from the Advanced Options window. The settings for the DOS and Windows programs are adjusted for you. This chapter describes how to install programs after system installation and change their settings to suit your needs. For example, after your programs are installed, you might want to change the way the program object appears on your desktop; (see "Program Object Settings" on page 185).

Installing New Programs

After you have installed OS/2 2.1 and your existing programs have been migrated into the OS/2 2.1 environment, you will probably want to install new programs as the need arises. The installation procedure that you follow depends on whether the program is an OS/2, DOS, or Windows program.

OS/2 Programs

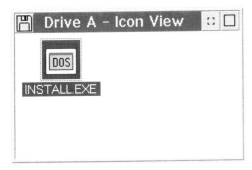

To install an OS/2 program:

1. Insert the first diskette for the program into a diskette drive (for example, drive A).
2. Open the Drive A object. If the diskette is not in drive A:
   a. Open **OS/2 System**.
   b. Open **Drives**.
   c. Open the appropriate drive object.
3. Open the program-file object used for installation (for example, INSTALL.EXE).
4. Follow the instructions that came with the program to complete the installation.
5. Remove the diskette from the drive.
6. Point to the title-bar icon of the drive window.
7. Double-click.
8. Point to the title-bar icon of the OS/2 System window, if open.
9. Double-click.

177

Or

1. Place the first diskette for the program into a diskette drive (for example, drive A).
2. Open **OS/2 System**.
3. Open **Command Prompts**.
4. Open either **OS/2 Window** or **OS/2 Full Screen**.
5. Type the letter of the drive containing the diskette (for example, A:); then press Enter.
6. Type the command used by the program to install (for example: INSTALL); then press Enter.
7. Follow the instructions that came with the program to complete the installation.
8. Remove the diskette from the drive.
9. Type **EXIT**; then press Enter to close the OS/2 window.
10. Point to the title-bar icon of the Command Prompts window.
11. Double-click.
12. Point to the title-bar icon of the OS/2 System window.
13. Double-click.

Note: If a program object was not created during the installation, see "Creating a Program Object" on page 181.

DOS Programs

> **Attention!**
>
> The OS/2 CONFIG.SYS file might be overwritten with incompatible information during the installation of some DOS programs. If this occurs, refer to "Recovering the CONFIG.SYS File" in the *OS/2 2.1 Installation Guide*.

Note: DOS_AUTOEXEC is a new DOS setting that allows you to define a file that runs instead of the default AUTOEXEC.BAT file. This setting is used to set up the environment variables for programs running in a DOS session.

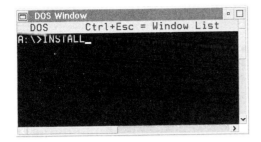

To install a DOS program:

1. Insert the first diskette for the program into a diskette drive (for example, drive A).
2. Open **OS/2 System**.
3. Open **Command Prompts**.
4. Open either **DOS Full Screen** or **DOS Window**.
5. Type the letter of the drive containing the diskette (for example, A:); then press Enter.
6. Type the command used by the program to install (for example: INSTALL); then press Enter.
7. Follow the instructions that came with the program to complete the installation.
8. Remove the diskette from the drive.
9. Type **EXIT**; then press Enter to close the DOS window.
10. Point to the title-bar icon of the Command Prompts window.
11. Double-click.
12. Point to the title-bar icon of the OS/2 System window.
13. Double-click.

Note: If a program object was not created during the installation, see "Creating a Program Object" on page 181.

Windows Programs

> **Attention!**
>
> The OS/2 CONFIG.SYS file might be overwritten with incompatible information during the installation of some Windows programs. If this occurs, refer to "Recovering the CONFIG.SYS File" in the *OS/2 2.1 Installation Guide*.

Note: DOS_AUTOEXEC is a new WIN-OS/2 setting that allows you to define a file that runs instead of the default AUTOEXEC.BAT file. This setting is used to set up the environment variables for programs running in a WIN-OS/2 session.

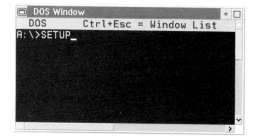

To install a Windows program:

1. Insert the first diskette for the program into a diskette drive (for example, drive A).
2. Open **OS/2 System**.
3. Open **Command Prompts**.
4. Open a **DOS Full Screen**.
5. Type the letter of the drive containing the diskette (for example, A:); then press Enter.
6. Type the command used by the program to install (for example: SETUP); then press Enter.
7. Follow the instructions that came with the program to complete the installation.
8. Remove the diskette from the drive.
9. Type **EXIT**; then press Enter to close the DOS window.
10. Point to the title-bar icon of the Command Prompts window.
11. Double-click.
12. Point to the title-bar icon of the OS/2 System window.
13. Double-click.

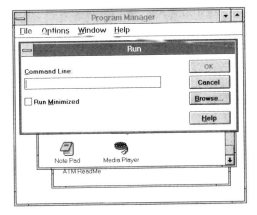

If the instructions require you to install the program from the Program Manager:

1. Insert the first diskette for the program into a diskette drive (for example, drive A).
2. Open **OS/2 System**.
3. Open **Command Prompts**.
4. Open **WIN-OS/2 Full Screen**.
5. Select **File**.
6. Select **Run**.
7. Type the letter of the drive followed by the command used to install the program, (for example: A:\SETUP); then press Enter.
8. Follow the instructions that came with the program to complete the installation.
9. Remove the diskette from the drive.
10. Point to the title-bar icon of the Program Manager.
11. Double-click.
12. Point to the title-bar icon of the Command Prompts window.
13. Double-click.
14. Point to the title-bar icon of the OS/2 System window.
15. Double-click.

Note: If a program object was not created during the installation see "Creating a Program Object" on page 181.

Creating a Program Object

A program object is used to start a program from the Workplace Shell. Some programs automatically place a program object on the desktop or in a folder on the desktop during their installation.

If a program installed on your system does not have a program object on the desktop or in a folder on the desktop, you can create one.

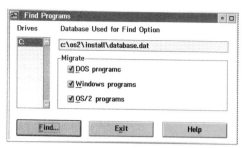

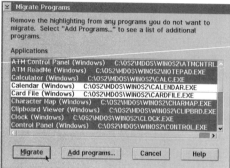

To create a program object:

1. Open **OS/2 System**.
2. Open **System Setup**.
3. Open **Migrate Applications**.
4. Remove the check mark from the program types that you do not want to migrate by clicking on them.
5. Select **Find**. If your program is not found, see "Migrate Applications" on page 69 for information about adding a program to the list.
6. Deselect any program names that you do not want a program object for.
7. Select **Migrate**.
8. Select **Exit**.
9. Select **Yes**.
10. Point to the title-bar icon in System Setup.
11. Double-click.

The new program object is placed in one of the following folders:

OS/2 Programs	Contains migrated OS/2 programs
Additional OS/2 Programs	Contains migrated OS/2 programs
WIN-OS/2 Groups	Contains folders of Windows programs
Windows Programs	Contains migrated Windows programs
Additional Windows Programs	Contains migrated Windows programs
DOS Programs	Contains DOS programs
Additional DOS Programs	Contains migrated DOS programs.

Note: Some Windows groups contain DOS programs. After migration, these DOS program objects are placed in the WIN-OS/2 Group folder and DOS folder.

To use the newly-created program object:

1. Open the folders that correspond with the type of program object that was created.
2. Open the program object.

Adding a Program Choice to the Pop-Up Menu

If you want another method of accessing a program, you can add the program as a new menu choice on the pop-up menu of any folder. For example, the desktop pop-up menu can be enhanced to add the "Reversi" item.

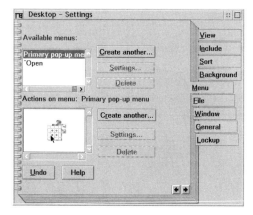

To add a program to a pop-up menu:

1. Point to an empty area on the desktop.
2. Click mouse button 2.
3. Select the arrow to the right of **Open**.
4. Select **Settings**.
5. Select the **Menu** tab.
6. Point to a program object (for example, the Reversi object in the Games folder).
7. Press and hold mouse button 2.
8. Drag the program object to the **Actions on menu** list box.
9. Release mouse button 2.
10. Point to the title-bar icon.
11. Double-click.

The next time you display the desktop folder pop-up menu, "Reversi" will be one of the available menu choices. If you select this choice, the Reversi game is displayed.

Note: When you open a program object from the pop-up menu of a folder object, the name of the object is passed to the program object. This may cause an error when the object is opened. To avoid errors, display the pop-up menu for the program object, select the arrow to the right of **Open**, and then select **Settings**. Type % in the **Parameters** field.

Program Object Settings

Every object in the Workplace Shell interface has *settings* Settings are properties or characteristics of the object that determine the way it runs and looks. You can view or change these settings using the settings notebook for the object. The Settings notebook looks like a multi-page book with tabs attached to the edge of its pages. The tabs divide the notebook into sections. Each section can contain multiple pages. You can switch from section to section using the tabs, and you can move between pages using the arrows on the lower-right corner of the notebook.

Viewing Program Object Settings

To view the settings of a program object:

1. Point to the object.
2. Click mouse button 2.
3. Select the arrow to the right of **Open**.
4. Select **Settings**. The Settings notebook appears.
5. Select each of the following tabs in the notebook:
   - Program
   - Session
   - Association
   - Window
   - General

Program

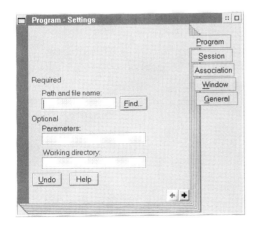

Use this page to specify a working directory for the selected object. When you do this, you control how the program starts each time you open the program object.

Note: Windows programs do not use the **Working Directory** field.

Session

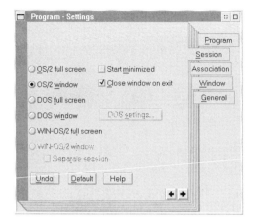

Use this page to select the appropriate session for a program object. The type of session determines how the program runs. The types are OS/2, DOS, and WIN-OS/2 full screen and window.

Notes:

1. If **WIN-OS/2 window** or **WIN-OS/2 full screen** is selected, then a **WIN-OS/2 settings** push button is displayed instead of a **DOS settings** push button.

   Selecting this push button displays the list of DOS or WIN-OS/2 settings for the session. By fine tuning these settings, you can improve the way a program runs in the session.

2. If you change your WIN-OS/2 or DOS settings, you must save them with the **Save** push button.

Association

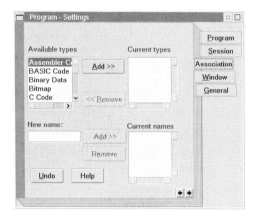

Use this page to create a special link (an association) between the current program object and one or more data-file objects.

For more information on associating program objects and data-file objects, see "Associating Data-File Objects with Program Objects" on page 188.

Window

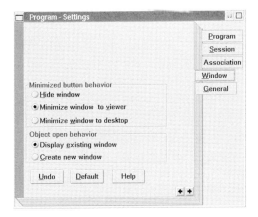

Use this page to change the system default for what happens when you select the minimize button in the title bar of a program object. The system default is that an object is placed in the Minimized Window Viewer folder.

The Minimized Window Viewer folder provides quick access to windows that you have minimized.

General

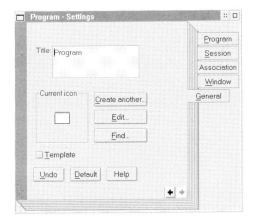

Use this page to:

- Change the name (title) of the current object.
- Change the current icon that represents the object by dragging an icon from anywhere on the desktop and dropping it on the General page of the notebook.
- Create a new icon for the object.
- Change (edit) the icon for the object.
- Find the names of program objects that create other icons.
- Create a template of the object.

Changing Program Object Settings

You can change the settings for a program object to modify the way that it looks or runs.

When a change is made, the change takes place immediately. You do not have to save the changes. To change the settings back, select:

Undo   To change the settings back to their previous setting.

Default   To change the settings back to their default settings (settings made during installation).

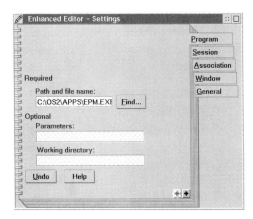

To change the settings for a program object:

1. Point to a program object.
2. Select mouse button 2.
3. Select the arrow to the right of **Open**.
4. Select **Settings**. The Settings notebook appears.
5. Select each tab and make the desired changes. For information about the fields in the notebook, select the **Help** pushbutton located on each page of the Settings notebook.

Associating Data-File Objects with Program Objects

The data-file objects that you work with on a daily basis can be associated with program objects. This means that when you open a data-file object, the program it is associated with opens at the same time. For example, you can link every spreadsheet data-file object to the spreadsheet program object. Then, whenever you open a spreadsheet data-file object, the spreadsheet file is displayed in the open spreadsheet program.

If you do not create an association for a data-file object, the object is associated to the OS/2 System Editor by default. A data-file object is displayed in the System Editor until it is associated with another program object.

Note: If you need more than one copy of the data-file object, create a template of the object (see "Creating a Template of an Object" on page 153).

Associating a Data-File Object with a Program Object

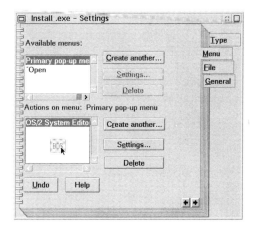

To associate a data-file object with a program object:

1. Point to the data-file object.
2. Click mouse button 2.
3. Select the arrow to the right of **Open**.
4. Select **Settings**.
5. Select the **Menu** tab.
6. Select **Open** in the **Available menus** selection list.
7. Point to the program object that you want to associate with this data-file object.
8. Press and hold mouse button 2.
9. Drag the program object to the **Actions on menu** field.
10. Release mouse button 2.
11. Point to the title-bar icon.
12. Double-click.

Associating Multiple Data-File Objects with a Program Object

You also can associate multiple data-file objects with the same program object. For example, if you have many existing data files of the same type or extension, you can associate them to one program object. Then, each time a data-file object of that type or extension is opened, the program object also is opened.

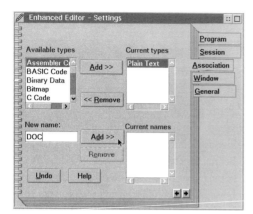

To associate multiple data-file objects with the same program object:

1. Point to the program object that you want to associate to a group of data files.
2. Click mouse button 2.
3. Select the arrow to the right of **Open**.
4. Select **Settings**.
5. Select the **Association** tab.
6. To associate the data file using the file type:
   a. Select a file type in the **Available types** selection list (for example, Plain Text).
   b. Select **Add**. You can add as many file types as you want.
   c. The added file types are shown in the **Current types** field.

To associate the data files using the file extension:

7. Type the extension of the file, in the **New name** field (for example, DOC, TXT, or SCR).
8. Select **Add** You can add as many file extensions as you want.
9. Select **Add**
10. Point to the title-bar icon.
11. Double-click.

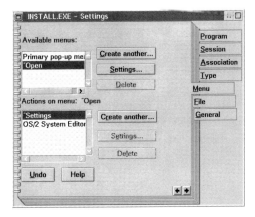

To make an associated program object the default menu choice for a data-file object, do the following:

1. Point to the data-file object.
2. Click mouse button 2.
3. Select the arrow to the right of **Open**.
4. Select **Settings**.
5. Select the **Menu** tab.
6. Select **Open** in **Available menus**.
7. Select **Settings** to the right of the Available menus selection list.
8. Select the down arrow in the **Default action** field.
9. Select the name of the program object from the list.
10. Select **OK**.
11. Point to the title-bar icon.
12. Double-click.

The next time you open the data-file object, it is displayed in the default program object.

Opening an Associated Object from a Pop-Up Menu

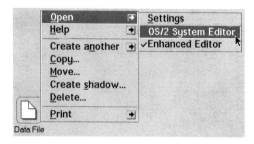

To open the data-file object in a program object other than the default one:

1. Point to the data-file object.
2. Click on mouse button 2.
3. Select the arrow to the right of **Open**.
4. Select a program name that does not have a check mark next to it. The data file opens in the selected program object.

Chapter 18. Using Windows Programs

WIN-OS/2

The feature of the OS/2 operating system that provides Windows program support is called *WIN-OS/2*. WIN-OS/2 allows Windows programs to use many of the features of OS/2, such as multitasking, running programs in windows, and sharing information between programs. This chapter presents an overview of WIN-OS/2.

WIN-OS/2
Groups

The WIN-OS/2 Groups folder contains two folders-WIN-OS/2 Main and Accessories folders. The WIN-OS/2 Main folder contains a set of Windows programs that let you organize files and directories, configure hardware, and view the contents of the WIN-OS/2 clipboard. Each program has a set of help menus to assist you with using the program.

To open the WIN-OS/2 Main folder:

1. Open **WIN-OS/2 Groups**.
2. Open **WIN-OS/2 Main**.
3. Open the program you want to use.

File Manager

File
Manager

The File Manager is a tool you use to organize files and directories. You use File Manager to move and copy files, start applications, connect to network drives, print documents, and maintain disks.

Control Panel

Control
Panel

The Control Panel is a program you use to modify your system while working with WIN-OS/2. Each option that you can change is represented by an icon in the Control Panel window.

Print Manager

Print
Manager

The Print Manager is a program you use to manage printing. You can print your documents to a local or network printer. A local printer is connected directly to your computer. If you are using a network printer, you can connect to a network printer to print your documents. For more information, see Chapter 16, "Printers and Plotters" on page 155.

Clipboard Viewer

Clipboard
Viewer

The Clipboard Viewer is a tool you use to see the contents of the WIN-OS/2 clipboard. When you cut or copy information from a program, it is placed into the clipboard. You then paste this information from the clipboard into other documents or programs. For more information, see "Using the Clipboard and Dynamic Data Exchange Features" on page 205.

WIN-OS/2 Setup

WIN-OS/2
Setup

The WIN-OS/2 Setup is a tool you use to install or change WIN-OS/2 network drivers and set up programs.

Adobe Type Manager (ATM) Control Panel

ATM Control
Panel

The ATM is a program you use with PostScript Type 1 font packages. You use the ATM Control Panel to add and remove fonts, change the font cache size, use pre-built or resident font software and turn the ATM program on or off. For more information, see Chapter 19, "Adobe Type Manager for WIN-OS/2" on page 211.

WIN-OS/2
Groups

The WIN-OS/2 Accessories folder contains a set of Windows programs that let you create drawings, play multimedia files, and keep track of your appointments. Each program has a set of help menus to assist you with using the program.

To open the WIN-OS/2 Accessories folder:

1. Open **WIN-OS/2 Groups**.
2. Open **WIN-OS/2 Accessories**.
3. Open the program you want to use.

Media Player

Media
Player

The Media Player is a program you use to play multimedia files, such as sound or animation, and control hardware devices, such as a videodisc player.

Clock

Clock

The Clock is a tool you use to view the system date and time. You can display the Clock in either analog or digital mode.

Character Map

Character
Map

The Character Map is a tool you use to insert extended characters into documents. Character Map only works with Windows programs.

Card File

Card File

The Card File is a tool you use to organize and manage information, such as names, addresses, and phone numbers.

Calendar

Calendar

The Calendar is a program you use to keep track of your appointments.

Calculator

Calculator

The Calculator is a program you use to perform simple calculations or solve scientific mathematical problems.

Write

Write

Write is a word processor you use to create and print documents.

Sound Recorder

Sound
Recorder

The Sound Recorder is a tool you use to play, record, and edit sound files. Before you use this tool, you must use the WIN-OS/2 Control Panel to install and configure the appropriate sound hardware and device driver.

Paint Brush

Paint Brush

The Paint Brush is a tool you use to create drawings.

Object Packager

Object
Packager

The Object Packager is a tool you use to create icons that represent an embedded or linked object and insert them into documents.

Note Pad

Note Pad

The Note Pad is a text editor you use to edit small text files.

Locating Windows Programs

During the installation of OS/2 2.1, if you had Windows programs already installed on your hard disk, you were prompted to migrate these programs. Migrate means to make the programs ready to operate using OS/2 2.1. Windows programs that were migrated during installation can be found on the desktop. During installation, the following folders were created for you to store your Windows programs.

WIN-OS/2
Groups

When you run the Migrate Applications program for existing Windows programs, the WIN-OS/2 Groups folder is created and placed on the desktop. The WIN-OS/2 Groups folder contains folders of Windows application programs *groups*. A group is a set of Windows programs that are related.

For example, if you have CorelDraw for Windows installed, when you run the Migrate Applications program, a folder for all the CorelDraw programs is created and placed in the WIN-OS/2 Groups folder. Now you have access to all the CorelDraw programs in one folder. For more information about migrating programs, see "Migrate Applications" on page 69.

Windows
Programs

The Windows Programs folder contains Windows programs that have settings preselected to optimize the performance of your program. Windows programs that do not belong to any group are migrated to the Windows Programs folder.

Additional
Windows
Programs

The Additional Windows Programs folder contains Windows programs that have default settings for your programs. If these programs do not run correctly, you can specify other settings.

Setting the WIN-OS/2 Mode

WIN-OS/2 can run in two operating modes:

- *Standard* mode is used to run programs written for Microsoft Windows Versions 3.0 and 3.1.
- *Enhanced compatibility* mode is used to run programs that require Microsoft Windows Versions 3.0 and 3.1 enhanced.

Note: All Windows Version 3.0 and 3.1 standard mode programs will run in a WIN-OS/2 enhanced compatibility mode session.

You can specify a mode for a WIN-OS/2 session or Windows program by changing the WIN-OS/2 run mode setting. For Windows programs that require Microsoft Windows Version 3.1 enhanced mode, set the WIN_RUN_MODE setting to **3.1 Enhanced Compatibility**.

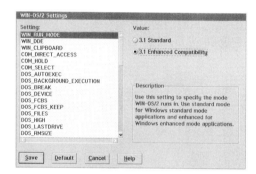

To set the mode:

1. Display the pop-up menu for the Windows program object.
2. Select the arrow to the right of **Open**; then select **Settings**.
3. Select **Session**.
4. Select the **WIN-OS/2 settings** push button.
5. Select the **WIN_RUN_MODE** setting.
6. Select the **3.1 Enhanced Compatibility** radio button.
7. Select **Save**.

Note: See "Incompatible Programs" on page 317 for important information on program mode support.

Changing WIN-OS/2 Settings

When your Windows programs were migrated to OS/2 2.1 during installation, the WIN-OS/2 settings were adjusted for you to provide optimum performance. These settings define characteristics such as memory size, keyboard rate, and program speed. You can change these settings using the Settings notebook. See Chapter 17, "Preparing Your Programs" on page 177.

When you change the value of a setting before you start a session, the changes affect all programs running in that session. When you change the value of a setting while the session is running, the changes affect only the programs you run in that session. If you want the changes to remain whenever you start a specific session or program, you must save the changes.

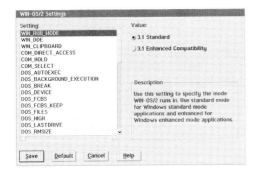

To change WIN-OS/2 settings:

1. Display the pop-up menu for the object.
2. Select the arrow to the right of **Open**; then select **Settings**.
3. Select **Session**.
4. Select the **WIN-OS/2 settings** push button.
5. Select the setting you require from the list.
6. Adjust the value of the choice, as appropriate.
7. Select **Save**.

To change settings for a WIN-OS/2 full-screen session while it is running:

1. Display the pop-up menu for the open session.
2. Select **DOS Settings**.
3. Select the setting you require from the list.
4. Adjust the value or the choice, as appropriate.
5. Select **Save**.

Running Windows Programs in WIN-OS/2 Sessions

Windows programs, like OS/2 programs, run in a *session* on the desktop. Most Windows programs are set up during installation of the OS/2 operating system to run in a WIN-OS/2 window session. If you start one or more Windows programs, they will run in this single WIN-OS/2 window session. The first program started in this window session determines the setting for all other programs running in this session. To exit from a window session, you must exit from each program in the session. Some Windows programs cannot run in a WIN-OS/2 window session. These programs are set up to run in a WIN-OS/2 full-screen session.

Windows programs also can be run in a WIN-OS/2 window separate session. You might want to use a separate session for your programs that have specific requirements. You can run more than one separate session at a time.

Note: You cannot change settings for any of the programs currently running in a WIN-OS/2 window or separate session while the session is running. The settings push buttons are not available.

Running Windows Programs from the Desktop in a Window Session

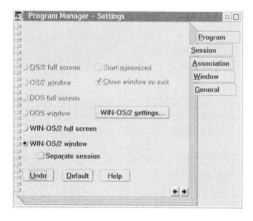

To change a Windows program object so that the program always runs in a WIN-OS/2 window session on the desktop alongside an OS/2 program:

1. Display the pop-up menu for the Windows program object.
2. Select the arrow to the right of **Open**; then select **Settings**.
3. Select **Session**.
4. Select the type of session: **WIN-OS/2 window**.

To run a Windows program from the desktop in a WIN-OS/2 window session:

1. Open the WIN-OS/2 Groups, Windows Programs, or Additional Windows Programs folder.
2. Open the program object.

To run more than one Windows program in a WIN-OS/2 session, repeat the above steps as needed.

Running Windows Programs from the Desktop in a Window Separate Session

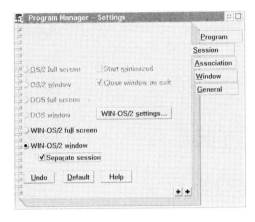

To change a Windows program object so that the program always runs in a separate WIN-OS/2 window session on the desktop alongside an OS/2 program:

1. Display the pop-up menu for the Windows program object.
2. Select the arrow to the right of **Open**; then select **Settings**.
3. Select **Session**.
4. Select the type of session: **Separate session**.

To run a Windows program from the desktop in a WIN-OS/2 window separate session:

1. Open the WIN-OS/2 Groups, Windows Programs, or Additional Windows Programs folder.
2. Open the program object.

To run more than one Windows program in a WIN-OS/2 session, repeat the above steps as needed.

To end a WIN-OS/2 window session, close each program in the Window List. When you exit the last program, the WIN-OS2 window session ends.

Note: Do not close the WIN-OS/2 window session unless you have exited each program in this session. Closing this session automatically exits each program. This also applies to the WIN-OS/2 Program Manager when it is running in a WIN-OS/2 window session.

Running Windows Programs in a Full-Screen Session

The WIN-OS/2 full-screen session uses the WIN-OS/2 Program Manager to run programs. You can include a program in a WIN-OS/2 Program Manager group, and then run that program by selecting it from the appropriate WIN-OS/2 Program Manager group window.

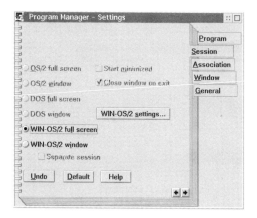

To change a Windows program so that it always runs in a WIN-OS/2 full-screen session, do the following:

1. Display the pop-up menu for the Windows program object.
2. Select the arrow to the right of **Open**; then select **Settings**.
3. Select **Session**.
4. Select the type of session: **WIN-OS/2 full screen**.

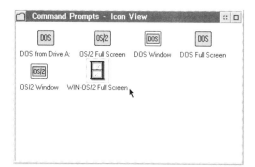

To run your Windows programs in a WIN-OS/2 full-screen session:

1. Open **OS/2 System**.
2. Open **Command Prompts**.
3. Open **WIN-OS/2 Full Screen**.
4. Open the program object.

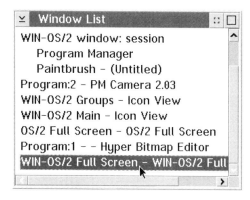

To return to the OS/2 desktop without exiting your WIN-OS/2 full-screen session, select the **OS/2 Desktop** icon at the bottom of the WIN-OS/2 full-screen session screen. You can return directly to your WIN-OS/2 session by selecting the program or session name from the OS/2 Window List.

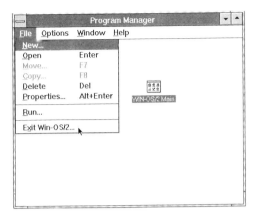

To exit a WIN-OS/2 full-screen session, select **Exit WIN-OS/2** from the **File** menu on the WIN-OS/2 Program Manager menu bar. You also can select **Close** from the WIN-OS/2 Program Manager system menu.

To switch between tasks in a WIN-OS/2 full-screen session:

1. Press Ctrl+Esc to display the Task List for WIN-OS/2.
2. Select the task you want as the active program.

Note: If pressing Ctrl+Esc does not display the Task List, you need to change the **KBD_CTRL_BYPASS** (Control-key bypass) setting to CTRL_ESC.

To switch between sessions, press Alt+Esc. The next session might be an OS/2, DOS, or WIN-OS/2 session.

Using the Clipboard and Dynamic Data Exchange Features

You use the WIN-OS/2 Setup object to set up the clipboard and the dynamic data exchange (DDE) features. For more information about the WIN-OS/2 Setup object, see "WIN-OS/2 Setup" on page 85. The clipboard feature shares information between sessions. You can copy or cut information from one session or program to the clipboard and then paste the same information from the clipboard to a different session or program. The DDE feature causes changes made in one data file or session to cause the same changes to be made in another data file or session.

The clipboard and DDE can be set to *Public* or *Private*. When the clipboard is set to Public, information can be shared with OS/2, DOS window, and WIN-OS/2 sessions. When the DDE is set to Public, information can be shared with OS/2 and WIN-OS/2 sessions. DDE Information cannot be shared with DOS sessions. When the clipboard or DDE is set to Private, sharing data between sessions is restricted. This means that only information for those programs running in that single session can be shared. When OS/2 2.1 is installed, the clipboard and DDE are set to Public.

OS/2 2.1 has an OS/2 clipboard and DDE and a WIN-OS/2 clipboard. The WIN-OS/2 settings, WIN-CLIPBOARD and WIN_DDE, are set to On for a public clipboard or DDE. To make them private, set them to Off.

Changing the Clipboard and DDE to Private for All WIN-OS/2 Sessions

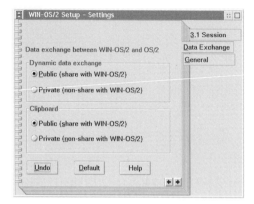

Use **WIN-OS/2 Setup** to select the clipboard and DDE settings for *all* your WIN-OS/2 sessions. To change the default clipboard or DDE setting for WIN-OS/2 sessions:

1. Display the pop-up menu for the Desktop folder.
2. Open **System setup**.
3. Open **WIN-OS/2 Setup**.
4. Select **Data Exchange**.
5. Select the **Private** radio button for **Dynamic Data Exchange** and **Clipboard**.
6. Close the WIN-OS/2 Setup Settings notebook.

Note: If you change the settings for the clipboard or DDE while a program is running in a WIN-OS/2 session, the settings for the program will take effect immediately.

Changing the Clipboard or DDE to Private for a WIN-OS/2 Separate Session

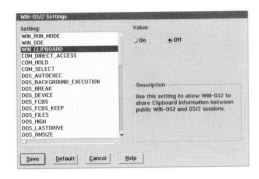

To change the clipboard and DDE settings for a single program, running in a WIN-OS/2 separate session, use the pop-up menu of the program object:

1. Display the pop-up menu for the program object.
2. Select the arrow to the right of **Open**; then select **Settings**.
3. Select **Session**.
4. Select the **WIN-OS/2 settings** push button.
5. Select **WIN_CLIPBOARD** or **WIN_DDE** from the list.
6. Select the **Off** radio button.
7. Select **Save**.
8. Close the Settings notebook.
9. Restart the program by opening the program object.

Copying or Cutting Information to the Public Clipboard

You can *cut* (move) or *copy* (duplicate) information. When you cut or copy something, it is placed in the public clipboard until you *paste* (put it somewhere else) or you write over it by cutting or copying something else to the public clipboard.

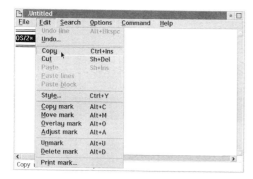

To copy or cut (move) information to a public clipboard to a program:

1. Mark the information you want to copy or cut:
   a. Point to the beginning of the text or graphics you want to copy or cut.
   b. Press and hold mouse button 1.
   c. Drag the mark to the end of the text or graphics you want to copy or cut.
   d. Release mouse button 1. The information is marked.
2. Select **Edit**.
3. Select either **Copy** or **Cut**.

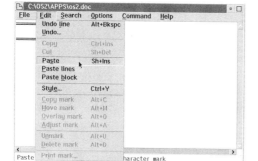

To paste information from a clipboard:

1. Open the data file where you want to put the information.
2. Move the mouse pointer to where you want the information to appear.
3. Use the **Paste** choice from the **Edit** menu to insert the information.

Note: If you are using a DOS window or OS/2 window, display the pop-up menu to see the Mark, Copy, and Paste menu choices.

Copying to and from DOS and OS/2 Sessions

Sometimes when you start a program from a DOS or OS/2 command prompt, the program runs in a window that contains a menu bar and has cut, copy, and paste functions available. To learn how to cut, copy, and paste to and from such a program, use the information that came with the program.

Sometimes, however, a program that runs in a DOS or OS/2 window might not have a menu bar or support cut, copy, and paste functions. Then the pop-up menu for the window contains specific choices that enable you to copy text or graphics to and from those windows. The data is transferred in and out of the windows through the OS/2 clipboard.

You can copy text or graphics from any DOS or OS/2 window to the OS/2 clipboard. Likewise, you can copy any text or graphics from the OS/2 clipboard to any DOS or OS/2 window. A cut procedure is not available.

The text or graphics you copy from the clipboard can come from another DOS or OS/2 window, a WIN-OS/2 session, or any program that has cut, copy, and paste functions available.

Copying or Moving Information between Two Programs in the Same WIN-OS/2 Session

To copy or move information between two programs or documents in the same WIN-OS/2 session, use the Cut, Copy, and Paste procedures defined for your Windows program.

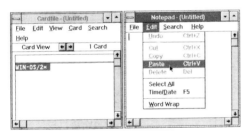

To copy or move clipboard information:

1. Mark the information you want to copy or move:
   a. Point to the beginning of the text or graphics you want to copy or move.
   b. Press and hold mouse button 1.
   c. Drag the mark to the end of the text or graphics you want to copy or move.
   d. Release mouse button 1. The information is marked.
2. Select **Edit**.
3. Select either **Copy** or **Cut** to put the information into the WIN-OS/2 clipboard.
4. Open the data file where you want to put the information.
5. Select the location where you want the information to appear.
6. Select **Edit**.
7. Select **Paste** to insert the information.

Starting an OS/2 or DOS Program in a WIN-OS/2 Session

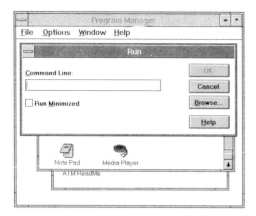

You can start a DOS or an OS/2 program in a WIN-OS/2 session. To start an OS/2 or DOS program in a WIN-OS/2 session:

1. Open **Windows Programs**.
2. Open **Program Manager**.
3. Select the File menu on the WIN-OS/2 Program Manager menu bar and then select **Run**. The Run pop-up window appears.
4. Type the program file name, including the path, in the **Command Line** field.
5. Select **OK**.

Note: If you do not know the file name of the program or its path, select the **Browse** push button from the Run pop-up window. The Browse window appears with a list of file names and directories.

You also can find the program path and file name by selecting the program from the WIN-OS/2 File Manager program.

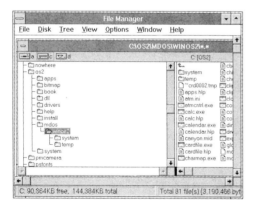

To start the WIN-OS/2 File Manager program:

1. Open the **WIN-OS/2 Groups** folder.
2. Open **WIN-OS/2 Main**.
3. Open **File Manager**.
4. Select the appropriate drive and directory for your program.
5. Open (double-click) the file that starts your program.

Chapter 19. Adobe Type Manager for WIN-OS/2

ATM Control
Panel

The Adobe Type Manager (ATM) produces the sharpest possible font types on screen and on the printed page. Because it incorporates PostScript outline font technology, the ATM program eliminates jagged fonts so that your screen can display high-quality typefaces of any size or style. The ATM program also enables even inexpensive printers to print PostScript language fonts that are crisp and smooth.

ATM is included with OS/2 2.1 and ATM fonts are handled automatically for OS/2 applications. You can install additional ATM fonts using the Font Palette, see "Font Palette" on page 64. OS/2 2.1 also includes the Adobe Type Manager for WIN-OS/2 so that your Windows programs can use the same fonts as your OS/2 programs.

OS/2 2.1 also includes the IBM Core Fonts which are automatically copied onto your hard disk during installation, unless you specify otherwise. To make these fonts available to your WIN-OS/2 applications, you must add the fonts to ATM. Follow the instructions for "Adding Fonts to Your System" on page 213. At step 5 specify C:\PSFONTS\PFM as the source directory.

Note: If you want to use the fonts for both WIN-OS/2 and OS/2 programs, you must install the font files using both the Font Palette and the ATM Control Panel. For more information about using the Font Palette, see "Font Palette" on page 64.

This chapter explains how to open the ATM Control Panel in the WIN-OS/2 environment of OS/2 and how to use it.

ATM Control Panel

The ATM program works with PostScript Type 1 font packages. You can use the ATM Control Panel to add and remove fonts, change the font cache size, use pre-built or resident font software, and turn the ATM program on or off. When you change any of the choices in the ATM Control Panel, except the **Use Pre-Built or Resident Fonts** choice, you must exit and then restart your WIN-OS/2 session for your changes to take effect.

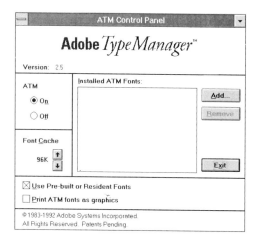

To open the ATM Control Panel:

1. Open **WIN-OS/2 Groups**.
2. Open **WIN-OS/2 Main**.
3. Open **ATM Control Panel**.

    The ATM Control Panel appears.

Adding Fonts to Your System

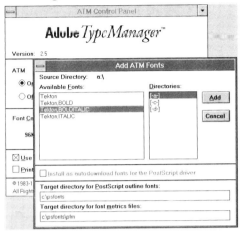

To add fonts to your system:

1. Open the **ATM Control Panel**.

2. Select the **Add** push button. The Add ATM Fonts pop-up window appears.

   The top portion of the pop-up window lets you locate the directory or diskette where the fonts currently reside. The Available Fonts selection list lists the names of the outline fonts in the current directory. The bottom portion of the pop-up window allows you to specify the directory in which the fonts will be installed.

3. In the **Target directory for PostScript outline fonts** field, you can accept the default, C:\PSFONTS, or type the name of the directory to which you want to copy the font outline files. If the directory name you enter does not correspond to an existing directory, ATM will create a new directory. Any directory name you type automatically appears in the **Target directory for font metrics files** field. You can accept this name or enter the name of another directory for the font metric files.

4. If you have diskettes containing fonts, insert the appropriate diskette according to the type of PostScript fonts you are adding:

   - If you are adding Revision 3 Adobe Type Library font software or Revision 2, 3.5-inch-diskette Adobe Type Library fonts, insert the *Font* diskette or the *Printer Font* diskette, respectively.

   - If you are adding Revision 1 Adobe Type Library fonts, insert the *Program* diskette.

   - If you are adding non-Adobe fonts, insert the diskette containing the font metric files (.PFM or .AFM).

5. Select the drive or directory containing the fonts from the Directories selection list.

6. Select the fonts you want to add by selecting **Add**. You can select as many fonts as you want. If you want to select all of the fonts in the selection list, select the first font in the list, scroll to the end of the list, and then press and hold down the Shift key while selecting the last font. If you want to select specific fonts in the list, hold down the Ctrl key as you click on the names of the fonts you want to add.

   Note: You should install each style of a font you want to use. For example, if you are installing the Times font, you should install Times.BOLD, Times.ITALIC, and Times.BOLDITALIC. However, if disk space is limited, you can install the regular typeface and ATM will approximate the other styles. Keep in mind, however, that ATM will not approximate the other styles if you are printing to a PostScript printer.

7. At this point, depending on the type of fonts you are adding, the program might prompt you for outline font files (.PFB). If the program does not prompt you for any additional files, go on to the next step. Otherwise, do one of the following:

   • If you are using an Adobe Type Library package with multiple font diskettes, insert any supplemental diskette included in the package and select the appropriate drive or directory in the Directories selection list.

   • If you are adding non-Adobe fonts, Revision 1 Adobe fonts, or Revision 2, 5.25-inch-diskette Adobe fonts, insert the *Printer Font* diskette (that is, the diskette containing the font outline files) and select the appropriate drive or directory in the Directories selection list.

   After the fonts have been loaded, the new fonts appear in the Installed ATM Fonts selection list in the ATM Control Panel.

8. Select the **Exit** push button to complete the font installation. A pop-up window appears, asking whether to restart the WIN-OS/2 session or return to the current WIN-OS/2 session. You must restart the WIN-OS/2 session to use the new fonts.

Removing Fonts from Your System

To remove fonts from your system:

1. Open the **ATM Control Panel.**
2. Select the fonts you want to remove from the Installed ATM Fonts list.
3. Select the **Remove** push button.

   The ATM Confirmation pop-up window appears for each selected font asking you to confirm that you want to remove the font.

4. Select **Yes** to remove the font. To remove the remaining fonts without confirming each one, select the **No confirmation to remove fonts** field.

Note: Removing a font does not delete the corresponding .PFB and .PFM files from the hard disk.

Using Pre-Built or Resident Bit-Map Fonts

When pre-built fonts (soft fonts) or resident bit-map or outline fonts (cartridge fonts or fonts built into the printer) are available, the ATM program will use them if you select **Use Pre-Built or Resident Fonts** in the ATM Control Panel.

In some situations, however, you might not want the ATM program to use pre-built or resident fonts.

- If your application supports autokerning, the ATM fonts will be kerned but the pre-built or resident fonts will not.

- Some typefaces might have a different appearance if you use pre-built or resident fonts. This situation is most apparent with the Courier font printed to a Hewlett-Packard** LaserJet printer.

- If you change the printer resolution, the ATM text changes accordingly, but the pre-built or resident fonts will not.

Changing the Font Cache Size

The size of the font cache determines the amount of system memory available to store font information. The default setting for the font cache is 96KB. You can set the font cache from 64KB to 32 000KB.

If you are using many typefaces or sizes, you might want to increase the font cache size to improve performance. Experiment with the font cache size parameter to see how it affects performance.

If your applications seem unusually slow when you scroll, change pages, or display fonts, your font cache size is probably too small.

To change the font cache size:

1. Open the ATM Control Panel.

2. Select the Up Arrow in the **Font Cache** field to increase the size, or select the Down Arrow to decrease the size.

3. Select the **Exit** push button. A pop-up window appears, asking whether to restart the WIN-OS/2 session or return to the current WIN-OS/2 session. You must restart the WIN-OS/2 session for your change in the font cache size to take effect.

Turning the ATM Program On or Off

To turn the ATM program on or off, select the **On** or **Off** radio button in the ATM Control Panel. A pop-up window appears, asking if you want to restart the WIN-OS/2 session or return to the current WIN-OS/2 session. You must restart the WIN-OS/2 session for your changes to take effect.

Removing the ATM Program from Your System

In rare instances, you might want to remove the ATM program from your system.

To remove ATM from your system:

1. Delete the ATM Control Panel from the Main group.

2. Use the OS/2 System Editor to open the SYSTEM.INI file in the OS2\MDOS\WINOS2 directory.

   Change the line:

   ```
   SYSTEM.DRV=ATMSYS.DRV
   ```

   to:

   ```
   SYSTEM.DRV=SYSTEM.DRV
   ```

   Delete the line:

   ```
   ATM.SYSTEM.DRV=SYSTEM.DRV
   ```

3. Save the file and exit the editor.

4. Delete the ATM16.DLL or ATM32.DLL file and the ATMSYS.DRV files from OS2\MDOS\WINOS2\SYSTEM.

5. Delete the ATM.INI and ATMCNTRL.EXE files from C:\OS2\MDOS\WINOS2.

6. Delete the files with the extensions PFM and PFB from the directories in which you installed them.

Printing on PCL Printers

For optimal performance, print through a parallel port (LPT).

ATM can use pre-built fonts (soft fonts) or resident fonts (cartridge fonts or fonts built into the printer) when the exact font size and style are available. This reduces the amount of printer memory required to print some pages and might improve printing performance. The Adobe Font Foundry program (included with all Adobe Type Library packages) can be used to generate such soft fonts; the ATM Control Panel can then be used to turn this feature on and off.

Printing on PostScript Printers

If you are using ATM with a PostScript printer, PostScript soft fonts are automatically downloaded when you print; you might want to download fonts that are not resident in your printer prior to printing. Downloading fonts before printing can increase printing performance. This feature is especially useful if you frequently use the same fonts on your PostScript printer.

Resolving ATM Problems

This section contains solutions to problems you might encounter when using the ATM program. You might also want to refer to the README file on your ATM program (OS2\MDOS\WINOS2\README.ATM) for troubleshooting information that is not included in this book. Use a text editor to open and read the file.

ATM Disabled

Problem: The ATM startup icon is crossed out, or the ATM Control Panel shows that the program is "inactive".

Solution: Make sure that:

- Fonts appear in the ATM Control Panel
- Your SYSTEM.INI file contains the following entries:

    SYSTEM.ATMSYS.DRV

    ATM.SYSTEM.DRV=SYSTEM.DRV

Jagged Characters

Problem: Characters appear jagged on screen or when the document is printed, or both.

Solution: Make sure that:

- You are using a PostScript language Type 1 font program, such as those provided with ATM.

- The ATM program is turned on in the ATM Control Panel. (Make sure that ATM is not labeled "inactive" in the ATM Control Panel. If ATM is active, the program's version number appears in the Control Panel.)

- Your printer is set for the highest resolution in its Setup pop-up window.

Problem: Characters appear jagged on screen but print correctly on a PostScript printer.

Solution: For each PostScript language printer font, install the corresponding outline-font program using the ATM Control Panel.

ATM Fonts Missing

Problem: The ATM fonts do not appear in the Font menu of your application.

Solution: Reselect your printer from within the application.

Also verify that the font metrics (.PFM files) and PostScript language outline-font programs (.PFB files) are installed correctly. If necessary, add the fonts again using the ATM Control Panel.

Printing Is Slow

Problem: Computer or printer performance seems slow.

Solution: Increase the size of the font cache. The default setting is 96KB. For graphic arts applications, you might want to use a font cache size of 128KB or larger.

Error Messages

Problem: A memory error occurs when you open an application with the ATM program turned on.

Solution: The current system configuration does not leave enough memory for your application. Try decreasing the ATM font cache size, decreasing the number of files specified in your CONFIG.SYS file, removing any networking software, or increasing the DPMI memory limit in the WIN-OS/2 settings for your WIN-OS/2 session.

Problem: A PCL printer indicates an "out of memory" error condition.

Solution: If you have the correct soft font or cartridge font installed, make sure that **Use Pre-Built or Resident Bit Map Fonts** is selected in the ATM Control Panel. Also, consider adding more memory to your printer.

Chapter 20. Using a Network

Network

If your system is part of a local area network (LAN), you have a
Network object on your desktop.

The Network Group Folder

When you open the Network object, another object, the *network group* folder,
appears.

That network group folder has the name assigned to the particular network you
use. You can have more than one network group folder inside the Network folder
if your system is connected to more than one network. Then, each folder has a
different name.

The network group folder contains the server objects. Server objects contain
network resources, such as network folders, data-file objects, program objects, and
printer objects. When you use network objects, you might be asked to type your
user identification and password.

221

Viewing Network Objects

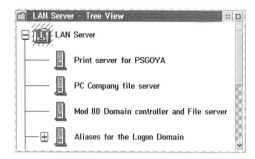

To view the objects available to you on the network:

1. Open the Network folder on your desktop. The Network folder is displayed. It contains objects that represent the networks you have access to.
2. Open a network object to display the contents of the folder. If this is the first time you have opened this folder, display the pop-up menu for the folder by pointing at the folder and then clicking mouse button 2.
3. Select **Refresh**. The network servers you have access to are displayed.
4. Open a server to view the network folders and network printers.

Accessing a Network

Typing your user identification information is called *login* or *logon*.

A network administrator usually oversees the operation of the LAN and is responsible for giving you access authorization, such as a user identification and password, to use the network.

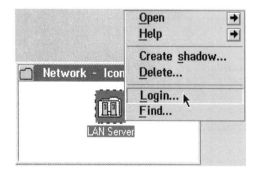

If you want to log in before being prompted:

1. Display the pop-up menu for the folder or printer object you want to use by pointing at the folder and then clicking mouse button 2.
2. Select **Login**.

Note: If you intend to leave your system unlocked and unattended for a period of time, be sure you display the pop-up menu for the network folder object and select **Logout**.

Using Non-LAN-Aware Programs

Some programs are not LAN-aware, which means they will not run from a Network folder or they cannot access files from a network folder. For example, some programs can access data only on disk drives that have letter names, such as A or C. Using the OS/2 operating system, you can display the pop-up menu of a network directory and select **Assign drive** if you need a drive letter for it.

Some programs do not provide a way for you to print on a network printer. These programs recognize printer objects by the port they are connected to, such as LPT1 (line printer 1). To assign a port, display the pop-up menu for the printer object by pointing at the object and then clicking mouse button 2. If you need a port for one of these resources, you can select **Assign port**. For more information, refer to "network, using an assigned port" in the Master Help Index.

Accessing Objects on Another Network

You can create an object to represent a server, network folder, or network printer on another network.

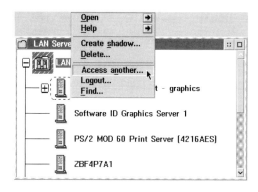

To create an object that enables you to reach the other network's resources:

1. Display the pop-up menu for the type of item you want to access.
2. Select **Access another**. A window appears. This window enables you to fill in details about the object you are trying to access.

After you create the object, you might need to select **Login** from its pop-up menu before you can use the object.

What is *multimedia*? Multimedia is the combined use of various media in applications, such as text, graphics, sound and motion video to enhance the communication of information.

This section describes the multimedia applications and features that are part of OS/2 2.1 and how to use them. If you have not installed multimedia yet, see "Installing Multimedia Features" in the *OS/2 2.1 Installation Guide*.

Chapter 21. Multimedia Features

Multimedia
Features

The Multimedia folder contains the following applications that allow you to experience multimedia on your system.

System Sounds

Sound

Use the Sound object to attach sounds to system events.

Digital Video

Digital
Video

Use the Digital Video media player to play movies on the desktop.

Compact Disc

Compact
Disc

Use the Compact disc application to play your favorite music CDs.

Digital Audio

Digital
Audio

Use the Digital Audio application to play, record, and edit sound files.

MIDI

MIDI

Use the MIDI media player to play MIDI songs.

Multimedia Setup

Multimedia
Setup

Use the Multimedia Setup application to control settings for multimedia devices.

Multimedia Data Converter

Multimedia
Data
Converter

Use the Multimedia Data Converter application to convert multimedia files to a different format.

Volume Control

Volume
Control

Use the Volume Control application to set the system wide volume level for multimedia applications.

Readme

README

Read the Readme file for items of interest concerning MMPM/2.

Chapter 22. Multimedia Applications

Multimedia

This chapter describes the multimedia applications. Refer to the online help information for assistance in using them. After you have installed multimedia, you can start the various applications by opening the Multimedia folder and selecting the program objects.

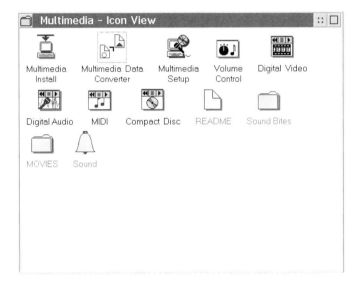

When you install multimedia, you add the capability to attach sounds to system events and have the sounds play whenever the events occur. This capability is provided by an extension to the OS/2 Sound object.

The Sound object is located in System Setup in the OS/2 System folder. A shadow of the Sound object is copied to the Multimedia folder.

Use system sounds to alert and inform you of activities on the system. A set of system sounds is included and already associated with system events. You can make different associations using these sounds, or you can create your own sounds.

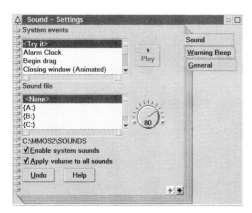

OS/2 System Sounds Events

- Information message
- Warning message
- Error message
- Opening a window
- Closing a window
- Picking up an object
- Dropping an object
- System startup
- System shutdown
- Shredding an object
- Alarm clock ringing
- Printer error message
- Desktop lockup

Use the **Play** button to test a sound file before it is associated with a system event. Use the volume dial to set the volume level of the sound. If **Apply Volume to all sounds** is checked, whatever volume level you set is automatically applied to all system sounds.

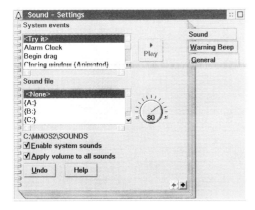

To associate sounds with events:

1. Open  in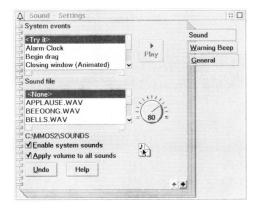
2. Select an event from the list of system events.
3. Select a sound from the list containing sound files.

To test a sound before you associate it with an event:

1. Select **<Try it>** in **System events**.
2. Select a sound from the sound files list.
3. Select the **Play** button to play the selected sound.

Use **Digital Audio** in ![] to record your own sounds. If you do not have a sound adapter, you can associate a system event with a tune file created with the OS/2 Tune Editor as follows:

1. Open OS/2 System.
2. Open Productivity.
3. Open ![]

Using the Tune Editor, create tune files and put them in a folder. Then:

1. Select an event from the list of system events.
2. Open the folder containing the tune files.
3. Point to a tune file.
4. Press and hold mouse button 2.
5. Drag the tune to the notebook page.
6. Release mouse button 2.

MMPM/2 also provides support for playing a sound file from an OS/2 command file. This feature is useful for alerting you when a location in the file is reached that requires you to do something.

Support for playing and recording sound files from command files is implemented in the PLAY.CMD and RECORD.CMD files, located in the \MMOS2 directory. When you type the name of either of these command files at the command prompt, a description of the syntax is displayed.

To use the PLAY.CMD and RECORD.CMD files, you must have the basic REXX support installed on your system. The REXX multimedia function used in the PLAY.CMD and RECORD.CMD files is described in the online publication *Controlling Multimedia Devices with REXX.*

Digital Video

 If you installed the Software Motion Video feature, you can play movie files.

View high-resolution digital movies on your desktop without any additional hardware requirement. With the addition of an audio adapter, you can enjoy an audio track that is fully synchronized with the video.

MMPM/2 brings you a standard resolution of 320x240 at 15 frames per second, using the Ultimotion** compression type. This is based on a system configuration with a 25Mhz 386 processor and SVGA or XGA video support. Movie playback is scaled to whatever system is being used. The amount of scalability depends on the amount of data put into the video at the time of its creation, and the processing capabilities of your computer. Ultimotion supports both 256 and 65,000 colors, providing clear images and data transfer rates within standard CD-ROM capabilities (150 kilobytes per second).

OS/2 supports the AVI file format for movie files.

To play a movie:

1. Select a data object.

2. Open .

3. Drag the data object to the Digital Video program object and release it.

4. Select and enjoy the movie.

Note: Different methods can be used for compression by AVI format files, and not all compression types are supported. If a compression type is not supported, an error message is displayed when you attempt to load the file.

Compact Disc

If you have a CD-ROM drive and install multimedia support, you can use the Compact Disc application to play music CDs.

Start the application. If a CD is not present in the drive, a graphic is displayed, prompting you to load a CD.

After you insert a CD in the drive, numbered buttons representing the tracks are displayed.

To the left of the buttons are a number and a minutes:seconds (MM:SS) value. The number is the track currently selected for play, and the MM:SS value is the position in the track. For example, in the picture above, track 3 is selected, and the position in the track is at the beginning. If you are familiar with the track order on the CD, you can go directly to your favorite track by pressing a track button.

Use the buttons below the track buttons to play and browse the tracks sequentially:

1. Select ▶ to play the current track.

2. Select ◀◀ to go to the beginning of the track.

3. Select ◀◀ again to go to the previous track.

4. Select ▶▶ to go to the next track.

5. Select ▶▶ to move forward in the current track.

6. Select ◀◀ to move backward in the current track.

7. Select ‖ to toggle between stopping and playing.

8. Select ■ to stop playing the current track.

9. Select ▲ to eject the currently loaded CD electronically.

Shuffling the Tracks

When you first load a CD, its tracks are shown in numerical order. For variety, you can play tracks in a random order.

To play the tracks in random order:

1. Select the title bar icon to display the pop-up menu.
2. Select **Options**.
3. Select **Shuffle Tracks**.

You can shuffle the tracks again to create a new random order.

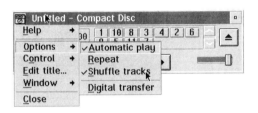

To restore the numerical order, deselect **Shuffle Tracks**.

Disabling a Track

You can play only your favorite tracks by disabling the tracks you do not want played.

To disable a track:

1. Press and hold the **Shift** key.
2. Point to the track button.
3. Click mouse button 1 to disable the track.

Dashes replace the track button number, indicating the track is no longer selected for playing. To reinstate the track, click mouse button 1 on the disabled track button. To select the track so it is the next one played, click mouse button 1 again.

Editing the Window Title

When you first load a CD, the window title is shown as Untitled - Compact Disc.

You can change the title so it includes the name of your CD:

1. Select the title bar icon to display the pop-up menu.
2. Select **Edit Title**.
3. Select the entry field in the **Edit Title** window.
4. Type a name, up to 32 characters in length.
5. Select **Save**.

After you save the name, it is displayed as part of the window title whenever your CD is loaded.

Settings for CDs

The Compact Disc application remembers the title and disabled tracks associated with a particular CD each time you load the CD.

Settings on the **Options** menu affect any currently loaded CD.

- **Shuffle tracks** shuffles the track play order.
- **Repeat** plays enabled tracks repeatedly.
- **Automatic play** automatically plays the CD.

Compact Size

To save room on the desktop, you can select a compact size that displays only buttons for stop, pause, play, track selection, and scanning.

To change the window to the compact size:

1. Select the title bar icon to display the pop-up menu.
2. Select the **Window** submenu.
3. Select **Compact Size**.
4. Select **Default Size** to change back to the original size.

Digital Audio

The Digital Audio application has play and record functions for digital audio files. It also has powerful editing functions. These functions are available to users in two different views: **Player/Recorder** and **Editor**.

Playing a Sound

To play sound files, select **Player/Recorder** on the **View** menu. You can play sounds stored in a variety of digital audio formats (for example, PCM, ADPCM, MU-LAW and A-LAW).

To play a sound:

1. Select **File** on the menu bar.

2. Select **Open** and choose a file to play.

3. Select [▶] to begin playing the file.

4. Select [❙❙] to toggle between stopping and playing.

5. Select [■] to stop playing.

Recording a Sound

When you use the Digital Audio application to record, files are recorded in the PCM format. These files typically have a .WAV extension.

The term "wave" or "waveform" refers to the digital representation of a sound wave. PCM is an abbreviation for Pulse Code Modulation, which is the recording method used by most audio devices to encode sound wave samples.

You can set PCM-format values with the Type menu. Format values are set only for new files after they are created and before any sound is put into them by recording or editing. If you do not select values from the Type menu, the defaults supported by your sound adapter are selected.

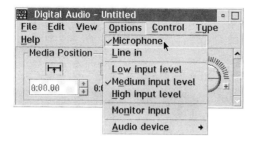

To record into a new file using the microphone:

1. Select **Options**.

2. Select **Microphone**.

3. Select **File**.

4. Select **New** to create a new file.

5. Select **Type**.

6. Select format values.

7. Select ⬜ to start recording. While recording is in progress, the record button blinks.

8. Select ⬜ to stop recording.

9. Select ⬜ to hear what you recorded.

Most sound adapters have two input jacks: microphone and line in. The line-in jack can connect the sound adapter with audio output from another device, such as a CD-ROM device.

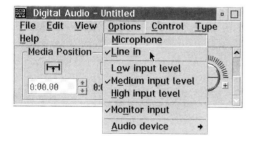

To set up a line-in device for recording:

1. Ensure that the device is connected to the line-in jack.
2. Select **Options**.
3. Select **Line in**.
4. Select **Options**.
5. Select the desired input level.
6. Select **Options**.
7. Select **Monitor input** if you want to hear what is recorded.

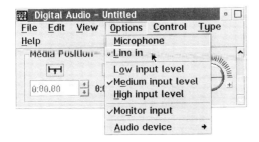

To record into an existing file:

1. Select **Options**.

2. Select the input device.

3. Select **File**.

4. Select **Open** to open an existing file.

5. Select the position in the file where recording is to start.

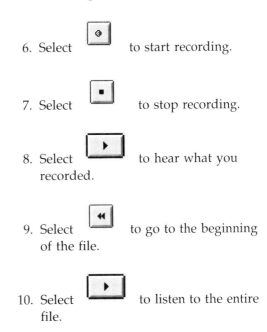

6. Select   to start recording.

7. Select   to stop recording.

8. Select   to hear what you recorded.

9. Select   to go to the beginning of the file.

10. Select   to listen to the entire file.

Settings on the Type menu cannot be selected after you load an existing file. Digital Audio selects the values that were set when the file was recorded and disables the other values.

Editing a Sound

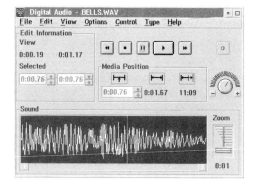

For editing operations, select **View**. Then select **Editor**.

Editing operations are done using a graphical representation of a sound file in the editing window.

1. Select **File**.

2. Select **New**.

3. Select ⬜ to record a new file.

4. Select ⬜ and observe the cursor movement as the sound file plays.

5. Use the Zoom slider to enlarge the sound graph.

6. Mark an area of the sound graph for editing.

7. Select ⬜ to hear the marked sound.

8. Select the **Selections** spin buttons to adjust the marked area.

9. Select **Edit**.

10. Select the desired edit command.

Marking a Sound Clip: Some edit commands on the **Edit** menu require you to mark (select) an area on the sound graph that the command will affect. For example to use the **Delete** command, you have to mark the area you want to delete.

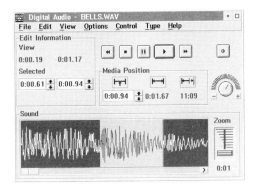

You can mark the entire file or only a section. To mark the entire file, select **Edit**; then select **Select all**.

To mark a section using the mouse:

1. Point to the start of the sound graph area you want to mark.
2. Press and hold mouse button 1.
3. Drag the cursor and highlight the area.
4. Release the mouse button when the desired position is reached.

Adjusting a Marked Area: As you listen to the sound file play, you can watch the cursor move through the sound graph and associate sounds in the file with variations you see in the graph. This process helps you identify the area in the sound graph you want to edit.

To adjust a marked area in hundredths of seconds, use the **Selection** spin buttons.

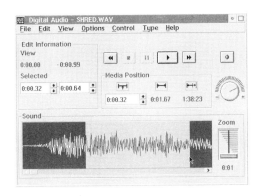

There are several ways to change the minutes-seconds-hundredths value in a spin button:

- Tab to the spin button field and type a value directly into it. Use a colon (:) between minutes and seconds, and a period (.) between seconds and hundredths.
- Select an arrow to scroll the value in the field up or down, changing it by hundredths of seconds.
- Mark a portion of the value in the field and scroll the portion up or down. For example, you can mark the seconds portion and scroll it to change only the seconds value.

Copying a Sound

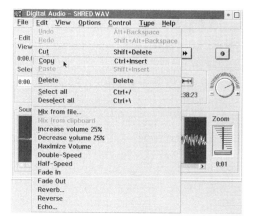

To copy a sound into another file:

1. Mark a sound to be copied to the clipboard.
2. Select **Edit**.
3. Select **Copy**.
4. Select **File**.
5. Select **Open** to load another file.
6. Select the desired position for the sound.
7. Select **Edit**.
8. Select **Paste**.

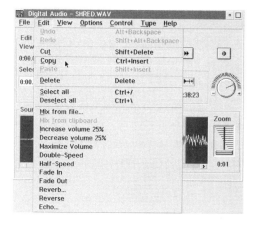

To copy a sound to another location in the same file:

1. Mark a sound to be copied to the clipboard.
2. Select **Edit**.
3. Select **Copy**. The sound in the marked area is copied to the clipboard.
4. Select anywhere on the sound graph to deselect the marked area.
5. Select the location on the sound graph where the sound is to be copied.
6. Select **Edit**.
7. Select **Paste** to copy the sound from the clipboard to the new location.

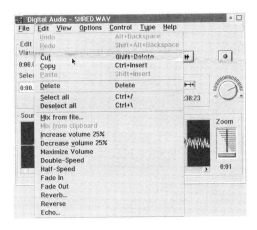

To move a sound to another location in the same file:

1. Mark the sound to be moved in the current file.
2. Select **Edit**.
3. Select **Cut**. The sound in the marked area is removed from the file and is copied to the clipboard.
4. Select the new location on the sound graph.
5. Select **Edit**.
6. Select **Paste**.

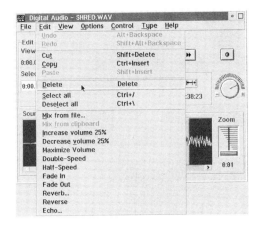

To delete a sound:

1. Mark the sound to be deleted in the current file.
2. Select **Edit**.
3. Select **Delete**.

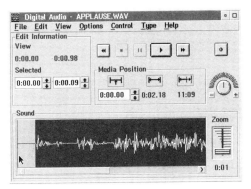

There are times when you might want to remove the silence, indicated by a flat line, at the beginning or end of a recording. An easy way to do this is to:

1. Point to the start of the silence within the file.
2. Press and hold mouse button 1.
3. Drag the cursor to the beginning or end of the file.
4. Release the mouse button.
5. Select **Edit**.
6. Select **Delete**.

Audio Special Effects

The Digital Audio application has a wide variety of special effects, which can be used to operate on a marked area of sound. Special effects are described in the following table.

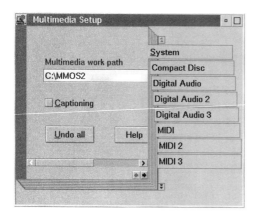

If you are using special effects on large digital audio files, ensure that the swapper path is on a disk that has enough space. Or you can use Multimedia Setup to change the multimedia work path to the appropriate disk.

Special Effect	Description
Mix from file	Mixes a specified file with the marked sound.
Mix from clipboard	Mixes a sound in the clipboard with the marked sound.
Increase volume 25%	Increases the volume of the marked sound 25%.
Decrease volume 25%	Decreases the volume of the marked sound 25%.
Maximize volume	Increases the amplitude of the marked sound as much as possible without clipping it.
Double-speed	Doubles the playback speed of the marked sound and raises its pitch.
Half-speed	Halves the playback speed of the marked sound and lowers its pitch.
Fade In	Gradually increases the marked sound volume from silence to its original level.
Fade Out	Gradually decreases the marked sound volume from its original level to silence.
Reverb	Makes the marked sound reverberate, as if it were recorded with a reverberating microphone.
Echo	Makes the marked sound echo, as if it were recorded in an echo chamber.
Reverse	Causes the marked sound to be played backward.

Mixing Two Sounds Together

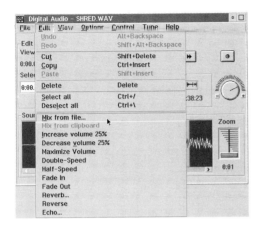

To mix a marked sound with another file:

1. Mark the sound in the current file to be mixed with another sound file.
2. Select **Edit**.
3. Select **Mix from file**.
4. Type or select the name of the sound file to be mixed with the marked sound clip.

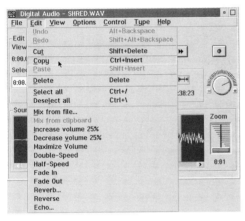

To mix a marked sound with clipboard contents:

1. Mark a sound in the current file for copying to the clipboard.
2. Select **Edit**.
3. Select **Copy**.
4. Select **File**.
5. Select **Open** to load another file.
6. Mark the sound in the open file to be mixed with clipboard contents.
7. Select **Edit**.
8. Select **Mix from Clipboard**.

Changing the Volume of a Sound Clip

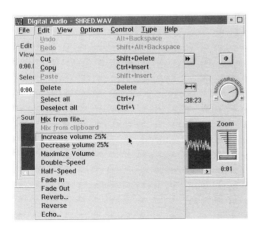

To change the volume of a sound clip:

1. Mark the sound you want to make louder.
2. Select **Edit**.
3. Select **Increase volume 25%**.

Or

1. Mark the sound you want to make softer.
2. Select **Edit**.
3. Select **Decrease volume 25%**.

Playing MIDI Files

 MIDI files contain sounds that are stored in a format used by musical equipment such as synthesizers and drum machines. MIDI files have a .MID extension and are played on a sequencer device by the Media Player.

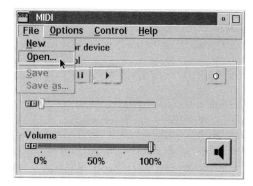

To play a MIDI file:

1. Open  in

2. Select **File**.

3. Select **Open**.

4. Point to a data object.

5. Press and hold mouse button 2.

6. Drag the data object to the program object.

7. Release mouse button 2.

8. Select and listen to the melody.

Volume Control

 Use the Volume Control application to set the volume level of all sound-producing media devices connected to your computer system. For your convenience, a copy of this application is installed on the desktop and in the Multimedia folder.

The volume control provides several ways to change the volume.

Change the volume slowly

1. Position the mouse pointer on the plus button (+) or minus button (–).
2. Hold down mouse button 1 to spin the volume level value.
3. Click the mouse button to change the volume level value by 1.

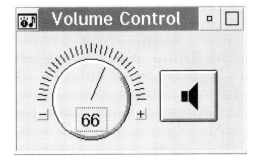

Change the volume at a moderate rate

1. Move the mouse pointer to the dial upper half.
2. Hold down mouse button 1 to move the indicator line to the mouse pointer.
3. Move the indicator line back and forth.

or

1. Move the mouse pointer to the dial lower half.
2. Hold down mouse button 1.
3. Move the mouse pointer left or right to change the volume.
4. Release the mouse button when the desired level is reached.
5. Click the mouse button inside the dial to change the volume level value by 10.

Change the volume fast

1. Position the mouse pointer anywhere on the volume increment marks surrounding the dial.
2. Press mouse button 1 to change the volume level immediately.

Volume Control works similar to an amplifier in a stereo system. For example, if other application programs (such as Digital Audio) are controlling specific devices, adjusting the Volume Control has the following effects:

- Decreasing the Volume Control decreases the volume for a device, even if the controlling application program has set the volume of the device to the maximum level.
- Increasing the Volume Control increases the volume for a device up to the level set by the controlling application program.

You can control the volume of an external device regardless of the volume settings shown by the Volume Control or other applications. For example, the volume of a device connected to an audio amplifier or powered speakers can be raised or lowered (using volume controls on the devices) even if the Volume Control settings are unchanged. The exceptions are if the Volume Control is set to 0 or if the audio is muted.

Once a volume level has been set externally (using volume controls on the devices), the Volume Control application can be used to lower or raise the level.

Setting the Volume Control to a given level will affect devices differently, depending upon the capability and volume level setting of the particular devices. Therefore, some devices may appear to change volume level more rapidly than others. For example, suppose you are simultaneously playing a MIDI device with a low volume setting and a CD player with a high volume setting, and you use Volume Control to reduce the volume to 50%. Because Volume Control scales the volume level of all devices at the same rate, the MIDI device might become inaudible while the CD player can still be heard.

Also, some devices support only two volume settings, On or Off. In this case, adjusting the Volume Control will have no apparent effect on the volume of the device.

Multimedia Data Converter

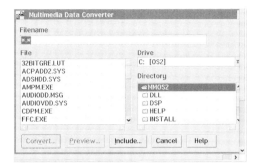

Use the Multimedia Data Converter application to convert certain multimedia files to a different format. For example, you can convert files from an IBM M-Motion image format to an OS/2 bitmap format.

The following table lists some of the file-name extensions supported by the Multimedia Data Converter.

Extension	Description	Type
_IM and !IM	IBM AVC* still video	Image
VID	IBM M-Motion still video	Image
BMP	OS/2 1.3, 2.0	Bit map
DIB	Microsoft device independent bit map	Bit map
RDI	RIFF device independent bit map	Bit map
VOC	Creative Labs voice file	Audio
_AU, _AD	IBM AVC ADPCM digital audio	Audio
WAV	RIFF WAVE digital audio	Audio

Note: Not all image files use these file extensions or have file extensions. The table above summarizes some of the more common extensions used in the industry.

Multimedia Setup

Multimedia
Setup

Use the Multimedia Setup application to change the settings of multimedia devices connected to your computer.

Devices are represented by notebook tabs in the Multimedia Setup window. You can select a device tab and:

- Associate files with a device.
- Change the name of a device.
- Change device-specific information.

Some devices have tabs for setting device-specific information. For example, you can select the MAPPER tab to control the way MIDI files are played. You can:

- Specify the MIDI device type
- Activate or deactivate specific channels

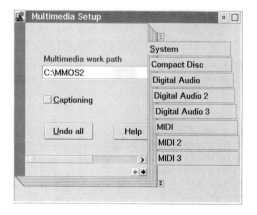

The Multimedia Setup application also has a system tab for setting system-wide values for applications. The system tab allows you to set the captioning flag. Captioning is the ability of an application to provide a visual representation of sound. Most commonly, captioning is text that accompanies spoken words.

You can turn the captioning setting on or off. Any applications that provide captioning can query this setting to determine whether you want to have captioned information displayed.

Some applications allow users to add a feature to the application by running a special file called a macro. Excel** and Lotus 1-2-3** applications have this capability. OS/2 multimedia provides users of these applications with macros that enable them to annotate their work sheets with audio. When you install multimedia, macro files for Lotus 1-2-3 and Excel are copied to the \MMOS2\MACROS directory.

Audio annotation is an effective way to communicate information related to a financial work sheet. For example, suppose you are working with a group of people on an accounting project. You are using complex formulas in your work sheets that need to be explained to members of the group. Audio annotation enables you to add the information where and when it is needed.

Using the audio-enabling macro, you can associate a sound file with any cell in the work sheet. You record the sound files with a simple recorder provided by the audio-enabling macro. And when you select a cell that has audio, its sound file plays.

This chapter describes the steps needed to incorporate the MMPM/2 audio enabling macro into Excel and Lotus 1-2-3 environments.

Adding Audio to an Excel 3.0 Work Sheet

There are two ways you can use the audio-enabling macro for Excel 3.0. You can:

- Define the macro to the application so it runs automatically.
- Request the macro each time you want to annotate a work sheet.

Setting Up the Macro to Run Automatically

To have the work sheet run the macro automatically:

1. Activate the work sheet.
2. Select **Formula**.
3. Select **Define Name**.
4. In the **Name** field, type a name that starts with Auto_Open. For example:

   AUTO_OPEN_MYAUDIO

5. In the **Refers to** field, type **Audio.xlm!InitializeApp**
6. Select **OK**.

Use the above procedure once. Thereafter, the macro runs automatically when you open the application. For more information about running the macro automatically, refer to the *Excel User's Guide*.

Requesting the Macro

Use the following procedure to run the macro only when you use the audio feature. Whenever you want to use the macro, you must repeat the procedure.

1. Load the work sheet you are going to annotate.
2. Ensure that the work sheet is saved and unprotected.
3. Select the **File** menu.
4. Select **Open**.
5. Type the macro name **\MMOS2\MACROS\AUDIO.XLM** in the entry field.
6. Select **OK** to load the macro.
7. Reselect your original work sheet to activate it.
8. Select **Macro**.
9. Select **Run**.
10. Select **Audio.XLM!InitializeAudio**.
11. Select **OK**.

When you type the macro name and select **OK** to load it, a small window appears in the corner of your work sheet. This window is the actual macro containing the instructions for enabling audio. The macro is protected and cannot be used as a work sheet. If you attempt to use the macro as a work sheet, you get the message "Active document is not a work sheet."

When you reselect the work sheet you intend to annotate, the work sheet is activated, and the macro window is hidden.

Activating the Work Sheet

Whether you set up the macro to run automatically or request it each time you use it, you must *activate* the work sheet in order to annotate it. In addition, the work sheet must be saved, open, and unprotected. For example, if you are creating a new work sheet, you must remember to save it before you load the macro.

If you attempt to annotate a protected document, "Active document is protected" is displayed. Similarly, if you select a protected cell to annotate, the message "Active cell is protected" is displayed.

Annotating Work Sheet Cells with Audio

After the macro is run, Audio is added as a choice on the application menu. Choices on the **Audio** menu include:

- Play
- Record
- Show
- Hide
- Delete
- Stop
- Initialize work sheet

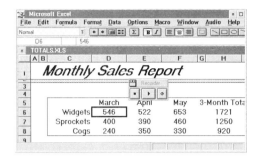

To display the recorder:

1. Select a cell on a work sheet.
2. Select **Audio**.
3. Select **Record**.

A miniature recorder appears on top of the work sheet.

To annotate a work sheet cell:

1. Select [   ] to record.

2. Select [   ] to stop recording.

3. Select [   ] to hear what you recorded.

When you first annotate a work sheet, an audio file is created that will hold all the audio elements for the cells in the active work sheet. The audio file has the same name as the work sheet except it has a .BND extension. For example, if the active work sheet you are annotating is EXPENSES.XLS, its associated audio file is named EXPENSES.BND. These two files must be in the same directory.

Upon completion of each annotation, an audio element is added to the .BND file, and the selected cell is shaded.

If a cell you select to annotate already has audio, a message is displayed, giving you the choice to record over the existing message or to end the recording operation. If an error occurs during recording, the message "There was an error in the record function" is displayed.

During the annotation process the recorder is visible, and you can select the recorder buttons to record and play back audio. However, if you load an already annotated work sheet and just want to play the audio, you can use the Audio menu.

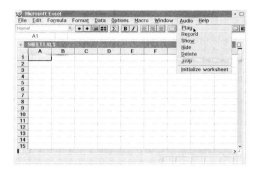

To play an audio cell:

1. Select a cell on a work sheet.
2. Select **Audio**.
3. Select **Play**.

If the cell you select has audio, the audio element is played. If the cell does not have audio, the message "Selected cell does not have audio annotation" is displayed. If you cannot access the audio element, the message "There was an error accessing the recorded file" is displayed.

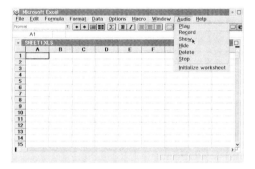

To show all audio-annotated cells:

1. Select **Audio**.
2. Select **Show**.

If there are cells that have audio, each of these cells is shown, one by one, as selected and shaded.

If there are cells that have audio, each of these cells is shown, one by one, as selected and unshaded.

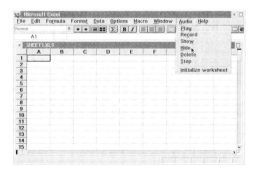

To hide all audio-annotated cells:

1. Select a cell on a work sheet.
2. Select **Audio**.
3. Select **Hide**.

If the cell you select to delete has audio, its audio element is deleted from the .BND file associated with the work sheet. If the cell does not have audio, the message "Selected cell does not have audio annotation" is displayed.

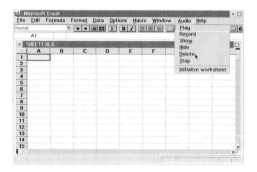

To delete audio from a work sheet cell:

1. Select a cell on a work sheet.
2. Select **Audio**.
3. Select **Delete**.

If the work sheet is not synchronized with the .BND file, the message "Delete was unsuccessful." is displayed. As a result, the Show choice still shows this cell as having audio.

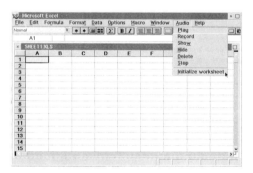

To remedy this situation:

1. Select **Audio**.
2. Select **Initialize work sheet**.

The **Initialize work sheet** choice synchronizes the cells on the work sheet that have audio annotation with the sound elements in the .BND file. If there are elements that have no corresponding cell names, the elements are deleted from the .BND file. If there are annotated cells that have no corresponding elements, the cells are no longer annotated. This will preserve the integrity of the Show and Hide choices as well as save disk space.

This option must be run for each work sheet that is going to access the audio enabling macro.

Adding Audio to a Lotus 1.1 or 2.0 1-2-3 Work Sheet

With the exception of the initialization procedure and the requirement that an environment variable be set, the description for using the audio-enabling macro with Lotus 1-2-3 is the same as that for Excel.

Initializing Audio Capabilities

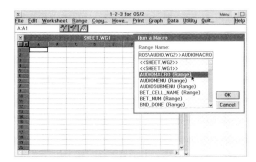

To initialize audio capabilites:

1. Select **File**.
2. Select **Open**.
3. Select a Lotus 1-2-3 work sheet.
4. Select **File**.
5. Select **Open**.
6. Type \MMOS2\MACROS*.*
7. Select **AUDIO.WG2** if using Lotus 1-2-3 1.1

   or

   Select **AUDIO2.WG2** if using Lotus 1-2-3 2.0.
8. Minimize the **AUDIO.WG2/AUDIO2.WG2** work sheet.
9. Press **ALT+F3**. The Run a Macro window is displayed.
10. Select **<<AUDIO.WG2>>** or **<<AUDIO2.WG2>>**.
11. Select **AUDIOMACRO (Range)**.

When you initialize audio capabilities, the **Audio** menu choice is added to the menu, and the work sheet cells are synchronized with audio elements in the .BND file associated with the work sheet.

For information about running macros automatically, refer to *Lotus 1-2-3 Functions and Macros*.

Environment Variable

The 123 macro requires the NCDEBUG=4000 environment variable to be set.

While most users might not require the information in this section, it can be a useful reference if a software or hardware problem occurs. It describes:

- What to do when you have a problem
- Tuning the performance of your system
- Software support, including information about the OS/2 clipboard and Dynamic Data Exchange (DDE)
- Hardware support, including information about high-resolution displays and CD-ROM drives
- Printing support, including information about installing and configuring printer drivers

Chapter 24. Solving Problems

This chapter will assist you if a problem occurs while you are using OS/2 2.1

It provides information you can use to try to solve the problem yourself and tells you how you can obtain assistance using electronic support.

If you need further assistance, refer to the inside front cover of this book for information about calling IBM for technical support.

Note: When you are having a problem, a message might be displayed on the screen. The message might come from OS/2 2.1 or a program you are using. Try to correct the problem by following the information in the message. Messages from OS/2 2.1 will have a **Help** push button you can select for additional assistance. For more information about help for messages, refer to "Displaying Help for OS/2 Messages" on page 49.

How to Use This Chapter

The following sections contain problem-solving information about specific topics. They are:

- Installation of OS/2 2.1
- The Workplace Shell interface
- Printers
- DOS sessions
- WIN-OS/2 sessions
- OS/2 programs
- Diskette, hard disk, and CD-ROM drives
- Mouse
- Communications
- TRAP, INTERNAL PROCESSING ERROR, and program trap

Each topic contains a table with a problem or question listed on the left and a possible solution or answer on the right. A solution to a problem might include referring to related information in this book or the *OS/2 2.1 Installation Guide*.

If you are directed to call the IBM OS/2 Technical Support Team for assistance in solving your problem, you can use the forms in Appendix G, "Recording Information about Your Computer" on page 463 to record specific information that will be useful to the support team. For example, it will be helpful if you record any message that was displayed on the screen when your problem occurred.

Installation of OS/2 2.1

Following is a table you can use to solve problems that occur while you are trying to install OS/2 2.1.

Problem	Action
• OS/2 2.1 did not install. You did not see a window that states installation is completed. • OS/2 2.1 installed successfully, but the OS/2 2.1 desktop did not display after you pressed Enter to restart your system.	Refer to the following: • "Read Me First" in the diskette package of the OS/2 2.1 operating system box • "Before You Begin" and "Diagnosing System Problems" in *Installation Guide* • Chapter 29, "Hardware Support" on page 361

The Workplace Shell

Following is a table you can use to solve problems that occur while you are using the Workplace Shell.

Problem	Action
After installation of OS/2 2.1, the desktop was not displayed. (Refer to "Part 1: Getting Started with OS/2 2.1" on page 1 to see a figure of the desktop.)	Refer to the following: • "Read Me First" in the diskette package of the OS/2 2.1 Operating System box • "Before You Begin" and "Diagnosing System Problems" in *Installation Guide* • Chapter 29, "Hardware Support" on page 361
When you start the computer, the screen is blank except for the mouse pointer moving around.	If your computer has a preinstalled version of the OS/2 operating system, re-create your .INI files using the procedure in "Re-creating the .INI Files" on page 435. If your computer does *not* have a preinstalled version of the OS/2 operating system, change the desktop back to the way it was when OS/2 2.1 was installed. Refer to "Reverting to the Original Desktop" on page 434.

Problem	Action
The desktop is blank, objects are missing, you cannot delete an object, or you have another problem that involves objects.	Run the CHKDSK (check disk) program until the results indicate there are no errors. To run CHKDSK, do the following:
	1. Insert the *Installation Diskette* into drive A.
	2. When prompted, insert *Diskette 1*.
	3. When prompted, press Esc.
	4. Insert *Diskette 2*.
	5. Type the following for a File Allocation Table (FAT) file system:
	`CHKDSK /F`
	Or type the following for a High Performance File System (HPFS):
	`CHKDSK /F:3`
	For more information about CHKDSK, select **Command Reference** in the Information folder. (If Command Reference is not installed, you can install it. Refer to "Adding online documentation after installation" in the Master Help Index.)
	If your problem is not resolved, go to the next problem in this table.
One or more of the objects in the OS/2 System folder are gone.	Rebuild the desktop by using the procedure in "Rebuilding the Desktop" on page 433.
There is a problem when you open the Drives folder. Either the folder opens and closes immediately, or you have more than one icon for the same drive object.	Refer to "Re-creating the .INI Files" on page 435. Follow steps 1 and 2; then follow steps 8–10.

Problem	Action
• The desktop is missing objects or there is more than one icon for the same object. • One or more desktop folders are empty. • After you shut down the computer and start it again, the objects on the desktop are not displayed the same as when you shut down. • Desktop folders open and then close immediately.	Rebuild the desktop by using the procedure in "Rebuilding the Desktop" on page 433. If that does not fix the problem, re-create your .INI files using the procedure in "Re-creating the .INI Files" on page 435.

You cannot delete an object.	Follow the procedure in "Deleting an Object" on page 22.
	
	If you still cannot delete the object, do the following:
	
	1. Create a folder.
	2. Drag the object you want to delete to the new folder and drop it.
	3. Drag the folder to the Shredder and drop it.
	
	If you cannot shred the folder, do the following:
	
	1. At an OS/2 command prompt, type:
	
	   `CD DESKTOP`
	
	2. After the DESKTOP directory opens, type:
	
	   `RD`
	
	Then press the Spacebar once and type the name of the folder.

You have tried all of the above and you still have a problem with the desktop.	Look at the other tables in this chapter for assistance. Then, if you still have a problem, refer to the introductory information in Appendix G, "Recording Information about Your Computer" on page 463 and then to "How to Get Technical Assistance or Electronic Support for OS/2 2.1" on page 289.

Printers

Following is a table you can use to solve problems that occur while you are trying to print.

For more information about printers, refer to Chapter 28, "Printer Support" on page 349.

Problem	Action
An error, such as the following, is displayed on the screen when you try to print: • SYS0004–Cannot write to LPT1 • PMV8007–The printer is switched off or LPT1 not responding	Verify that you have a printer object for the printer. Also verify that it has been set up properly.
Text files print correctly, but graphics files contain meaningless data or garbled text.	If the system utilizes Direct Memory Access (DMA), refer to "PS/2 Direct-Memory-Access Parallel Ports" on page 350.
• One or more ports on the Output page of the Settings notebook for a printer object are in use (cross-hatched), but no printer is associated with those ports. • Multiple printer queues appear in an application, but there is only one printer object defined on the desktop.	The OS2 2.1 .INI files (OS2.INI and OS2SYS.INI) have been damaged. Re-create the .INI files, using "Re-creating the .INI Files" on page 435.
There is no output from a PostScript printer.	Verify that the default printer driver has the letters PSCRIPT in its name. For example, an HP Laserjet IIID PostScript printer must use the PSCRIPT.HP Laserjet IIID PS 52_2 printer driver as the default, *not* the LASERJET.HP Laserjet IIID driver. **Note:** A file that is not formatted for PostScript cannot be printed from a command-prompt session. If you try to print from a command-prompt session, you might see the buffer light on the printer flash, but no output will be produced.

Problem	Action
Your printer is not on the list of supported printers.	You might be able to run the printer in an emulation mode of an OS/2 printer driver. Refer to the user manual that came with the printer to determine if the printer can be configured with an emulation-mode setting.
• Your printer does not have an emulation mode that is supported by an OS/2 printer driver. • You have a DOS program that uses its own internal printer driver.	Use the IBMNULL.DRV printer driver, which is installed by default when you install a printer. This driver supports printers that receive straight ASCII data. If you have a DOS program that uses its own internal printer drivers, use the IBMNULL.DRV printer driver on the OS/2 desktop. This ensures that data from the program is not altered. **Note:** If the printer does not support ASCII data, the program must provide required ESC sequences that will set the printer to the correct print mode. DOS programs normally provide the required sequences.
The first one or more characters of your printout are incorrect.	1. Verify that the installed printer driver is the correct one for your printer. 2. Verify that the printer emulates the selected printer driver 100 per cent. (Some printers do not fully implement emulation.)
You cannot print from a DOS program while you are using a *dongle* (security key).	The DOS print function and a dongle both access a parallel port. OS/2 2.1 does not support simultaneous access of one parallel port by two processes, such as print and security. When you stop using the parallel port for the security process, DOS printing can start.
You cannot print using automatic print-sharing devices.	OS/2 2.1 does not support these devices because of the mechanism the devices use to assign the printer to an operating system.

Problem	Action
From a DOS full-screen session, you cannot print graphics by pressing Print Screen.	DOS contains a GRAPHICS.COM file in the CONFIG.SYS file. That file enables you to print graphics by pressing Print Screen. The DOS emulation mode in OS/2 2.1 does not provide the GRAPHICS.COM file or emulate its function. Instead, OS/2 2.1 provides support for Extended Graphics Array (EGA) ASCII characters when you press Print Screen. A DOS program should use its own printer drivers to provide the capability to use Print Screen to print graphics.
You have tried all of the above and you still have a problem with your printer.	Look at the other tables in this chapter for assistance. If you still have a problem, refer to Appendix G, "Recording Information about Your Computer" on page 463 and then refer to "How to Get Technical Assistance or Electronic Support for OS/2 2.1" on page 289.

DOS Sessions

Following is a table you can use to solve problems that occur while you are using DOS sessions.

Problem	Action

You cannot install a DOS program.	Do the following:
	
	1. Open a DOS full-screen session.
	2. Follow the installation instructions from the program manufacturer. For example, you might be instructed to type the following:
	
	    `A:INSTALL`
	
	  and then press Enter.
	
	Refer to Chapter 26, "Software Support" on page 297 for information about running specific DOS programs.

The program does not run correctly.	1. Verify that you migrated the program to your OS/2 desktop. Refer to the migrating information in "Locating Windows Programs" on page 199. 2. Refer to Chapter 26, "Software Support" on page 297 to see if any special settings are required for your program.
The program cannot be migrated.	Create a program object for the program. To find out how to do this using the Templates folder, refer to "Creating a Program Object" on page 153. Then refer to Chapter 26, "Software Support" on page 297 to see if any special settings are required for your program.
The program runs extremely slowly.	Refer to "Improving Program Compatibility" on page 320 for information about improving the performance of your DOS programs.
You cannot print from your program.	Verify that you can print from an OS/2 session. If you can, install the IBMNULL.DRV printer driver and set it as the default. To find out how to do this, refer to Chapter 28, "Printer Support" on page 349.

Problem	Action
The program will not run on a network.	Download the program and try to run it without the network. If it does not run, the problem is probably related to the network. Ask your network administrator for assistance.
The image file you created to use with a previous version of the OS/2 operating system does not work correctly with OS/2 2.1.	Create a new DOS image file, using OS/2 2.1. To find out how to do this, refer to "Running a Specific Version of DOS" on page 323.
The message Incorrect DOS version is displayed on the screen when you try to run a program.	Modify the DOS_VERSION DOS setting for the program object by adding its executable file name to the setting. To find out how to do this, refer to the information about the Session tab in "Session" on page 186.
You have tried all of the above and you still have a problem using DOS sessions.	Look at the other tables in this chapter for assistance. If you still have a problem, refer to Appendix G, "Recording Information about Your Computer" on page 463 and then refer to "How to Get Technical Assistance or Electronic Support for OS/2 2.1" on page 289.

WIN-OS/2 Sessions

Following is a table you can use to solve problems that occur while you are using WIN-OS/2 sessions.

Problem	Action
You cannot install a Windows program.	Do the following: 1. Open the Windows Programs folder. 2. Open the Program Manager folder. 3. Select **File**. 4. Select **Run**. 5. Insert the first installation diskette in drive A. 6. Follow the installation instructions from the program manufacturer. For example, you might be instructed to type the following: `A:INSTALL` and then press Enter. Refer to Chapter 26, "Software Support" on page 297 for information about running specific Windows programs.
The program does not run correctly.	1. Verify that you migrated the program to your OS/2 desktop. Refer to the migrating information in "Locating Windows Programs" on page 199. 2. Refer to Chapter 26, "Software Support" on page 297 to see if any special settings are required for your program.

Problem	Action
The program runs only if no other Windows program is running.	Try to run the program in a WIN-OS/2 window separate session. Do the following: 1. Open the folder on the desktop that contains the object you want to run in a WIN-OS/2 window separate session. Depending on how the program was migrated, the object might be in any one of the following folders: WIN-OS/2 Groups, WIN-OS/2 Programs, or Additional Windows Programs. 2. Open the Settings notebook for the program object. 3. Select the **Session** tab. 4. Select the **Separate session** check box.
You cannot print from your program.	1. Verify that you can print from an OS/2 session. 2. Verify that your WIN-OS/2 printer driver is installed correctly. Refer to Chapter 28, "Printer Support" on page 349. 3. Verify that the correct printer port is assigned. For example, if your printer is attached to LPT1, verify that **LPT1.OS2** is selected.
You have a problem using a communications or a fax program that runs from your COM port.	The baud rate for the program might be set too high. Set the baud rate lower (for example, to 4800).
You have a problem communicating with a host computer. For example, you lose the connection with the host or a file does not transfer completely when you run a program in the background.	Run the program in a WIN-OS/2 window session in the foreground. If you still have a problem, do the following: 1. Display the pop-up menu for the WIN-OS/2 window session. 2. Select the arrow to the right of **Open**. 3. Select **Settings**. 4. Select the **Session** tab. 5. Select **WIN-OS2 settings**. 6. Select **IDLE_SENSITIVITY**. 7. Set the value to 100.

Problem	Action
A program running in a WIN-OS/2 full-screen session stops running or printing when you switch to another full-screen session.	Run the program in a WIN-OS/2 window session. To find out how to do this, refer to "Running Windows Programs in WIN-OS/2 Sessions" on page 201.
The program will not run from a network drive.	Ask your network administrator for assistance.
Graphics will not paste between a Windows program and an OS/2 Presentation Manager program.	Some graphics file formats, such as certain types of metafiles, cannot be exchanged between Windows programs and OS/2 Presentation Manager programs.
You have tried all of the above and you still have a problem running WIN-OS/2 sessions.	Look at the other tables in this chapter for assistance. Then, if you still have a problem, refer to Appendix G, "Recording Information about Your Computer" on page 463 and then refer to "How to Get Technical Assistance or Electronic Support for OS/2 2.1" on page 289.

OS/2 Programs

Following is a table you can use to solve problems that occur while you are using OS/2 programs.

Problem	Action
A program does not run and you do not know if it ever ran in a previous version of the OS/2 operating system.	1. Verify that the program is an OS/2 program, not a DOS or Windows program. 2. If it is an OS/2 program, contact the program manufacturer and ask if your version of the program is intended to run on OS/2 2.1.
A program ran before but it suddenly stopped.	1. If you recently added any hardware or software to your computer, changed your CONFIG.SYS file, or made changes in a Settings notebook, try to restore the computer and operating system to its previous state. If the program runs again, the new change was responsible for the problem with your OS/2 program. 2. If you have not recently changed anything, as described in step 1, your .INI files might be damaged. Re-create your .INI files using the procedure in "Re-creating the .INI Files" on page 435.
You have tried all of the above and you still have a problem running an OS/2 program.	Look at the other tables in this chapter for assistance. Then, if you still have a problem, refer to Appendix G, "Recording Information about Your Computer" on page 463 and then refer to "How to Get Technical Assistance or Electronic Support for OS/2 2.1" on page 289.

Following is a table you can use to solve problems that occur while you are using diskette drives, hard disk drives, or CD-ROM drives.

Problem	Action
You have more than two hard disk drives and you cannot set up a primary partition on one of the hard disk drives.	With OS/2 2.1, you can have a primary partition on two hard disk drives; however, the BIOS in your computer determines which two hard disk drives can have primary partitions.
Your hard disk drive has more than 1024 cylinders, but you cannot access the entire drive space.	If you have a non-IBM controller and device driver, contact the manufacturer of the device driver to ask if your level of the driver supports more than 1024 cylinders.

Problem	Action

There is a problem with a hard disk controller.	1. Determine the controller manufacturer, model number, and type. Also determine which device driver is installed for the controller (for example, FD7000EX.ADD).
	2. Verify that the installed device driver is the correct one. Refer to the table in "SCSI Adapters and Device Drivers" on page 362, or contact the technical support line of the manufacturer of the controller.
	3. Verify that the BASEDEV= statements are correct in your CONFIG.SYS file. Verify that the correct device driver is listed in a BASEDEV= statement. Also, verify that the correct device driver is the *only* device driver listed for that controller. For more information about BASEDEV= statements, open **Command Reference** in the Information folder.
	4. If you need technical support for a hard disk controller problem, have the following information available when you contact IBM:
	  • The controller type, manufacturer, and model number
	  • The name of the device driver installed for the controller
	  • The BIOS level of the system board
	  • A list of all BASEDEV= statements in your CONFIG.SYS file

There is a problem with a Quantum Hard Card or a secondary IDE controller.	Add the required switch settings (adapter number and IRQ level) to the IBM1S506.ADD device driver statement in your CONFIG.SYS file. If you need assistance with the switch settings or need a BIOS upgrade (for certain Quantum Hard Cards), contact Quantum.
There is a problem with a diskette drive.	Verify that the switch settings are correct for the IBM1FLPY.ADD device driver statement in your CONFIG.SYS file. To determine the correct switch settings, refer to "OEM Diskette Drives" on page 372.

Problem	Action
There is a problem with a CD-ROM drive.	1. Verify that the CD-ROM drive and its adapter are properly secured in the computer. 2. Determine the CD-ROM drive manufacturer and model number, the manufacturer of the adapter, and the name of the device driver that is installed. 3. Verify that the installed device driver is the correct one. Refer to the table in "SCSI CD-ROM Support" on page 363, or contact the technical support line of the manufacturer of the CD-ROM adapter.
You have tried all of the above and you still have a problem with a diskette, hard disk, or CD-ROM drive.	Look at the other tables in this chapter for assistance. Then, if you still have a problem, refer to "How to Get Technical Assistance or Electronic Support for OS/2 2.1" on page 289. Have the following ready when you ask for technical support: 1. A list of all device drivers installed on your system, such as the drivers for diskette drives, hard disks, mouse, and display. Refer to "General Information" on page 464. 2. A complete description of the circumstances surrounding the occurrence of the problem. For example, describe the function you were trying to perform and what you had been doing before you started that function.

Mouse

Following is a table you can use to solve problems that occur with your mouse.

Problem	Action
Your mouse does not work when connected to COM3 or COM4.	OS/2 2.1 only supports connection to COM1 or COM2, at the standard input/output (I/O) address and interrupt request (IRQ) setting. Refer to "Understanding COM Ports" on page 374 for more information.
Your Logitech** mouse does not work after performing a dual boot to DOS.	Before performing the dual boot, open a DOS window or full-screen session and type the following: MOUSE PC Or, if the mouse is connected to COM2, type: MOUSE 2 PC If the previous command does not work, turn your computer off and back on again to allow the mouse to reset. **Note:** You must use the MOUSE.COM that came with the mouse, or the command will not work.
When you move your mouse, the mouse pointer on the screen does not move.	Verify that each device on your computer that uses an IRQ setting is not conflicting with another IRQ setting. Refer to "Understanding COM Ports" on page 374 for more information.

Problem	Action

You do not know which statements to put in your CONFIG.SYS file so your mouse can run properly.	The correct CONFIG.SYS statements for running a mouse are as follows:
	
	• For a serial mouse:
	
	`DEVICE=C:\OS2\MDOS\VMOUSE.SYS`
	`DEVICE=C:\OS2\POINTDD.SYS`
	`DEVICE=C:\OS2\PCLOGIC.SYS SERIAL=COMx`
	`DEVICE=C:\OS2\MOUSE.SYS TYPE=PCLOGIC$`
	
	C is the drive on which OS/2 2.1 is installed, and COMx is either COM1 or COM2.
	
	• For a Microsoft or IBM mouse:
	
	`DEVICE=C:\OS2\MDOS\VMOUSE.SYS`
	`DEVICE=C:\OS2\POINTDD.SYS`
	`DEVICE=C:\OS2\MOUSE.SYS`
	
	C is the drive on which OS/2 2.1 is installed.

You have a 3–button mouse and error SYS1201 is displayed on the screen.	OS/2 2.1 supports only the 2–button mode on a 3–button mouse. If your mouse has a switch to change to a 2–button mode, change the switch.
You have an erratic pointer in your WIN-OS/2 programs.	Set the following DOS settings: • MOUSE_EXCLUSIVE_ACCESS DOS setting to **On** • IDLE_SENSITIVITY to 100 • IDLE_SECONDS to 20
Your mouse is not recognized on a non-IBM machine that has a mouse port with an attached mouse.	Your mouse might be incompatible with the mouse port because of the chip on the mouse adapter. Attach the mouse to a serial port. If the mouse still does not work, try a different mouse with the mouse port.
Both the mouse and the keyboard stop working.	If you have AMI BIOS, you might have an old version. Refer to the information about AMI BIOS in *OS/2 2.1 Installation Guide*.

Problem	Action
You have tried all of the above and you still have a problem with your mouse.	Look at the other tables in this chapter for assistance. Then, if you still have a problem, refer to Appendix G, "Recording Information about Your Computer" on page 463 and then refer to "How to Get Technical Assistance or Electronic Support for OS/2 2.1" on page 289.

Communications

Following is a table you can use to solve problems that occur with communications.

Problem	Action
The port is not recognized or does not work.	If the program is a DOS communication program, set DOS settings as follows: ``` COM_HOLD: On COM_DIRECT_ACCESS On or Off COM_SELECT specific COMx DOS_DEVICE: C:\OS2\MDOS\COMDD.SYS (+) HW_ROM_TO_RAM: On HW_TIMER: On IDLE_SECONDS 60 IDLE_SENSITIVITY 100 ``` The (+) means that DOS_DEVICE (COMDD.SYS) might not be the only one required, depending on the program. For example, the Intel** SatisFAXtion** board requires a device driver loaded into each DOS session that will use that adapter. C indicates the drive on which OS/2 2.1 is installed.
The port is not recognized or does not work.	The COMDD.SYS driver is usually required only for earlier DOS communication programs. Do not use COMDD.SYS for every DOS communication session; use it only if it resolves the problem.
The port is not recognized or does not work.	Verify that you are sending the correct parameters to the COM.SYS driver in the CONFIG.SYS file. Some computers must have the serial ports (COM1 and COM2) defined to COM.SYS in the CONFIG.SYS file. If you are using a serial mouse, do not specify the communication port of the mouse. Refer to "Understanding COM Ports" on page 374.
The port is not recognized or does not work.	If you receive an error message during startup, COMx was not installed because the interrupt was already in use. Check for an IRQ conflict with other device drivers or hardware. Refer to "Understanding COM Ports" on page 374 for more information.
The port is not recognized or does not work.	To provide a higher priority to all communication programs, change the following parameters in the CONFIG.SYS file: ``` PRIORITY_DISK_IO: NO MAXWAIT: 1 ```

Problem	Action
The port is not recognized or does not work.	Some DOS programs will open all the COM ports. Use the COM SELECT DOS setting for all DOS communication sessions. COM_SELECT allows the DOS session to select only one communication port to be used by the session. The communication ports that are not selected will be hidden from the DOS session.
	The DOS_SELECT setting is effective in preventing DOS programs from taking over all the communication ports. For example, the DOS program LapLink Pro** attempts to control all these ports. If you want to run LapLink Pro and another program that accesses a communication port at the same time, you must change the value for COM_SELECT to something different from the default, which is ALL. For example, you could select the value COM1 or NONE.
Your OS/2 program stops.	Ensure that your COM port works in a stand-alone DOS session. Use the MODE command to turn off the IDSR, ODSR, and OCTS parameters. For example, to change COM3, type: `MODE COM3 OCTS=OFF ODSR=OFF IDSR=OFF`

Your OS/2 program is losing data.	Do one or both of the following:
	• Lower the baud rate
	• To provide a higher priority to all communication programs, change the following parameters in the CONFIG.SYS file:
	`PRIORITY_DISK_IO:     NO`
	`MAXWAIT:              1`

Problems occur when you use a FAX program that uses a COM port.	Fax programs must operate at less than 9600 bps. Use an OS/2 program for high-speed faxing.
Communication problems are occurring in a program that uses QBASIC or BASIC CTTY.	Set the DOS settings DOS_DEVICE to the following: `C:\OS2\MDOS\COMDD.SYS` C indicates the drive on which OS/2 2.1 is installed. Dow Jones Link software requires this setting.
You have tried all of the above and you still have a problem with communications.	Look at the other tables in this chapter for assistance. Then, if you still have a problem, refer to Appendix G, "Recording Information about Your Computer" on page 463 and then refer to "How to Get Technical Assistance or Electronic Support for OS/2 2.1" on page 289.

TRAP, INTERNAL PROCESSING ERROR, and program trap

Following is a table you can use to solve problems when your system stops running or your program is ended by OS/2 2.1.

For any of the error situations described below, you can restart your system by pressing Ctrl+Alt+Del, or you can turn the computer off and back on again.

Note: When you call the IBM OS/2 Technical Support Team, you might be asked if you have a *dump* diskette so you can run the dump utility. You cannot create a dump diskette after the system stops; you must have already created it. For more information about the dump utility, refer to Appendix I, "The OS/2 2.1 Memory Dump Process" on page 483.

The IBM support phone number is listed on the inside front cover of this book.

Problem	Action
The system stops and the message on the screen starts with TRAP.	1. Complete the form in "TRAP Messages" on page 478 to record the information *exactly* as it is displayed on the screen. 2. Record a description of what you were doing when the trap occurred. 3. If you have a dump diskette, it would be helpful if you start the dump utility before you call IBM for assistance. 4. Call the IBM support telephone number and provide the information you prepared about the TRAP error.
The system stops and the screen displays INTERNAL PROCESSING ERROR at the top of a message.	1. Complete the form in "INTERNAL PROCESSING ERROR Messages" on page 479 to record the information *exactly* as it is displayed on the screen. 2. Record a description of what you were doing when the trap occurred. 3. If you have a dump diskette, it would be helpful if you start the dump utility before you call IBM for assistance. 4. Call the IBM support telephone number and provide the information you prepared about the INTERNAL PROCESSING ERROR.

Problem	Action
The system stops and your keyboard and mouse do not respond.	1. Press Ctrl+Esc or Alt+Esc and wait a few seconds to see if the system responds. 2. Determine if you can move your mouse but cannot select any object when you press mouse button 1. 3. Press the Caps Lock and Num Lock keys to see if their status lights come on. 4. Record a description of what you were doing when the trap occurred. If any messages were displayed on the screen, be sure to record the message text. 5. If you have a dump diskette, it would be helpful if you start the dump utility before you call IBM for assistance. 6. Call the IBM support telephone number and provide the information you prepared about the problem.

Problem	Action
An error message is displayed in a box with text followed by two choices. This indicates that OS/2 2.1 detected a program error and has ended the program.	1. Complete the form in "Hard Error Messages" on page 480 to record the information *exactly* as it is displayed on the screen. 2. Record a description of what you were doing when the trap occurred. 3. Call the IBM support telephone number and provide the information you prepared about the program trap. **Note:** Unless you have the statement TRAPDUMP=ON in your CONFIG.SYS file, it is not useful to run the dump utility after a hard error has occurred. However, if you have a dump diskette available and you can re-create the situation that caused the hard error message to be displayed, the system can create an automatic dump as the problem reoccurs. To find out how to produce the dump automatically, refer to Appendix I, "The OS/2 2.1 Memory Dump Process" on page 483. If you are able to produce an automatic dump, have the dump diskette available when you call the support number.

Refer to the inside cover of this book for information about getting technical assistance for problems with OS/2 2.1.

Also, in the United States, Puerto Rico, and Canada, electronic support is available for OS/2 2.1. In the United States and Puerto Rico, there is an electronic method of getting new OS/2 device drivers.

OS/2 Electronic Support (U.S. and Puerto Rico only)

Electronic support enables you to access current OS/2 technical information, exchange messages with other OS/2 users, and submit program defects to IBM. Electronic support is available to users with a modem and a telephone line through the IBM OS/2 Bulletin Board System (BBS) or CompuServe**.

For information about registration and access to the IBM OS/2 BBS, call 1-800-547-1283.

For CompuServe membership information, call 1-800-848-8199.

If you already are a CompuServe member, type GO OS2SUP at the ! prompt to access the IBM OS/2 forum.

OS/2 Electronic Support (Canada only)

Electronic support enables you to access current OS/2 technical information and exchange messages with other OS/2 users. Electronic support is available to users with a modem and a telephone line through a BBS.

In Canada, you can connect directly to the OS/2 BBS nearest you by selecting one of the following numbers:

- 1-416-946-4255
- 1-514-938-3022
- 1-604-664-6466

Set your modem and communication software to the following: no parity bit, 8 data bits, 1 stop bit.

OS/2 Electronic Device Driver Distribution Mechanism

There are three methods of device-driver distribution. The primary methods include incorporation of selected drivers in OS/2 releases and delivery of device drivers with the associated hardware devices. The third method, the OS/2 Electronic Device Driver Distribution Mechanism, is a program intended to complement the primary methods.

The Electronic Device Driver Distribution Mechanism is designed to provide efficient distribution of OS/2 device drivers by allowing device drivers to be distributed independently of any release of the OS/2 operating system.

The IBM and non-IBM device drivers are provided to licensees of the OS/2 operating system under this program **"as is," with no warranty of any kind.** IBM plans to add device drivers to the program as they become available. You can regularly contact your Electronic Device Driver Distribution Mechanism channel for new and updated OS/2 device drivers.

The Electronic Device Driver Distribution Mechanism is available only in the United States and Puerto Rico.

Obtaining an OS/2 Device Driver

For licensees of OS/2 2.1, the National Support Center (NSC) has expanded its facilities to allow direct user access to the device-driver file sections.

The NSC Bulletin Board is available 24 hours a day on a toll-call basis, with no access charge to the bulletin board. To access the bulletin board, call 1-404-835-6600.

The NSC Bulletin Board contains the OS/2 device drivers in a format suitable for downloading. Each device driver downloaded comes with its own Terms and Conditions, either from IBM or the hardware vendor.

IBM and non-IBM OS/2 device drivers are available from IBM without charge. However, you are responsible for all telephone toll charges incurred when electronically downloading the device drivers.

Requirements for the asynchronous electronic connection to the NSC Bulletin Board are:

- A modem that supports 1200 baud or more that is set to:

  - Eight data bits
  - One stop bit
  - No parity
  - Standard transmission speed from 1200 to 9600 baud

- Communication software capable of supporting XMODEM file-transfer protocols

- A switched telephone line

Information regarding the installation of OS/2 device drivers is contained in the OS/2 product documentation.

Supplemental Distribution: If you do not have the required modem for electronic distribution and you cannot obtain an OS/2 device driver from an IBM Authorized Personal Computer Dealer Advanced Products or an Authorized Industry Remarketer-Personal Computers, you can contact your IBM Marketing Representative to obtain available OS/2 device drivers.

Additional Information

The Electronic Device Driver Distribution Mechanism plans to include selected device drivers for non-IBM hardware devices. These device drivers are obtained by IBM from the hardware developer and are included in the IBM distribution mechanism as a convenience to IBM customers. Hardware developers remain responsible for their own distribution of OS/2 device drivers for their hardware devices. Inclusion of non-IBM device drivers in the IBM product is not intended as an endorsement of any non-IBM product.

IBM will not guarantee the compatibility or functionality of the non-IBM device drivers or hardware devices with OS/2 2.1. You should contact the hardware developer directly about the suitability of the device drivers for your equipment and requirements.

You can direct questions regarding this delivery mechanism or existing device-driver distribution to your IBM Authorized Personal Computer Dealer Advanced Products, IBM Authorized Industry Remarketer-Personal Computers, or IBM Marketing Representative.

The device drivers offered and this distribution method can be modified or withdrawn at any time at the discretion of IBM.

Chapter 25. System Performance Considerations

The minimum memory requirement for OS/2 2.1 is 4MB. The recommended memory requirement is 6MB. Some systems use 128KB or more for read-only memory (ROM) to random access memory (RAM) remapping, so less than the minimum required memory is available. On these systems, you might need another 512KB–1MB to satisfy the minimum requirements. Check your system to see if it offers a way to recapture the memory so that you can regain the minimum requirement.

Memory Management

Users concerned with response times when using some system functions, such as loading programs, starting sessions, and switching between sessions, can improve performance by increasing system memory. If you are running on a constrained system (small hard disk, 16MHz or less processor, 4MB of memory), an additional 2MB of memory will improve performance. In the entry memory system (4MB), the recommended file system is the FAT file system (see Appendix D, "The OS/2 File Systems" on page 437).

Determining the Disk Cache Size

The disk cache is a facility that has the potential for dramatic performance gains. The disk cache allows a portion of the system storage to be used as an additional hard disk buffer. A disk cache size is preselected by the system based on installed memory, disk size, and file systems installed. The default for the entry memory system (4MB) is a cache size of 128KB. The default for a memory system with 8MB is a cache size of 512KB. Any memory set aside for the disk cache is memory that is taken away from the free memory available for programs. Therefore, it is recommended that as much memory as possible be dedicated to the cache size after taking into account the normal operating requirements of your system. This requires that you have a good understanding of the working set of requirements of your system. For example, a computer with 6MB or more of RAM should use a disk cache size of 256KB. For more information on tuning the size of the disk cache, see DISKCACHE in the online *Command Reference*. For information about using the DISKCACHE command to automatically check your drives after an improper shutdown, see "Customizing Your CONFIG.SYS for Startup" on page 91.

Understanding Memory Swapping

Memory over commitment occurs when a program uses more memory than is actually available in the computer. The operating system handles memory over commitment by copying memory to the system *swap file*. The swap file

(SWAPPER.DAT) is used to temporarily store data segments that the system moved out of main storage. Although a program cannot control swapping, you can specify whether the system can swap memory by including the MEMMAN command in the CONFIG.SYS file. For more information about MEMMAN, see the online *Command Reference*.

The system automatically preallocates the SWAPPER.DAT file based on the size of installed memory. The location of the SWAPPER.DAT file can be specified by including the SWAPPATH command in the CONFIG.SYS file. To tune the size of the swap file, see the information about SWAPPATH in the online *Command Reference*.

Ignore any CHKDSK errors that might be reported on the SWAPPER.DAT file. These error indications are normal.

Saving Hard Disk Space

Hard disk space is a very important asset. There are many ways to save hard disk space, and one of them is to be sure to install only the functions you need. If you have installed the optional productivity aids and games, and later only want a subset of these, delete their program files from the OS2\APPS and OS2\APPS\DLL subdirectories (see Appendix F, "Removing Programs" on page 453). Also, delete TUTORIAL.HLP in OS2\HELP\TUTORIAL subdirectory, if you no longer need the tutorial. The WIN-OS/2 and DOS environments also can be deleted if support is not needed; or one of the text editors (OS/2 ships two text editors) can be deleted.

Improving Performance

On memory constrained, low-end systems, the performance when opening folders and starting sessions can be improved by disabling animation. Animation is the process of drawing boxes on the screen that appear to grow in size, culminating in an open folder or session. This gives a nice appearance when systems are performing well. If you are running on a 80386 SX system and are overcommitted in memory, performance is improved if animation is disabled.

To disable desktop animation, open the System Setup object in the the OS/2 System folder. Open the System object, and go to the page with the Window bookmark. This screen allows you to select Disable Animation.

Tip ───

To improve system performance:

- Close opened programs when you are not going to use them again.
- Close folders that you do not need.
- Move commonly used functions out of folders and onto your desktop; then close the folders that contained the objects.

───

OS/2 Programs

OS/2 applications are designed to run in the native OS/2 environment. Because of this, special settings and configurations to support these applications are not required. Well written OS/2 applications take advantage of OS/2 at the application program interface (API) level. Users do no need to make explicit changes for OS/2 applications.

DOS Programs

You can improve the performance of some DOS application programs by adjusting the DOS settings. If the program does not require extended or expanded memory, change the EMS_MEMORY_LIMIT and XMS_MEMORY_LIMT values to zero. This will provide maximum performance.

The recommended settings for games played in a DOS session are:

> HW_TIMER On
> VIDEO_8514A_XGA_IOTRAP Off
> VIDEO_RETRACE_EMULATION Off

Notes:

1. Run games in full-screen sessions.

2. Increase the IDLE_SECONDS and IDLE_SENSITIVITY settings. This will improve the DOS performance at the expense of multitasking performance.

3. The VIDEO_8514A_XGA_IOTRAP setting is available for all adapters, not just 8514A and XGA adapters.

Some DOS programs use polling techniques to poll the system for work. An example is a program that appears to be idle at an input prompt, but is in fact polling the keyboard looking for keystrokes. Use the **IDLE SENSITIVITY** DOS setting to detect this occurrence and suspend the program while it is polling. For more information on changing DOS settings, see "Program Object Settings" on page 185.

Windows Programs

If you choose to migrate your Windows programs (at installation time or later using the Migrate Applications program), most Windows programs will run in one WIN-OS/2 session. If you set up a Windows program and do not migrate it, the program runs in its own WIN-OS/2 session.

In low-memory configurations, you can run multiple Windows programs in one WIN-OS/2 session. This reduces both memory and swapper-file requirements.

With a WIN-OS/2 window session, a new session is created every time you double-click on an active object.

MMPM/2 Programs

If you installed OS/2 2.1 and would like to install Multimedia Presentation Manager/2 (MMPM/2), you might need additional memory. The following table shows the memory requirements for OS/2 2.1 with MMPM/2 installed.

Table 2. Minimum memory requirements for OS/2 2.1 with MMPM/2	
4MB	System sounds and low quality audio
5MB	High quality audio (22kHz or greater, 16-bit stereo)
6MB	System sounds, low quality audio, and video playback
7MB	System sounds, high quality audio (22kHz or greater, 16-bit stereo), and video playback

The following table shows the hard disk space that is required for MMPM/2 *in addition to* the space required for OS/2 2.1.

Table 3. Minimum hard disk space requirements for MMPM/2	
3MB	Audio only
6MB	Video playback and audio

Chapter 26. Software Support

Most DOS, Windows, and OS/2 programs run under OS/2 2.1 without any modification. A few need special attention. This chapter contains unique application program compatibility information and other useful tips and techniques that might be helpful in specific situations. This chapter also contains information about running Windows programs in WIN-OS/2 sessions.

Attention

Some of the information in this section is intended for the more advanced user or for the user already familiar with various functions provided with OS/2 2.1.

Application Program Compatibility

The following list provides information about the compatibility of specific programs with OS/2 2.1. This information is version specific; later versions of the same program might operate correctly. Some program manufacturers already have resolved incompatibility issues and have fixes available; these are noted.

After Dark (Windows)

- To run this program in a WIN-OS/2 window session, change the object's settings to hide or minimize the program object to the desktop.
- This program places a terminate and stay-resident (TSR) reference in the AUTOEXEC.BAT file when it is installed. To run in a WIN-OS/2 window session, remove this reference from the AUTOEXEC.BAT file.

Aldus PageMaker** (OS/2)

- Pasting a bit map into this program produces a blank or incorrect black and white bit map.

- If you experience incorrect output when spooling standard format files to the printer, change the Printer object settings. To do this, take the following actions:

  1. Display the pop-up menu of the Printer object on the desktop.
  2. Select **Open**, then **Settings**, then **Queue Options**.
  3. Ensure that **Printer specific format** is selected.

Aldus Persuasion** 2.0 (Windows)

- Use a parallel port to print.

Arts & Letters** Graphics Editor 3.1 (Windows)

- To run in a WIN-OS/2 window, change the settings so that the program minimizes to the desktop.
- The directory created by Arts & Letters is named A&L. The ampersand character (&) is a reserved character of the command shell, CMD.EXE. To change to the A&L directory with the CD command, you must use one of two methods of quoting the directory name. The first method is to prefix the & in A&L with a ^ (caret, shift 6):

```
CD A^&L
```

The second method is to surround the entire directory name with quotation marks (" "):

```
CD "A&L"
```

- If you are running Arts & Letters and you get a system error (a GDI trap), you must restart the operating system before running the program again. This is because the program left a portion of itself running when it ended and will not start a new copy of itself while that portion is running. This also means that when you restart the computer, Arts & Letters will start again automatically. It is recommended that you close the copy that is opened on system startup and start the program from its object when you intend to run it in a window.

Arts & Letters Composer (OS/2)

- In SVGA mode, when a portion of a picture is copied to the clipboard as a metafile, it is not visible when you view the clipboard. This problem occurs for both VGA and TSENG** ET4000 SVGA display resolutions. This works correctly in XGA resolution.
- In SVGA mode, when stretching or flipping bit map segments that are pasted into the application from the clipboard, program traps might occur in the 1024 x 768 x 256 TSENG ET4000 and XGA display resolution. This problem also occurs in XGA resolution.

AutoCAD** (OS/2)

- Some of the background colors are set to a very pale color that does not show up well on XGA displays.

AutoManager 4.0 (DOS)

- The version of the program that uses extended memory uses an unsupported DOS memory extender. Use the real-mode version of the program.
- The program expects COMMAND.COM to be in the root directory of drive C. Copy COMMAND.COM from the C:\OS2\MDOS directory to C:\.

Borland C++ 2.0 and 3.0 (DOS)

- Set the DPMI_DOS_API DOS setting to Enabled.

Borland Paradox** (DOS)

Change the following DOS settings:

- Set the DPMI_DOS_API to Enabled
- Set the DPMI_MEMORY_LIMIT as high as 6.

Borland Turbo Debugger for Windows (Windows)

- Run the program in a WIN-OS/2 full-screen session.
- The screen is temporarily damaged when this program is called from Turbo C++**. The screen is restored on the first repaint. (A repaint can be forced by clicking the mouse on several different windows.)

Borland Turbo Pascal** 7.0 (DOS)

Change the following DOS settings:

- DPMI_DOS_API_DOS to Enabled
- Set DPMI_MEMORY_LIMIT_ to 6

Castle Wolfenstein (DOS)

- Set the VIDEO_RETRACE_EMULATION setting to Off.
- Set the IDLE_SECONDS setting to 60.
- Set the IDLE_SENSITIVITY setting to 100.

Central Point Backup** for DOS 7.1 (DOS)

- Meaningless characters are displayed when running in a DOS window session. Run this program only in a DOS full-screen session.

Central Point PC Tools** Deluxe 7.1 (Windows)

- The backup feature of this program performs in a manner similar to Central Point Backup for Windows (see 318), which is in the list of programs that do not work correctly with OS/2 2.1. If you experience difficulty backing up on a diskette, back up on an alternate device, such as a network drive or a tape drive.

Tip: You might need to install this program under a specific DOS session.

Commander Keen (DOS)

- Set the VIDEO_RETRACE_EMULATION DOS setting to Off.

Commute (Windows)**

- When this program is installed under WIN-OS/2, the statement Keyboard.drv=commkbd.drv is added to the SYSTEM.INI file. Change this statement to Keyboard.drv=keyboard.drv.

Control Room 1.0 (DOS)**

- You must run this program in a DOS full-screen session for the screen blanking feature to work correctly.

CorelDRAW 2.0 (OS/2)

- If you do a large amount of printing while in this program, it is possible that you might run out of memory. To avoid this, periodically save your work and exit CorelDRAW; then restart the program and continue your work.
- In SVGA mode, sometimes the status words and the coordinate text under action bar menus of the client window are blacked out.

CorelDRAW 2.1 (Windows)

- To install this program:
  - Start a DOS session.
  - Run FFIX /date (note that "date" must be lowercase).
  - Type **A:** and press Enter.
  - Exit WIN-OS/2.
  - Run FFIX /u.
  - Type **install** and press Enter.
- Run the program in a WIN-OS/2 full-screen session.

Crosstalk (Windows)**

- Type **MODE COM**x **BUFFER=OFF** at the DOS command prompt, where x is the communications port you are using, before you run the program.

dBase IV 1.1 (DOS)**

- If you receive a `too many files open` error message, set the DOS_FILES DOS setting to 30. Set the DOS_VERSION DOS setting to DBASE.EXE,5,0,255. With Hyperdisk, set DOS_VERSION to DBASE1.EXE,5,0,255.

- When using Hyperdisk, you might have to adjust the EMS and XMS memory limits.
- With the multi-user version, the program must be run in a specific DOS session.

Describe (OS/2)

- In SVGA mode, when you use the hollow attribute for a letter of the alphabet, the letter will not display.
- In SVGA mode, after you insert text at the end of a document, the text at the end of the input line might be damaged. To correct this, scroll up and down to repaint the screen.
- In SVGA mode, when you print TIFF objects (bit maps) the resulting print might be skewed.

Designer (OS/2)

- The MIRRORS.DLL that comes with this program must be installed in the program directory, not in the C:\OS2\DLL directory, and the program must be started from this directory. This is because OS/2 2.1 comes with its own dynamic link library named MIRRORS.DLL.

Drafix CAD Version 1.11 (Windows)

- Run the program in a WIN-OS/2 full-screen session.

Drafix CAD Version 2.0 (Windows)

- Run the program in a WIN-OS/2 full-screen session.

DynaComm** Asynchronous OS/2 (OS/2)

- The dynamic link libraries (DLLs) included with this product cannot be in the same directory as the executable file. Put them in a separate directory and add that directory to the end of the LIBPATH.

Enhanced Editor (OS/2)

- The OS/2 Enhanced Editor supports up to 99 fonts.
- In the online help for the Enhanced Editor, it states that you should contact your IBM representative for detailed information on how to program the editor. Instead, obtain this information from the IBM bulletin boards.

F-117A Stealth Fighter 2.0 (DOS)

- Set the VIDEO_RETRACE_EMULATION DOS setting to Off.
- If the program appears to stop at a blank screen soon after you start it, press Esc and the program will continue. When you are past the opening screens, the program runs correctly.

F15 Strike Eagle III (DOS)

- Set the DOS_UMB setting to Off.
- Set the DOS_HIGH setting to On.

F19 (DOS)

- Set the HW_ROM_TO_RAM DOS setting to On and the VIDEO_RETRACE_EMULATION DOS setting to Off.

Fastback for Windows (Windows and OS/2)

- Use only Version 1.01, a no-charge upgrade from Fifth Generation Systems. To order, call 1-800-873-4384.
- In the Options menu in the program, make sure that the Media setting is set to the system default. (The other Media settings write to DMA device drivers, which have compatibility problems.)

Fastback Plus** 2.1 and 3.04 (DOS)

- If you experience difficulty backing up on a diskette, back up on an alternate device, such as a network drive or a tape drive.

FastLynx** 1.1 (DOS)

- To use the serial port with this program, remove the DEVICE=C:\OS2\MDOS\VCOM.SYS statement from the CONFIG.SYS file. The parallel port works correctly.
- Due to its high speed, the program sometimes fails to function. If this occurs, simply end the program; system integrity is not compromised. To minimize the possibility of this error condition, set the following DOS settings:
  HW_TIMER = On
  IDLE_SENSITIVITY = 100
  IDLE_SECONDS = 10

Form Publisher (Windows)

- Ensure that the program's printer driver is installed before running the program.

FormBase 1.2 (Windows)

- The SHARE statement is automatically added to the AUTOEXEC.BAT file during program installation. Use an editor to remove the SHARE command from the AUTOEXEC.BAT file.
- When running this program and Lotus 1-2-3 in the same WIN-OS/2 session, this program must be started first.

FotoMan** (Windows)

- Run the program in a WIN-OS/2 full-screen session.

Framework III** 1.1 (DOS)

- The program expects COMMAND.COM to be in the root directory of drive C. Copy COMMAND.COM from the C:\OS2\MDOS directory to C:\.
- Disable the program's print spooler; using it might cause an error.

Framework IV (DOS)

- You cannot save to a diskette drive. You can save to a hard disk drive only.

Guide (Windows)

- Should be run in a full-screen session only.

Harvard Draw (Windows)

- When installing this program under WIN-OS/2, you will receive an error message. Select **OK** and installation will be completed successfully.

Harvard Graphics** (Windows)

- When running this program in a WIN-OS/2 window session, the Color Selection windows are missing the Color Selection grid. Run this program in a WIN-OS/2 full-screen session.

HP New Wave 3.0 (Windows)

- Install the program under DOS. If you experience problems with program or session termination, include the UseOS2shield=0 in the SYSTEM.INI file, located in the OS2\MDOS\WINOS2 directory on your startup drive. If that does not help, run the program in a WIN-OS/2 full-screen session.

IBM 3363 Optical Drive

- The software for this product must be run in a specific DOS session that is started from drive A.
- You should run only a small number of other processes when using this product.

IBM PC LAN Support Program (DOS)

- If you close the DOS session that is running this program, you must first reset the token-ring adapter before you restart this session. To fix this problem, download RSTTOK.ZIP from the IBM BBS or from IBMFILES in CompuServe.

IBM PC/3270 Version 2.0 (DOS)

- First, the program must be migrated using the Migrate Applications program.
- Then, on the Session page of the Settings notebook, select the **DOS settings** push button.
  - Select **DOS full screen** or **DOS window**.
  - Set the VIDEO_MODE_RESTRICTION DOS setting to CGA.
  - Add D:[path]DXMA0MOD.SYS& and D:[path]DXMC0MOD.SYS& to the DOS_DEVICE DOS setting.
- Then, on the Program page of the Settings notebook.
  - Set the Path and File Name to *.
  - Set the Parameters to /K d:[path]PC3270.BAT.
  - Set the working directory to d:[path].

IBM PC/3270 V2.0 (Windows)

- First, the program must be migrated using the Migrate Applications program.
- Then, on the Session page of the Settings notebook, select the **WIN-OS/2 settings** push button.
  - Add /C PC3270WO.BAT to the DOS_SHELL WIN-OS/2 setting.
  - Add D:[path]DXMA0MOD.SYS, D:[path]DXMC0MOD.SYS, and D:[path]PCS802.SYS V=N. to the DOS_DEVICE WIN-OS/2 setting.
  - Set the DOS_SHELL setting to /C PC32700WO.BAT.
  - Select **WIN-OS/2 window Separate session** or **WIN-OS/2 full screen**.
- Then, on the Program page of the Settings notebook:
  - Set the path and file name to d:[path]PC3270.EXE.
  - Set the working directory to d:[path].

Icon Author (Windows)

- In XGA high resolution, the graphics (in the demo program only) are scaled to only a portion of the screen and text is drawn in normal size.

Intel SatisFAXtion (DOS)

- The program must be run in a specific DOS session.
- If SatisFAXtion software is loaded into each DOS session, it might cause the fax to stop if another DOS session is started. Set up one DOS session to be used for faxing, and load the device driver and executable files only into that DOS session. To do this, take the following steps:
  1. Edit the AUTOEXEC.BAT file.
  2. Cut the last two lines referring to the Intel SatisFAXtion board to the clipboard and save the file (using DOS Command File for the file type).

3. Open a new file.
4. Paste the last two lines into the new file.
5. Save the new file as FAX.BAT, using DOS Command File as the file type.
6. Edit the CONFIG.SYS file and cut the last two lines relating to the Intel SatisFAXtion board to the clipboard (cut only the last line if you do not have a scanner installed).
7. Save the file using Plain Text as the file type.
8. In the Command Prompts folder, select a DOS Full Screen object, press the Ctrl key and mouse button 2 at the same time, move the mouse pointer to an empty area in the folder, and release the mouse button and the Ctrl key. This creates a copy of DOS Full Screen.
9. Put the mouse pointer over your new object and click mouse button 2.
10. Select the arrow to the right of **Open**, and select **Settings**.
11. Go to the Session page and select the **DOS settings** push button.
12. Go to DOS_DEVICE and click mouse button 1. Then, move the mouse to the dialog area and click on mouse button 1 (there should be a blinking cursor now).
13. Paste the text that you cut from the CONFIG.SYS file and select **Save**.
14. Go to the General page and replace the contents of the **Title** field with FAX (or whatever other title you choose).
15. If you want to edit the new session's object, go to the General page and select the **Edit** push button.
16. If you want to have this session start each time your system starts, move the object to the Startup folder.
17. Whenever you start this session, type FAX to run the FAX.BAT file before using the SatisFAXtion board.

> **Note:** Another way to start a session with FAX.BAT is to add the string
>
> ```
> /k fax.bat
> ```
>
> in the Parameters field of the Program page of the Settings notebook.

Use the fax board in only one session at a time.

- If you install the program using this procedure and you receive error messages, install the program under DOS.

King's Quest (DOS)

- Remove the DOS_HIGH statement, if one exists, from the CONFIG.SYS file or use the DOS settings for the object to turn DOS_HIGH off.

King's 6 (DOS)

- Edit the RESOURCE.CFG file and set the AUDIOSIZE size to 4(KB).
- Set the INT_DURING_IO setting to On.

LAN Support Program Device Drivers (DOS)

- If you opened a DOS session with the DOS LAN Support Program (LSP) device drivers and subsequently closed the session, you must ensure that the token-ring adapter is reset before using the LAN from another DOS session. To ensure that the token-ring adapter is reset, use RESETOKN.EXE or RESETOKN.SYS. These files can be retrieved from CompuServe by issuing GO OS2SUP and downloading RESTKN.ZIP from SECTION 17, IBMFILES, or they can be retrieved from the IBM National Support Center Bulletin Board System by downloading RESTKN.ZIP.
- The IBM token-ring adapter should be used by only one session at a time.

LANtastic** 4.0 (DOS)

- You might experience problems with this version of LANtastic. It will will only work in 8-bit mode, use Version 4.1 instead. For more information, contact the ARTISOFT BBS at 602-293-0065.

LANtastic 4.1 (DOS)

- Run this program in a specific DOS session. Set the DOS_STARTUP_DRIVE DOS setting to the location of the DOS kernel you want to start from.
- If you are using Artisoft AE-2 or AE-3 adapters, set your adapters to 8-bit mode, as described in the adapter documentation.

LapLink Pro (DOS)

- Type **MODE COM**x **IDSR=OFF ODSR=OFF OCTS=OFF** at the command prompt, where x is the communications port you are using, before you run the program.

LapLink** III 3.0 (DOS)

- It is preferable that you use the parallel port. To use the serial port with this program, set the DOS setting, COM_DIRECT_ACCESS to On.

Links 386 Pro (DOS)

- Set the DOS_DPMI_API setting to Enabled.
- Set the DPMI_MEMORY_LIMIT setting to 10.
- Set the DOS_UMB setting to Off.

Lotus 1-2-3 for Windows 1.0 and Lotus 1-2-3 Release 3.1 (DOS)

- If you plan to use this program, follow these steps:

1. Create a batch file called LOTUS.BAT which contains:

```
@ECHO OFF
CLS
PROMPT $p$g
PATH=X:\LOTUS
SET 123MEMSIZE=2048
...  (any other lines)
123.EXE   (last line in file)
```

2. Open the Templates folder from the desktop.
3. Move the mouse pointer to the object.
4. Press and hold mouse button 2.
5. Drag a program template to the desktop.
6. Display the pop-up menu for the program template by pointing at the object and then clicking mouse button 2.
7. Select the arrow to the right of **Open**. Select **Settings**.
8. In the **Path and file name** field, enter:

```
x:\path\lotus.bat
```

9. Select the **Session** tab and select the **DOS Full Screen** radio button. Select the **DOS Settings** push button.
10. Select or add the following DOS Settings:

```
DOS_UMB   On
DOS_HIGH  On
DOS_VERSION  INSTALL.EXE,3,40,255
                 123.EXE,3,40,255
                 LOTUS.EXE,3,40,255
                 123DOS.EXE,3,40,255
                 ZAP.EXE,3,40,255
                 INS.EXE,3,40,255
```

11. Select the **General** tab, and add:

```
Title -> Lotus 123 (or whatever you choose)
```

Close the notebook by selecting **Close** or double-clicking on the system menu.
12. Start the DOS session by opening the DOS Full Screen object.
13. From the A: prompt, type **INSTALL** to install the product.
14. Open the Lotus specific DOS session by double-clicking on the Lotus program object.

Lotus 1-2-3 Release 2.0 through 2.4 (DOS)

- All versions of Lotus 1-2-3 use expanded memory and look in the C0000-CFFFF range to find it. Expanded memory specification (EMS) requires a 64KB block of contiguous free memory in the address range from 640KB to 1MB for its page frame. You might have an adapter conflict.
- If Lotus does not start up after the instructions, (see the information about Lotus on page319).

If you plan to use this program follow these steps:

1. Open **Templates**.
2. Point to the **Program** template.
3. Press and hold mouse button 2.
4. Drag the template to the desktop.
5. Point to the program object.
6. Click mouse button 2.
7. Select the arrow to the right of **Open**.
8. Select **Settings**.
9. In the **Path and file name** field, type:

   d:\123R23\123.exe

10. Select the **Session** tab.
11. Select **DOS Full Screen**. Select the **DOS Settings** push button.
12. Select or add the following DOS Settings:

   ```
   EMS_MEMORY_LIMIT   4  (for Version 2.0 through 2.2)
                     12 (for Version 2.3 through 2.4)


   MEMORY_INCLUDE_REGIONS  C0000-CFFFF

   MEMORY_EXCLUDE_REGIONS  D0000-DFFFF
   ```

13. Select **Save**.
14. Select the **General** tab.
15. Type a title for the program:

   Lotus 2.3 (or whatever you choose)

16. Point to the title-bar icon.
17. Double-click.
18. Open the Lotus specific DOS session by double-clicking on the Lotus program object.

Lotus 1-2-3 Version 3.0 through 3.1 for DOS (DOS)

The install program checks to make sure it is running in a DOS session. If you plan to use this program in a DOS full-screen session follow these steps:

1. Using a text editor, create a 123.BAT file in the Lotus directory and include the following statements:

```
123MEMSIZE=2048 (This is the amount of memory needed to allocate
                 to the spreadsheet.  2,048 equals 2MB of ram).

CD\123R3    (The Lotus 1-2-3 directory name)

123 (or LOTUS)    (This starts the program)
```

2. Open **Templates**.
3. Point to a **Program** template.
4. Press and hold mouse button 2.
5. Drag the template to the desktop.
6. Point to the program object.
7. Click mouse button 2.
8. Select the arrow to the right of **Open**.
9. Select **Settings**.
10. In the **Path and file name** field, type:

    ```
    d:\123R3\123.bat
    ```

11. Select the **Session** tab.
12. Select **DOS Full Screen**.
13. Select **DOS Settings**.
14. Select or add the following DOS Settings:

```
DOS_FILES    40
DOS_VERSION  123.EXE,3,40,255
             123DOS.EXE,3,40,255
             LOTUS.EXE,3,40,255
             INSTALL.EXE,3,40,255
             TRANS.EXE,3,40,255

Note: If you do not want to run Install or Translate do not
      include the last two lines.
```

```
EMS_MEMORY_LIMIT    4 (for Version 2.0 through 2.2)
                   12 (for Version 2.3 through 2.4)

DPMI_MEMORY_LIMIT   4 (at least twice the EMS_MEMORY_LIMIT size)

DPMI_DOS_API   ENABLE

MEMORY_INCLUDE_REGIONS   C0000-CFFFF

MEMORY_EXCLUDE_REGIONS   D0000-DFFFF
```

15. Select **Save**.
16. Select the **General** tab.
17. Type a title for the program.

    Lotus 3.1 (or whatever you choose)

18. Point to the title-bar icon.
19. Double-click.
20. Open the Lotus specific DOS session by double-clicking on the Lotus
    program object.

Lotus Freelance Graphics for OS/2 (OS/2)

* If you experience installation problems, contact the Lotus Development
  Corporation. Lotus will provide a fix.

  You can also download FLGOS2.ZIP from the IBM BBS or from IBMFILES
  in CompuServe, or download INSTAL.ZIP from the Lotus section of
  CompuServe.

* If you experience problems with the color, change the palette from the
  Freelance menus. Instructions on how to do this can be found in the *Lotus
  Freelance Graphics for OS/2 User' Guide.* A set of new default palettes for
  Freelance Graphics is available. These can be retrieved from CompuServe
  by issuing GO OS2SUP and downloading PALETT.ZIP from SECTION 17,
  IBMFILES, or they can be retrieved from the IBM National Support Center
  Bulletin Board System by downloading PALETT.ZIP.

Lotus Freelance Graphics for Windows (Windows)

* The pointer to printer objects points to Screen Show instead of to the
  printer.

Lotus Magellan 2.0 (DOS)

* The UNDELETE function in the program uses physical-sector addressing,
  which is not supported. Use the OS/2 UNDELETE command.

Lotus Notes** (OS/2)

- To use Notes 2.*x*, you must delete the file QNC.EXE from the Notes program directory. This file is used only for debug support in the field. Therefore, its removal will not affect program execution.

MAGICorp** (Windows)

- Running this program with other programs in the same WIN-OS/2 session might cause a system halt. Run this program by itself in a WIN-OS/2 full-screen session.

Mathcad** 3.0 (Windows)

- To install this program:
    1. Start a DOS session.
    2. Run FFIX /date (note that "date" must be lowercase).
    3. Install the program (the installation program is a DOS program).
    4. Run FFIX /u.

Mathcad 3.1 (Windows)

- Set the XMS_MEMORY_LIMIT DOS setting to 0.
- Set the EMS_MEMORY_LIMIT DOS setting to 0.

MicroProse Civilization (DOS)

- Set the VIDEO_RETRACE_EMUL setting to Off. Set the HW_TIMER setting to On.

More Windows** (Windows)

- If you use the Full-Page Paper White mode or Full-Screen Color mode, the screen might be disrupted. Avoid using these modes.

MS Bookshelf** - CD-ROM Reference Library (DOS/Multimedia)

- The program requires version 6.14 of the mouse device driver, MOUSE.COM, which comes with the product.
- Use the INT_DURING_IO setting to avoid video and audio problems.
- The program will not install if the PATH statement in the AUTOEXEC.BAT file exceeds 254 characters. If this problem exists, do the following:
    1. Make a backup copy of the AUTOEXEC.BAT file.
    2. Edit the AUTOEXEC.BAT file and add the directory to install the program. For example, if you want to install the program on drive D, add D:\VIEWER to the PATH statement.
    3. Save the file; then start a WIN-OS/2 session to install the program.

MS** Chart 3.0 (DOS)

- Install the program's mouse driver and set MOUSE_EXCLUSIVE_ACCESS to On.

MS CodeView** (DOS/OS/2)

- When using the protect-mode version, CVP 2.2 (for OS/2), trace through the source code, rather than through the assembler language.
- In order for the program to work correctly, delete the PWBHLP.PXT help file.

MS CodeView for Windows Version 3.0 (Windows)

- Run the program in a WIN-OS/2 full-screen session.

MS Excel** for DOS 2.1 (DOS)

- Set the XMS_MEMORY_LIMIT DOS setting to 0.

MS Excel for OS/2 3.0 (OS/2)

- The Help index and the Keyboard Help windows operate incorrectly. Avoid using these functions.

Note: If you have a CD-ROM drive that is supported in OS/2, then OS/2 MSCDEX support can be used. It is part of the VCDROM.SYS.

MS Project for Windows 1.0 (Windows)

- Must be installed in a DOS session.

MS QuickC (Windows)

- Run the program in a WIN-OS/2 full-screen session.

Microsoft Word** (OS/2)

- You might have problems selecting items from the application menu, and the application appears to freeze. Call the Microsoft support number for their fix.

Mirrors** III

- Type **MODE COM*x* BUFFER=OFF** at the command prompt, where *x* is the communications port you are using, before you run the program.

National Geographic** Mammals (DOS)

- Run the program with the DOS Setting INT_DURING_IO set to On using a DOS image avoid choppy audio.

National Geographic Presidents (DOS)

- Run the program with the DOS Setting INT_DURING_IO set to On using a DOS image to avoid choppy audio.

Norton Backup** 1.2 (DOS)

- You might experience diminished performance when backing up to a diskette.

Norton Desktop (Windows)

- This program assumes that if it is not the first program loaded, another desktop is running. Include the UseOS2shield=0 statement in SYSTEM.INI (in the OS2\MDOS\WINOS2 directory on your startup drive).
- If you experience difficulty formatting a diskette, use the OS/2 FORMAT command. If you experience difficulty backing up on a diskette, back up on an alternate device, such as a network drive or a tape drive.
- Run the program in a WIN-OS/2 full-screen session.

Norton Utilities** 5.0 (DOS)

- The UNDELETE functions require physical-sector addressing, which is not supported. Use the OS/2 UNDELETE command.
- The utility programs that manipulate the hard disk (for example, UNDELETE, UNFORMAT, DISKTOOL, CALIBRATE, the Disk Doctor, and the Disk Editor) can cause a system halt. Some of these programs can be used on floppy diskettes.

PaintShow Plus 2.21 (DOS)

- Load the version of MOUSE.COM that comes with the program before starting the program.

Paradox** 3.5 (DOS)

- The version of the program that uses extended memory uses an unsupported DOS memory extender. Use the standard version of the program.

Peachtree Complete** III 5.0 (DOS)

- Set the DOS_FILES DOS setting to 60.
- The program's Lookup function does not list all the companies that have been entered into the program's list of companies; it displays meaningless characters.

Perform Pro 1.0 (Windows)

- Run the program in a WIN-OS/2 full-screen session.

PFS First Choice** (DOS)

- When the program is run in a DOS window, the mouse pointer does not reflect tool selection.
- Set the baud rate to 2400 or lower when using the communication feature.

PFS WindowWorks 1.75 (Windows)**

- Run the program in a WIN-OS/2 full-screen session.

Photostyler (Windows)

- Run the program in a WIN-OS/2 full-screen session.
- When an image is scanned or provided as input into a WIN-OS/2 window session and a menu that covers the image is selected, the first menu is not properly repainted when a second menu is selected. This problem occurs in SVGA mode.

PM Terminal Program

- Make sure that the asynchronous communications driver, SASYNCDB.SYS, is not commented out in a REM statement in the CONFIG.SYS file.

Prodigy (DOS)**

- Set the EMS_MEMORY_LIMIT setting to 0.
- Set the XMS_MEMORY_LIMIT setting to 0.

Publishers PowerPak 2.1 (Windows)**

- Create the directory
  C:\OS2\MDOS\WINOS2\POWERPAK
  before running the installation batch file.

Quattro Pro 3.0 (DOS)**

- Install printers from within the program, rather than during program installation.

Quicken (DOS)**

- Remove the DOS=HIGH statement, if one exists, from CONFIG.SYS or from the DOS_HIGH setting.

Risk (DOS)

- Do not use the program's shutdown function.

SantaFe Media Manager (DOS)

To install this program:
  - Start a DOS session.
  - Run FFIX /find (note that "find" must be lowercase).
  - Install the program.
  - Run FFIX /u.

- **Sherlock Holmes Consulting Detective Version 3 (DOS)**
  - Set INT_DURING_IO to ON.
- **SideKick** (OS/2)**
  - A printer must be installed and present on the desktop to use the Notepad.
- **Signmaster 5.11 (DOS)**
  - The plot/preview feature causes an illegal instruction to be issued.
- **Soft Term (OS/2)**
  - In the Send File and Receive File windows, the first time the drive is changed, the Directory window updates incompletely. After the first time, the Directory window works normally.
- **Sound Blaster** (DOS)**
  - The SBTEST utility program reports an incorrect DMA level during installation. Disregard the error message and continue with installation. The program will be installed correctly.
- **Space Quest IV (DOS)**
  - Set DOS_BACKGROUND_EXECUTION to Off so that the program stops when it is placed in the background.
  - Set up the program so that it does not use extra memory.
  - For best performance, run this program in a DOS full-screen session.
  - For computers with a Sound Blaster card, change to the drive and directory which contains Space Quest IV and enter

    ```
    SQ4FIX
    ```

    on the command line.
- **Stacker** 2.0 (DOS)**
  - This program does not run under OS/2 2.1. Stac** Electronics has announced an OS/2 2.1 compatible version of Stacker that will be released later in 1993. Contact Stac Electronics for more information.
- **Tetris for Windows (Windows)**

  - When running Tetris in a WIN-OS/2 window session, you might see icon color distortion on the desktop. This can be corrected by performing an action that causes the desktop to repaint itself. One such action is to select **Refresh** on the desktop pop-up menu.

- **The Way You Work (DOS/Windows)**
  - Install this program under DOS. When installed, the program can run in a DOS or WIN-OS/2 session.
- **Winfax Pro** (Windows)**
  - Run this program only in a WIN-OS/2 full-screen session.
  - If you are using (DDE), avoid switching from the WIN-OS/2 full-screen session in which you are running; switching from the WIN-OS/2 session to another session might break the DDE link.

- If you have transmission problems, try setting the line speed to 2400 baud.
- **Wing Commander** II (DOS)**
  - Set HW_TIMER to On.
  - If you are running on a slower computer, turn the sound option off.
- **WordPerfect** (DOS)**
  - Set the IDLE_SENSITIVITY setting to 100.
- **WordPerfect Office 3.0 (DOS)**
  - Install the keyboard-enhancement utility program manually, after program installation, by adding it to the CONFIG.SYS file.
- **WordPerfect 5.1 for DOS (DOS)**

  WordPerfect uses up a lot of system time while it is running in the foreground and background. To improve performance, change the following settings for the desktop:

  ```
  DOS_BACKGROUND_EXECUTION  Off
  VIDEO_RETRACE_EMULATION  Off
  IDLE_SENSITIVITY  100
  HW_ROM_TO_RAM  On
  ```

  Note: DOS_BACKGROUND_EXECUTION with the Off setting will suspend WordPerfect when it is in the background. Printing and auto-save will not occur while WordPerfect is suspended.

  For the following problems:
  - Black screen
  - WordPerfect will not open in a DOS session
  - SYS3176
  - Hanging while switching from WordPerfect in a DOS session to another session or to the desktop

    Change the WordPerfect settings by pressing SHIFT+F1, or by selecting **File** from the menu. Select the following:

    ```
    SETUP
    DISPLAY
    TEXT SCREEN TYPE
    IBM (VGA AND COMPATIBLE)
    ```

  - No mouse or an erratic mouse

    Change the WordPerfect settings by pressing SHIFT+F1, or by selecting **File** from the menu. Select the following:

    ```
    SETUP
    MOUSE
    MOUSE DRIVER (MOUSE.COM)
    ```

– Double mouse

Change the following DOS setting for the desktop.

```
MOUSE_EXCLUSIVE_ACCESS ON
```

- **Xtree** Pro Gold 2.0 (DOS)**
  – The Zip Manager feature cannot find the zip file it is to act upon. Avoid using this feature.

Incompatible Programs

The following identifies categories of programs that do not work correctly with OS/2 2.1:

- DOS extenders that require exclusive access to the 80386 control registers, such as the Virtual Control Program Interface (VCPI), are not supported because they would conflict with OS/2 2.1 operations. The DOS Protect-Mode Interface (DPMI) 1.0, the Expanded Memory Specification (EMS), and the Extended Memory Specification (XMS) are supported.

- Programs that directly address the physical disk sectors to perform disk-write operations are not supported. These operations would conflict with OS/2 2.1 operations. This category includes most DOS UNDELETE programs.

- WIN-OS/2 does not support real mode programs. Also, Windows enhanced mode programs that load specific Windows Version 3.1 virtual device drivers (.386 or .VXD) will not run in WIN-OS/2 enhanced compatibility mode. This mode uses an unsupported method. However, some of these programs will run in WIN-OS/2 standard mode. To run these programs, set the WIN_RUN_MODE setting to Standard.

- Some DOS or Windows games that use digitized sound might not work correctly. To fix this problem, change the DOS settings for the program to no sound.

- Programs that manipulate the 80386 control registers, such as 386 DOS debuggers, are not supported; this would conflict with OS/2 2.1 operations.

- Fax boards and programs that require (9600 baud or greater) are not supported. The following fax boards and programs contain timing sensitivities that might prevent reliable operation:
  – ATI** ETC
  – Cardinal FAX
  – Smartfax**
  – Twincomm 24/96

The programs listed here fit into one or more of the categories listed previously:

- Autocad XII (DOS)
- Bound Checker (DOS)
- Central Point Backup for Windows
- Close-Up (Windows)
- Comanche (DOS)
- Desert Storm CD-ROM (Windows)
- Distinct** Back-Up (Windows)
- DoDot 3.0 (Windows)
- Fax Concentrator (DOS)
- Magic-CV (DOS)
- Mathematica 2.0 (Windows)
- MusicPrinter Plus** 4.0 (DOS)
- Oracle** (DOS) (There is an OS/2 version of this program.)
- Perceive for Windows
- PharLap** DOS extenders prior to Version 4.0
- Realizer** 1.0 (Windows)
- Smartfax (DOS)
- Soft-ICE (DOS)
- Splash 1.01 (DOS)
- Turbo Debugger (DOS)
- Ultima VII (DOS)

- SYS2237 Error Message from Lotus 1-2-3 version 3.1

  Lotus 1-2-3 3.1 assumes that all 486 systems have a math coprocessor, for this problem, do the following:

  - Call Lotus Development Corporation at 800-343-5414, select the Upgrade Section, and ask for the math coprocessor fix.
  - Type the "-s" parameter in the 123.BAT file to indicate to Lotus 1-2-3 not to use a math coprocessor.

- Cannot install Lotus 1-2-3 error message

  You must run this program with DOS 3.3 or later. To install the program, do the following:

  1. Select the DOS_VERSION setting for either a DOS window or DOS full-screen session and add the following information:

     `INSTALL.EXE,5,00,255`

  2. Select **Save**.
  3. Close the notebook by selecting **Close** or double-clicking on the system menu.

4. Start the DOS session by opening the object.
5. From the A: prompt, type **INSTALL** to install the product.
6. Start OS/2 2.1 in Dual Boot or Boot Manager.
7. Start the session with a DOS diskette or create a specific DOS session.

   For information on creating a specific DOS session, see "Creating a DOS Image from a Startup Diskette" on page 323

- OS/2 EMS conflicts with DOS programs running in a DOS session

   Many DOS terminate stay resident (TSR) programs, or device drivers that are loaded high, use the expanded memory specification (EMS). Some examples of DOS programs are spreadsheets, word processors, databases, desktop publishing, and computer aided design (CAD) systems. The following problems might occur if EMS is not detected:

   - SYS3176 error
   - The DOS session locks up when starting up the program.
   - When starting up the program in a session, a flash of text relating to an adapter conflict appears before the program closes and goes back to the OS/2 desktop.
   - A session will close when it detects the TSR program terminating, in which case there is no chance for it to become resident. To load a TSR you must make a desktop program object from the Templates folder. Select the Program page of the Settings notebook; then type an * in the **Path and file name** field if it does not already exist. In the **Parameters** field type /**K** followed by the path and program name of the TSR program. For example,

      ```
      /K C:\FT\FTTERM.BAT
      ```

   - Very little expanded memory is used by the program even if the DOS setting was changed.

      In order to configure EMS support for a DOS session, a contiguous 64KB block of RAM is used as the EMS page frame and must be available within the Upper Memory Block (UMB) between 640KB and 1MB. This address range is between C0000-CFFFF, which is exactly 64KB of memory.

      All adapters whose ROM and RAM addresses are mapped between the C0000-CFFFF range, should be remapped to the D0000-DFFFF range. The most common adapters are video, network, modem, and emulation. Many IBM and Original Equipment Manufacturer (OEM) systems have their token-ring adapter mapped to the C0000-CFFFF region.

Improving Program Compatibility

The following provides techniques that improve program compatibility:

- For more reliable DOS communications performance on slower systems, the combined baud rate should not exceed 9600 bps (bits per second) for one or more concurrent DOS applications.

- You can improve the performance of DOS communications programs by using the 16550AFN UART communications chips.

- If you run a bulletin board or a DOS communications application that keeps timing out, change the DOS settings as follows. If the first settings change does not fix the problem, change the next settings, and so forth.

  1. HW_TIMER to On
  2. IDLE_SECONDS to 60, and IDLE_SENSITIVITY to 100
  3. COM_HOLD to On
  4. HW_ROM_TO_RAM to On
  5. If you lose data using DOS communications software, set the PRIORITY_DISK_IO setting to NO in your CONFIG.SYS file, and the IDLE_SENSITIVITY setting to 100% in the DOS settings for the object.

- Some DOS and Windows programs run correctly only in full-screen sessions. Any Windows program that does not use the Windows application program interface (API) function to change the video mode should be run in a WIN-OS/2 full-screen session.

- Some DOS and Windows programs must be installed or run in a *specific DOS session*. A specific DOS session is started from an actual version of DOS. For more information, refer to "specific version, starting" under DOS in the online Master Help Index.

- Some programs run in OS/2, DOS, or WIN-OS/2 sessions, but require that you install the program under DOS.

- DOS programs that use low level file-system calls cannot access HPFS disks.

- Code-page switching support is not available for graphics mode in DOS sessions.

- Some DOS and Windows programs use security keys as protection against copyright infringement. The security key is a 25-pin connector that is connected to the parallel port of the computer on which the program is executing. The program checks to see if the connector is attached and, if the connector is not present, the program is assumed to be an illegal copy. When more than one DOS session is running one of these programs, a SYS1799 error can result. This occurs because the programs that use these security keys do not de-allocate the parallel port if a second session is started for a program that also requires the security key. This error is the result of a direct I/O parallel port contention mechanism that protects the user from possible data corruption. To disable this mechanism:

1. Display the pop-up menu for the printer object by moving the mouse pointer to it and clicking mouse button 2.
2. Select the arrow to the right of **Open**; then select **Settings**.
3. Select the **Output** tab.
4. Open the LPT port that has the contention problem.
5. Select **Share access** to share the port between DOS sessions doing direct I/O to the parallel port.
6. Select **OK**.

- Some Windows Multimedia Extension programs might not work correctly after being migrated to OS/2 2.1. If this occurs, reinstall them under WIN-OS/2.

- If the SYS0005 error `ACCESS DENIED` occurs when starting DOS programs, follow this procedure:

1. Shut down the system.
2. Insert the *Installation Diskette* into drive A.
3. Restart the system.
4. When prompted, remove the *Installation Diskette*, insert *Diskette 1*, and press Enter.
5. At the Welcome to OS/2 screen, press Esc.
6. Remove *Diskette 1* and insert *Diskette 2*.
7. At the command prompt, type **CHKDSK C: /F** and press Enter.
8. If you receive the error `cross-linked extended attribute`, repeat the previous command until CHKDSK reports no errors.
9. After repeated attempts, if CHKDSK continues to report errors, note the names of the files related to the errors. Copy these files to a blank diskette and delete the files from the hard disk. Then, run CHKDSK again.
10. When CHKDSK reports no errors, copy the files back to their original location and restart your system.

Note: This problem usually occurs when an EADATA file is deleted from DOS.

Windows Application Programs

This section contains information about running a Windows program in a WIN-OS/2 window or full-screen session.

Improving Program Performance

The following are tips for using your computer more efficiently when running Windows programs in WIN-OS/2 sessions:

- If you are running Windows programs in WIN-OS/2 window sessions, you cannot have any statement in the AUTOEXEC.BAT file that prompts the user for input (for example, "Press any key to continue").

- Do not use the SETUP.EXE file shipped with Windows 3.1. Instead, use the SETUP.EXE file shipped with WIN-OS/2 to ensure your environment is properly configured for OS/2 2.1. Use the Selective Install program in OS/2 2.1 to change video device drivers for CGA, EGA, SVGA, VGA, XGA, and 8514, and for mouse device drivers. To start Selective Install, open **OS/2 System**, **System Setup**, then **Selective Install**.

- To decompress Windows device drivers supplied by equipment manufacturers, use the EXPAND.EXE utility program for WIN-OS/2 located on OS/2 2.1 *Diskette 9*.

- If a Windows program does not work correctly in a WIN-OS/2 session, it is likely that the program files were not all migrated properly. To fix the problem, you can reinstall the program using any WIN-OS/2 session. (Select **Run** on the File menu of the Program Manager and follow the program's instructions.) Or, if you know the specific files that are needed, you can copy them from the \WINDOWS directory to the \OS2\MDOS\WINOS2 directory.

- The value for VIDEO_SWITCH_NOTIFICATION should not be changed for an active WIN-OS/2 session.

- You cannot use the WIN-OS/2 Control Panel to change mouse buttons in WIN-OS/2 sessions. Change mouse button settings from the OS/2 desktop to affect the WIN-OS/2 mouse buttons in the WIN-OS/2 environment.

- If you install the US English version of OS/2 2.1, and you want to change the system configuration to another country or language, run Selective Install to make the changes effective for OS/2 2.1. To make the changes effective for WIN-OS/2, start WIN-OS/2 in a full-screen session, open the Control Panel, and use the **International** choice to make your changes.

- If you are running a WIN-OS/2 full-screen session with an XGA video device driver and your WIN-OS/2 objects are not clear, use the Control Panel to select another color scheme for the WIN-OS/2 Program Manager.

Using Clipboard and Dynamic Data Exchange

- If you cannot paste a bit map from the OS/2 clipboard to a WIN-OS/2 session, the program might not understand the device-independent bit map (DIB) format of the file. For example, icons created using the Icon Editor are not understood by some Windows programs, such as Microsoft Paintbrush. If your WIN-OS/2 session is started first, you can view the bit map in the OS/2 clipboard; however, you cannot paste it. The **Paste** menu choice is dimmed (unavailable).

- Metafiles in WIN-OS/2 and OS/2 are not compatible. If you copy a WIN-OS/2 metafile to a public clipboard, it will be sent to PM and vice versa.

- If you want to use dynamic data exchange (DDE) using the **Paste Link** choice on the File menu of a program, consider the following information.

    The clipboard should be set to Public. The client and server must negotiate the data format to initiate the DDE link. If this negotiation fails, some applications do not display any error message and no further action is taken. If this happens, try another menu choice (for example, **Link**), if available.

Running a Specific Version of DOS

Some programs require that you run a specific version of DOS rather than the DOS provided with the OS/2 operating system. There are multiple ways that this can be done:

- Install DOS before you install OS/2 2.1; then set OS/2 to run Dual Boot.
- Install OS/2 2.1 with the Boot Manager option; then install DOS.
- Use the DOS from Drive A object along with a DOS Startup diskette.
- Place a DOS image created from a DOS Startup diskette on your system.

Creating a DOS Image from a Startup Diskette

The instructions in this section explain how to place a DOS image on your system using a DOS Startup diskette. If you do not have a DOS Startup diskette, see "DOS from Drive A" on page 108 for information about creating one.

1. If you want to access the A: drive from the DOS Image, make the following changes to the DOS Startup diskette:

2. Edit the CONFIG.SYS file on your DOS Startup diskette and add the following information:

```
LASTDRIVE=Z
```

Note: The LASTDRIVE= statement can use any letter that is greater than the last physical drive on the system. If you use a LAN, make sure the LASTDRIVE= letter is greater than the letter you use to access the LAN.

3. Save and exit the file.
4. Edit the AUTOEXEC.BAT file on your DOS Startup diskette and add the following information:

```
PATH A:\;C:\OS2\MDOS;
C:\OS2\MDOS\FSACCESS M=A
```

Note: Any letter can be substituted for the letter M in the FSACCESS statement as long as the letter is not assigned to another drive or greater than the drive letter specified in the LASTDRIVE= statement. This drive letter will be the letter that you will use to access drive A while using the DOS Image. The specific DOS session will see the DOS image as A:

5. Save and exit the file.
6. Type **MD C:\VMB** and press Enter to make a directory for the DOS image.
7. Type **CD C:\VMB** and press Enter to change to the new directory.
8. Type **VMDISK A: DOS.IMG** and press Enter.
9. Type **Exit** and press Enter.
10. Open **Templates**.
11. Point to the Program file object.
12. Press and hold mouse button 2.
13. Drag the object to the desktop.
14. Type * in the Path field.
15. Select the Sessions tab.
16. Select either **DOS Window** or **DOS Full-Screen**.
17. Select **DOS Settings**.
18. Select the **DOS_STARTUP_DRIVE** setting.
19. Select the **Values** field.
20. Type **C:\VMB\DOS.IMG**.
21. Select **Save**.
22. Select the **General** tab.
23. Type a name in the **Title** field.
24. Point to the title-bar icon.
25. Double-click.
26. Point to the new object.
27. Double-click. The specific DOS version is displayed.
28. Press Ctrl+Esc; then point to the DOS version title.
29. Click mouse button 2; then select **Close**.

DOS Settings for a DOS Image

If you placed a DOS image on your hard disk drive you can fine tune th e settings so that your DOS applications run better with it. To change the settings:

1. Point to the object.
2. Click mouse button 2.
3. Select the **Settings** tab.
4. Select **DOS Settings**.
5. Change the following settings:
   - DOS_UMB to ON
   - DOS_HIGH to ON
   - XMS_MEMORY_LIMIT to: 2048 (minimum requirement)
6. If your DOS applications use DOS Protected Mode Interface (DPMI), change the following settings:
   - DPMI_MEMORY_LIMIT to 4 (minimum requirement)
   - DPMI_DOS_API to ENABLE
7. If your DOS applications or device drivers load High change the following settings:
   - EMS_MEMORY_LIMIT to 0
   - DPMI_MEMORY_LIMIT to 0
8. If your system has a LAN adapter or other adapter that uses RAM memory, change the following setting to match the adapters range:
   - MEM_EXCLUDE_REGIONS to adapter settings (D8000–DFFFF for an Ethernet Adapter)
9. Select **Save**
10. Point to the title-bar icon.
11. Double-click.

Chapter 27. Video Support

Computers can provide video support on the system board of the computer or on an adapter, depending on the type of computer you have. In this chapter the term *adapter* is used to describe both.

Display adapters (video adapters) are identified by the mode and resolutions that they can support. The greater the resolution and number of colors, the better the picture.

This chapter describes the different display adapters used with OS/2 2.1 and suggests ways of fine tuning their performance.

The OS/2 operating system supports the following kinds of display adapters:

Mode	Resolution
Color graphics adapter (CGA)	320 x 400 x 4 colors
Enhanced graphics adapter (EGA)	640 x 350 x 16 colors
Video graphics adapter (VGA)	640 x 480 x 16 colors
8514 adapter	1024 x 768 x 256
Extended graphics adapter (XGA)	1024 x 768 x 256
Super VGA (SVGA) adapter.	Installs to 640 x 480 x 16 colors can be switched to 1024 x 768 x 256 colors

The OS/2 operating system also supports the following SVGA chipsets:

Chipset	Resolution
ATI Technologies ATI28800	• 640 x 480 x 256 colors • 800 x 600 x 256 colors on 1MB of video memory • 1024 x 768 x 256 colors
Cirrus Logic CL-GD5422 and CL-GD5424	• 640 x 480 x 256 colors • 800 x 600 x 256 colors on 1MB of video memory • 1024 x 768 with 256 colors
Headland Technologies HT209	• 640 x 480 x 256 colors • 800 x 600 x 256 colors on 1MB of video memory • 1024 x 768 with 256 colors

Chipset	Resolution
IBM VGA256C	640 x 480 x 256 colors
Trident Microsystems TVGA8900B and TVGA8900C	• 640 x 480 x 256 colors • 800 x 600 x 256 colors • 1024 x 768 x 256 colors
TSENG Labs ET4000	• 640 x 480 x 256 colors • 800 x 600 x 256 colors • 1024 x 768 with 256 colors
Western Digital Imaging WD90C11, WD90C30, and WD90C31 (in WD90C30 compatibility mode)	• 640 x 480 x 256 colors • 800 x 600 x 256 colors • 1024 x 768 x 256 colors

Notes:

1. In the near future, 800 x 480 x 256 colors will be supported with .5MB of video memory.

2. Many adapters not supported in the OS/2 2.1 package are supported by the adapter manufacturer. Contact your adapter manufacturer for more information about driver availability.

Video Considerations for DOS Programs

OS/2 2.1 supports running programs in full-screen and window sessions. These sessions can run in either the foreground or in the background. OS/2, DOS, and Windows programs that use the text mode run successfully in either type of session in both the foreground and the background. However, some Windows and DOS programs that use the graphics mode might be suspended if they are not running in a full-screen session in the foreground. This is because the DOS program does not control the display hardware while it is in the background or in a window. OS/2 will either continue to run the program or suspend it based upon the resource requirements of the program. When OS/2 suspends a program, it saves the video state and restores it when the program returns to the foreground.

The following table lists considerations for running programs in graphics mode in a DOS window or in the background.

Table 4. Video Considerations for DOS	
Desktop Mode	**Considerations**
• Any adapter in VGA mode • SVGA adapters with 256 colors	All 256 color modes above 320 x 200 and all 16 color modes above 640 x 480 are suspended.
• XGA in XGA mode • 8514 adapter in 8514 mode	All 16-color modes and all 256 color modes above 320 x 200 are suspended.
• CGA adapters • EGA adapters	All sessions will suspend.

DOS Settings Used for Video

DOS Settings are used to fine tune a DOS session so that an application runs better.

There are eight DOS settings which affect the video environment for DOS applications under OS/2 2.1. Some of the settings affect full-screen DOS sessions only, some affect window DOS sessions only, and some affect both.

The DOS Settings and their default values are given below.

DOS Setting   **Default Value**

VIDEO_8514A_XGA_IOTRAP   ON

- If this parameter is set to ON, the switching of full-screen sessions is handled in a reliable and controlled manner.
- If this parameter is set to OFF, I/O trapping is not performed for the full-screen session. This allows DOS applications to directly access all functions of the video device for better video performance.

  This may cause problems if:
  - the video device registers are write-only and/or the application cannot save/restore the complete video state.
  - a VGA or SVGA DOS application is sensitive to timing; this might render the application unusable.
- This setting has no effect on DOS windows or a DOS full-screen session running in the background.

  Note: To solve performance problems with games played in a DOS session, set this parameter to OFF.

VIDEO_FASTPASTE   OFF

- If this parameter is set to ON, the speed at which a window DOS application receives input from the clipboard improves.
- This setting has no effect on DOS full-screen sessions.

VIDEO_MODE_RESTRICTION   NONE

- If this parameter is set to NONE, 64K of memory is set aside for video access.
- If this parameter is set to MONO or CGA, it limits the physical memory set aside for video from 64K to 16K for CGA or 4K for MONO. A DOS text-mode or CGA graphics-mode application can then use the additional memory.
- This setting affects DOS window and full-screen sessions.

Note: The VIDEO_MODE_RESTRICTION setting is not supported on some video adapters and might not function properly.

VIDEO_ONDEMAND_MEMORY ON

- If this parameter is set to ON, the video buffer is allocated while the full-screen session is running in the foreground. This improves the speed by which the session switches occur.
- If this parameter is set to OFF, the video buffer is allocated at the time the full-screen session is switched. This improves the performance of the DOS application slightly but slows down the session switch.
- This setting has no effect on DOS window sessions.

VIDEO_RETRACE_EMULATION ON

- If this parameter is set to ON, simulated vertical retrace is enabled. Some graphics-intensive DOS applications might experience video corruption with this setting. This might appear as intermittent snow at the top or other areas of the screen.
- If this parameter is set to OFF, the vertical retrace only occurs at the intervals requested at by the DOS application.
- This setting has no effect on DOS windows or DOS sessions running in the background.

VIDEO_ROM_EMULATION   ON

- If this parameter is set to ON, the virtual video drivers simulate a number of commonly used text-based video BIOS functions. Change this setting to OFF if the video BIOS for your device contains enhancements to the standard functionality.
- If this parameter is set to OFF, the text-based video BIOS functions are not simulated and you will not have the functions unless your video BIOS contains the enhancements.
- This setting has no effect on DOS window sessions.

VIDEO_SWITCH_NOTIFICATION OFF

- If this parameter is set to ON, the DOS application is notified whenever a session switches to or from a full screen. This may improve the save and restore speed of the video state for the application, but all corruptions that result from the session switch are the responsibility of the DOS application.
- If this parameter is set to OFF, the virtual video driver handles the save and restore of the session state for the application.
- This setting has no effect on DOS full-screen sessions.

VIDEO_WINDOW_REFRESH   1

- This DOS setting defines the time interval for repainting DOS windows. The higher the interval value, the less frequent the updates. This setting has no effect on updates that are a result of keyboard input or scrolling.
- This setting has no effect on DOS full-screen sessions.

Changing the DOS Settings for Video

To change the video DOS settings for an application:

1. Point to the object for the DOS application.
2. Click mouse button 2.
3. Select the arrow to the right of **Open**.
4. Select **Settings**.
5. Select the **Session** tab.
6. Select the **DOS settings** push button.
7. Change the DOS settings (see "DOS Settings Used for Video" on page 330).
8. Select the **Save** push button.
9. Point to the title-bar icon.
10. Double-click.

Video Considerations for Windows Programs

Whether a Windows application can run in a full-screen or window session is dependent upon the display adapter type as follows:

- CGA and EGA display adapters can run Windows applications only in full-screen sessions.
- VGA, XGA, 8514, and SVGA display adapters can run Windows applications in both WIN-OS/2 window and full-screen sessions.

Windows programs running either window or full-screen sessions can run in the foreground and the background regardless of the resolution and number of colors used. This is because OS/2 2.1 provides WIN-OS/2 display drivers that only write to the display when the session is in the foreground. They suppress all background operations that write to the display. This enables a Windows program to continue running while the session is in the background. When the session is in the foreground, the Windows program automatically redraws itself.

However, Windows full-screen display drivers that are not shipped with OS/2 2.1 might not be designed to suppress background writing to the display. A driver must be aware of the VIDEO_SWITCH_NOTIFICATION setting. If the driver does not suppress background writing to the display, corruption will occur. If you have a display driver that was not shipped with OS/2 2.1, it might cause a Windows program to be suspended under certain conditions. These conditions are similar to those described in Table 4 on page 329 for DOS programs.

Enabling SVGA in WIN-OS/2 Full-Screen Sessions

You can enable WIN-OS/2 full-screen sessions to run in high-resolution (1024 x 768) mode while the OS/2 desktop runs in VGA mode.

To enable WIN-OS/2 full-screen sessions for SVGA:

Note: Follow the instructions very carefully. Otherwise, you could cause your WIN-OS/2 sessions to become inoperable.

1. Install OS/2 2.1 for VGA (640 x 480).

2. Back up the SYSTEM.INI and WIN.INI files as follows:

   a. Open **OS/2 System**.
   b. Open **Command Prompts**.
   c. Open **OS/2 Full Screen**.
   d. At the C prompt, do the following:

      Type: **CD\OS2\MDOS\WINOS2** and press Enter.

      Type: **COPY WIN.INI WIN.BAK** and press Enter.

      Type: **COPY SYSTEM.INI SYSTEM.BAK** and press Enter.

3. Check the OS2\MDOS\WINOS2\SYSTEM directory for the desired high-resolution display device driver.

   - If the device driver is already on the system, go to step 4.
   - If the device driver is not found, use your OS/2 or Windows installation disk to copy the driver to the \OS2\MDOS\WINOS2\SYSTEM directory.

   For example, to use the OS/2 diskettes and install the 8514.DRV high-resolution device driver:

      a. Search the OS/2 installation diskettes for the WIN8514 and *G.FON files do the following:

      DIR A:WIN8514 and press Enter

      DIR A:*G.FON and press Enter

      Once you find the files, you have to unpack them. The files are packed with their standard target directory coded into the packed file.

      b. Copy the file to the system disk in the proper directory, using the UNPACK utility program:

      Type UNPACK A:WIN8514 and press Enter.

      Type UNPACK A:G.FON and press Enter.

      The SVGA driver and font files are now unpacked and in the correct directory.

4. Edit the SYSTEM.INI file and find the following line:

```
DISPLAY.DRV=VGA.DRV
```

This line specifies the device driver WIN-OS/2 uses in full-screen sessions.

5. Change this line to point to the high-resolution device driver that was unloaded in the steps above. In this example, the device driver is 8514.DRV. The modified line should look like the following:

```
DISPLAY.DRV=8514.DRV
```

6. Change the SYSTEM.INI font entries:

   • In SYSTEM.INI, these entries are:

```
FIXEDFON.FON=VGAFIX.FON
OEMFONTS.FON=VGAOEM.FON
FONTS.FON=VGASYS.FON
```

   • For 8514, these entries must be changed to:

```
FIXEDFON.FON=8514FIX.FON
OEMFONTS.FON=8514OEM.FON
FONTS.FON=8514SYS.FON
```

   • Save the changes to the SYSTEM.INI file.

7. Change the WIN.INI font entries

   • In WIN.INI, the entries are:

```
SYMBOL 8,10,12,14,18,24 (VGA RES)=SYMBOLE.FON
MS SANS SERIF 8,10,12,14,18,24 (VGA RES)=SSERIFE.FON
MS SERIF 8,10,12,14,18,24 (VGA RES)=SERIFE.FON
SMALL FONTS (VGA RES)=SMALLE.FON
COURIER 10,12,15 (VGA RES)=COURE.FON
```

   • For 8514, these entries must be changed to:

```
SYMBOL 8,10,12,14,18,24 (8514 RES)=SYMBOLG.FON
MS SANS SERIF 8,10,12,14,18,24 (8514 RES)=SSERIFG.FON
MS SERIF 8,10,12,14,18,24 (8514 RES)=SERIFG.FON
SMALL FONTS (8514 RES)=SMALLG.FON
COURIER 10,12,15 (8514 RES)=COURG.FON
```

   • Save the changes to the SYSTEM.INI file.

The system is ready to run Windows applications in WIN-OS/2 full-screen sessions high-resolution mode.

Super VGA

Resolutions above VGA (640 x 480 x 16 colors) are referred to as Super VGA (SVGA). The implementation of SVGA varies widely and requires different device drivers for different resolutions, adapters, and systems. All SVGA adapters and several of the more common SVGA chipsets are supported in VGA mode with the VGA driver provided with OS/2 2.1. For a list of the supported chipsets see Chapter 27, "Video Support" on page 327.

Note: Customers are encouraged to discuss SVGA problems with their display adapter manufacturer because they are best equipped to assist in correcting the problem.

Preparing to Switch to a Different Display Adapter

Because SVGA adapters are only compatible at the VGA level, the system must be restored to VGA in order to safely install a different display adapter.

To set your system back to VGA:

1. Open an OS/2 window or OS/2 full-screen command prompt.
2. Type **DSPINSTL**.
3. Press Enter to start the Display Install program. The Display Driver Install panel appears.

   Note: The DSPINSTL program is located in the \OS2\INSTALL directory on your hard disk drive.

4. Select **Primary Display**.
5. Select **OK**.
6. Select **Video Graphics Array (VGA)** from the list of drivers in the Primary Display Adapter Type window.
7. Select **OK** to verify this choice.
8. Type the location of the source directory. A: is the default.
9. Select **Install**. The appropriate files are copied to your hard disk drive.
10. When the installation is complete, shut down the system.

Your display adapter is restored and can work in VGA mode. If you want to install a new display adapter, complete the steps under "Installing a New Display Adapter" on page 337.

Installing a New Display Adapter

All display adapters must tailor their output to the capabilities of the display attached to the system. Unfortunately, there is no standard for communicating the capabilities of the display to the display adapter. The result is that many display adapters supply a program to define and select the type of display attached to the system. OS/2 2.1 responds to this situation by permitting the DOS display selection utilities provided by the manufacturers to be used to properly configure the system. OS/2 2.1 then configures the system in the same manner each time your machine is started.

If no display is specified, many display adapters make an assumption about the type of display attached to the system. This default setting is designed to work with the widest range of displays possible; thus, it is the safest choice.

During this installation procedure, you will be asked to make a decision about whether you want to use the defaults for your display type, or use the display adapter utility program provided by the manufacturer of the adapter. You should use the utility program provided by the manufacturer if any of the following apply:

- Your display adapter is produced by Diamond Computer Systems, Inc..
- Your display supports non-interlaced operation only.
- Your display does not support VESA standard refresh rates.
- Your display adapter requires software configuration to function properly in DOS.
- You want to configure your system to take advantage of the full refresh capabilities of your display.

Note: Using the utility program provided by the manufacturer requires exact knowledge about the capabilities of your display. If the wrong display type is selected, your system might not start.

If you have an SVGA adapter in your system, you must restore it to work in VGA mode before you can use the following instructions to install a different adapter in your system. See "Preparing to Switch to a Different Display Adapter" on page 336 for instructions.

To install a new display adapter:

1. Install the new display adapter using the manufacturer's instructions.
2. Restart your system.
3. Open an OS/2 window or OS/2 full-screen command prompt.
4. Type **DSPINSTL**.
5. Press Enter to start the Display Install program. The Display Driver Install panel appears.

6. Select **Primary Display**.
7. Select **OK**.
8. Select the correct display driver for your adapter.

   Note: If support for your adapter is included in OS/2 2.1, the proper display driver will already be selected. If your display driver manufacturer has supplied drivers and a .DSC file, these display drivers will also appear on this list, and the proper driver should be selected.

9. Select **OK** to verify the choice.
10. When the Monitor Configuration/Selection Utility window appears, select the choice that best meets your requirements.
11. Select **OK**.
12. If you selected Install Using Defaults for Monitor Type, go to step 16. If you selected Install Using Display Adapter Utility Program, continue with the next step.
13. Insert the utility program diskette into the diskette drive.
14. Type the name of the utility program and press Enter. If you are unsure of the name, select **Locate** to scan the diskette for the name of the program.
15. The utility program starts. Select the appropriate display type for your system.
16. You will notice screen flicker while the installation program sets the video modes for your adapter. When the Set Display Resolution window appears, select the resolution you want to use for the OS/2 and WIN-OS/2 sessions.
17. Select **OK**.
18. Follow the instructions on the screen.
19. When the installation is complete, shut down the system and restart to enable the new display adapter.

Recovering from an Incorrect Display Type Selection

If you performed the steps in "Installing a New Display Adapter" on page 337 and selected an incorrect display you can recover by restoring to VGA mode.

To restore to VGA mode:

1. Insert the OS/2 *Installation Diskette* into drive A. (If you have a preinstalled system, use the OS/2 utility diskettes.)
2. Restart the computer.
3. When prompted, remove the *Installation Diskette*, and insert *Diskette 1*; then press Enter.
4. When the first blue screen appears, press Esc. This opens an OS/2 full-screen session.
5. Change to the \OS2 directory on your hard disk drive.
6. Type **SETVGA C:** If OS/2 is installed on a different drive, substitute that drive letter for C.

7. Follow the instructions on the screen.
8. When the installation program is complete, remove the diskette from the diskette drive.
9. Press Ctrl+Alt+Del. Your system will restart in VGA mode. You can now reinstall an SVGA driver. See "Installing a New Display Adapter" on page 337 for instructions.

> **Note:** If the System Utilities were not installed during the OS/2 installation, you will not be able to perform this procedure. To recover, either get a copy of the RSPDSPI file and then try this procedure, or reinstall the OS/2 operating system and select VGA display.

Capturing the Display Configuration

Display and video mode configuration under OS/2 is controlled by the SVGADATA.PMI file. This file can be provided by the display adapter manufacturer or created using the SVGA utility.

The SVGA utility gets information from the SVGA chipset to set each video mode and captures the current state of the display adapter. This information is stored in the SVGADATA.PMI file and used when the system is started.

Both the SVGA.EXE and SVGADATA.PMI are located in the \OS2 directory.

Following is a list of valid SVGA entries:

SVGA ON generates the SVGADATA.PMI file which enables OS/2 SVGA support.

SVGA ON DOS
generates PMI information when executed outside the OS/2 DOS environment. This generates a SVGADATA.DOS file which can be renamed to .PMI and copied to the \OS2 directory. This entry might be required if your SVGA adapter uses DOS device drivers to configure the display. Trident adapters are an example.

SVGA ON INIT
generates default display information for some TSENG and Cirrus based display adapters.

SVGA OFF deletes the SVGADATA.PMI file, disabling OS/2 SVGA support.

SVGA STATUS
returns your graphics chipset, as it appears to OS/2.

Note: The SVGA utility might be affected by video configuration programs,

Terminate Stay Resident programs (TSR), and switches and jumpers on the display adapter. Configure your video adapter properly before using the SVGA utility to create the SVGADATA.PMI file.

Switching to a Display with Less Capability

Switching to a lower capability display after installing high resolution (SVGA) drivers might cause the system to start out of synchronization. Follow this procedure to switch to a display with less capability:

1. Open a DOS Full-Screen command prompt.
2. Run the DOS display configuration utility supplied with your SVGA adapter to properly configure your display adapter and display.
3. Change to the \OS2 directory on your hard disk.
4. Type **SVGA ON**.
5. Press Enter to start the SVGA utility. This utility saves the current state of your video configuration.
6. Shut down your system.
7. Restart your system to enable the new display.

Note: You can also use these instructions if you boot to a specific version of DOS. Substitute the following step for step 4. Type **SVGA ON DOS** and press Enter. When the SVGA utility finishes, type:

```
RENAME\OS2\SVGADATA.DOS \OS2\SVGADATA.PMI
```

Press Enter.

XGA Systems

The following information relates to specific situations with high resolution XGA displays.

XGA-2 Display Type Override

In order to correctly operate your display, OS/2 2.1 needs to determine the type and characteristics of the device by using a display identification number. Some displays have the same identification number but different characteristics. If OS/2 does not operate your display at the correct refresh rate or display mode, and you are running an XGA-2 adapter, do the following:

1. Open **OS/2 System**.
2. Open **System Setup**.
3. Open **System**.

The System Settings notebook appears.

4. Select the **Screen** tab. (The **Screen** tab appears in the System Settings notebook only if you have an XGA-2 display adapter.)

   The Screen page appears.

5. Select page 2. (You can go to page 2 by selecting the right arrow in the lower-right corner of the notebook.)

6. Select the appropriate display type using the list provided.

   Note: If an incorrect display type is selected, your display might be unusable after you restart your system.

7. Point to the title-bar icon.
8. Double-click.
9. Shut down and restart your system.

Recovering from an Incorrect Display Type Selection

If you performed the steps in "XGA-2 Display Type Override" on page 340 and your display is not usable, you can revert back to the previous display type. To erase the display type override information:

1. Insert the OS/2 *Installation Diskette* into drive A. (If you have a preinstalled system, use the OS/2 utility diskettes.)

2. Restart the computer.

3. When prompted, remove the *Installation Diskette*, and insert *Diskette 1*; then press Enter.

4. When the first blue screen appears, press Esc. This opens an OS/2 full-screen session.

5. Change to the C:\XGA$DMQS directory and delete the XGASETUP.PRO file. This erases all override information from your system.

6. Remove the diskette and restart your system by pressing Ctrl+Alt+Del. Your display now operates using its default settings.

Note: If you plan to change or replace your display, first delete the file XGASETUP.PRO from the XGA$DMQS directory and then turn off the system. If your new display does not operate correctly, repeat the preceding procedure.

Changing Screen Resolution and Number of Colors

To change the screen resolution or number of colors displayed for an XGA display adapter:

1. Open **OS/2 System**.
2. Open **System Setup**.
3. Open **System**.

4. Select the **Screen** tab.
5. Select the desired resolution and number of colors from the list.
6. Point to the title-bar icon.
7. Double-click.
8. Shut down and restart your system to make the new resolution and number of colors operational.

Note: The Windows XGA full screen driver does not support all the graphic modes handled by the OS/2 PM XGA driver. The full screen Windows driver does not support 1024 x 768 x 16 color. If this mode is selected, the OS/2 desktop will run at 1024 x 768 x 16 color, but the Windows full screen will operate in 1024 x 768 x 256 color mode.

VGA and Laptop LCD or Monochrome Plasma Displays

Laptop LCDs and computers with Monochrome Plasma displays use 16 shades of grey and operate similar to VGA displays.

You can optimize the color scheme for gray-scale usage, and also provide a good set of colors for a VGA desktop presentation on a laptop LCD or monochrome plasma display. To change the color scheme and create a more readable display image:

1. Use your Reference Diskette or hardware Setup program to set your hardware to VGA color, if possible.
2. Open **OS/2 System**.
3. Open **System Setup**.
4. Open **Scheme Palette**.
5. Select the monochrome scheme in the right-hand column.
6. Point to the title-bar icon.
7. Double-click.

Using an ATI Adapter with OS/2

ATI** makes various display adapters that are comparable with the IBM 8514/A display adapter. The ATI Graphics Ultra, 8514 Ultra**, and Graphics Vantage** can all be treated as IBM 8514/A adapters for the OS/2 2.1 installation process. However, if you have an ATI Graphics Ultra Pro, you must follow these steps before you install OS/2 2.1. The INSTALL utility used in the following steps will set your display to run as a VGA display so that OS/2 2.1 can be installed. After OS/2 2.1 is installed, you can run INSTALL utility again to select the correct display attached to the system.

To prepare your ATI Graphics Ultra Pro adapter for use with OS/2 2.1:

1. Start your system using DOS preferably from a diskette. You will need to start DOS again after OS/2 2.1 is installed because the ATI install utility only runs in DOS.
2. Type INSTALL at the DOS command prompt.
3. If your adapter has 1MB of video memory, select **SHARED**. If your adapter has 2MB of video memory, ensure that the aperture is properly configured.
4. Select **Monitor Setup**.
5. Select **Custom**.
6. Set the refresh rate for 640 x 480 to IBM DEFAULT.
7. Set the refresh of all other resolutions as appropriate for your monitor.
8. Save the configuration.
9. Install OS/2 2.1.

Note: Incorrectly following these steps might cause your system to hang with a black screen or corrupt your display with static.

Refer to the ATI documentation if you encounter problems configuring the Ultra Pro memory.

Tips for Specific Video Problems

Symptom	Tips
Minor video corruption with Headland (Video 7) display adapter.	You might experience minor video corruption when switching from an OS/2 full-screen session to the desktop using Alt+Esc. The video corruption usually does impair using the display. However, exiting the OS/2 session and restarting it might remove the corruption.
System problems with WIN-OS/2 and 8514 adapter	If you are running a WIN-OS/2 full-screen session with an 8514 adapter in a high-resolution mode, do not switch to a different session while the program is updating the screen or displaying an hourglass. The actual problem you experience (for example, video corruption, system hang) depends upon what the display driver is doing at the time of the switch.
Windows applications improperly drawn.	Windows applications that use color icons or color bit-map backgrounds must run in the foreground to be properly drawn. Do not switch from a Windows application while it is being started or before it completes drawing color icons and color bit-map backgrounds.

Symptom	Tips
Graphics in DOS application corrupted	Some DOS applications with graphics use a non standard VGA mode that the adapter can support, but the operating system cannot. These applications might be corrupted when displayed in a window. To avoid this problem run them in a DOS full-screen session.
Color corruption in DOS application	Some DOS applications experience color corruption when running in a window on a VGA desktop. This is a limitation of the VGA desktop because the color palette of the DOS session has to be translated to the Presentation Manager, and the VGA desktop does not offer enough colors to do a good translation. The best solution is to use a 256-color OS/2 2.1 driver or run the application in a DOS full-screen session.

Poor performance running Windows applications using an 8514 adapter	If your system has an 8514 adapter, you can improve the performance of your Windows applications by changing their settings. Open the Settings notebook for each Windows application and change the following WIN-OS/2 settings:
	
	    VIDEO_8514A_XGA_IOTRAP to OFF
	    VIDEO_SWITCH_NOTIFICATION to ON

Screen corruption occurs on XGA, when a Windows screen saver times out while in the background.	A Windows screen saver program that times out while in a background session might have a corrupted image being displayed when you switch back to the Windows session. The image refreshed by moving the mouse or pressing any key. You can eliminate this problem by changing your WIN-OS/2 settings for the screen saver application using the Settings Notebook. Change the settings to:
	
	    VIDEO_8514A_XGA_IOTRAP to ON
	    VIDEO_SWITCH_NOTIFICATION to OFF

Cannot use a Presentation Manager debugger without needing to restart the system upon exit.	Use an XGA or 8515/A adapter with the debugger. An access violation will occur when you exit the application, but you will not have to restart your system and you will not have system problems as a result of using the application.

Symptom	Tips
IBM SVGA Video drivers do not take full advantage of the video hardware.	IBM provided video drivers are generic drivers and are not optimized for any particular video adapter. These drivers provide generic SVGA and OS/2 support.
	If the adapter manufacturer has OS/2 video drivers available, they can be used instead of the generic ones provided by IBM. The manufacturer's drivers might provide better video performance because they are optimized for their video hardware.
	However, the drivers might not support all the functionality of the IBM OS/2 video drivers, such as Seamless, OS/2 Palette Management, Multimedia support, etc.
The graphics mode and refresh rates for the hardware are incorrect.	Most video adapters are sensitive to the characteristics and capabilities of the display attached to them. The video BIOS on these adapters detects and sets the hardware to support a desired graphics mode.
	Some adapters have configuration dip switches to select desired vertical refresh rates for high-resolution modes (800x600 and 1024x768). Others are shipped with DOS video-configuration utilities which allow selection of refresh rates. Usual refresh rates range from 56Hz to 72Hz non-interlaced or 88Hz interlaced. The display has to be capable of synchronizing to this frequency for proper mode set.
	Once the desired refresh rate has been set using either the dip switches or the video-configuration utilities, run the \OS2\SVGA.EXE utility to store the hardware setup in an \OS2\SVGADATA.PMI file. Type: **\OS2\SVGA ON**

Symptom	Tips
Resolution or refresh rate loses synchronization under OS/2 but not DOS.	Generate the \OS2\SVGADATA.PMI file under a DOS version. 1. Start DOS. 2. Type **\OS2\SVGA ON DOS** 3. Press Enter. 4. Type **RENAME \OS2\SVGADATA.DOS \OS2\SVGADATA.PMI** 5. Press Enter. 6. Restart OS/2. If this does not fix the problem, try selecting a different vertical refresh rate (refer to your adapter manual); then generate the PMI file again. If your display remains out of synchronization, or is stable and synchronized after restarting the system, but loses synchronization after a session switch, this may be due to your video adapter's hardware implementation. Some video adapter hardware cannot be fully saved and restored in all graphics modes for all refresh rates.
Video corruptions or traps occur while running DOS applications	If your display adapter chipset was not recognized correctly during installation, the \OS2\SVGADATA.PMI file might contain the wrong information. **Warning:** Do not do the following if you are using SVGA PM and WIN-OS/2 drivers because they require the SVGADATA.PMI file. Check to see that the information in the file corresponds to your display adapter chipset. If it is incorrect, run the \OS2\SVGA.EXE utility to remove the .PMI file. Type: \OS2\SVGA OFF
A notebook computer encounters problems when a DOS window is opened.	Some notebook computers get a TRAP D error or other problems when a DOS window is opened. This is caused by improper video register shadowing. To correct the problem: 1. Edit your C:\CONFIG.SYS file. 2. Change `DEVICE=C:\OS2\MDOS\VVGA.SYS` to `DEVICE=C:\OS2\MDOS\VSVGA.SYS` 3. Save the C:\CONFIG.SYS file. 4. Shut down and restart the computer.
The OS/2 operating system experiences video problems similar to those observed in the DOS environment.	When the BIOS video mode set fails, OS/2 experiences video problems similar to those observed in the DOS environment. For example, the video image on an ALR** Modular PS with a Flexview 2X SVGA display fails to occupy the entire screen in 1024 x 768 mode.

Symptom	Tips
Systems with two displays have problems switching from a DOS session.	Systems that have two XGA displays attached to them might have problems switching from a DOS session to the desktop. This problem is caused by the system not saving and restoring the video hardware registers correctly.
Certain DOS applications cause the system to trap, hang, or issue a SYS3176 error.	The address used by the display adapter conflicts with something else in the system. To remap the address of the display adapter on an IBM OS/2 2.0 Preload or IBM Value Point System: 1. Restart the computer and wait for the cursor to move from the upper-left corner of the display to the upper-right corner of the display. 2. While the cursor is in the upper-right corner of the display, press Ctrl+Alt+Ins. 3. When the IBM logo appears, press Enter. 4. Select **Configuration**. 5. Select **Change Configuration**. 6. Move the cursor to the display adapter. 7. Press F5 or F6 to change to a free memory range, possibly D0000–DFFFF. 8. Press F10 to save the configuration. 9. Press Ctrl+Alt+Del to restart your system. To remap the address of the display adapter on other IBM PS/2* Micro Channel* systems: 1. Place the Reference Diskette that came with the system into drive A. 2. Press Ctrl+Alt+Del. 3. Continue with step 3 on page 347. EISA and ISA bus architecture systems: Many of these systems have a built-in Diagnostics Setup and Configuration file. When the system is turned on, the screen displays a sequence of keys to press to start Setup. Some systems allow you to view and reconfigure, while others only allow you to view the configuration. Many adapters can only be reconfigured by setting dip switches on the adapter. Refer to the manufacturer's documentation that came with the adapter for more information and contact the place of purchase.

Chapter 28. Printer Support

On most *Industry Standard Architecture* (ISA), commonly referred to as AT bus computers, parallel ports are configured using either switches or jumpers. These computers and their adapters usually come with documentation that explains the interrupt request (IRQ) levels used.

Because AT bus computers do not allow hardware-interrupt sharing, each adapter must be configured to a separate IRQ level so it works properly. Some adapters, such as Sound Blaster, are factory configured to IRQ7, or their accompanying documentation recommend that you configure them to IRQ7. This might be the same hardware-interrupt level as the first parallel port on the computer. If you intend to print, this conflict must be resolved. Refer to "Unable to Print" on page 355. You might be able to use IRQ10 with Sound Blaster because it does not conflict with parallel ports (IRQ7 or IRQ5) or IRQ5 if LPT2 is not being used. Refer to "Setting COM Port Interrupt Request (IRQ) Levels" on page 375 for more information about possible parallel-port and IRQ settings.

Refer to the documentation for your adapters to configure the IRQ levels for your parallel ports and other adapters in your computer.

IRQ Settings

The following tables show standard parallel-port address and IRQ settings.

	AT Bus (ISA)	EISA	Micro Channel
LPT1	3BC/IRQ7	3BC/IRQ5 or IRQ7	3BC/IRQ7
LPT2	278/IRQ5	378/IRQ5 or IRQ7	378/IRQ7
OR			
LPT1	378/IRQ7	378/IRQ5 or IRQ7	378/IRQ7
LPT2	278/IRQ5	278/IRQ5 or IRQ7	278/IRQ7

	AT Bus (ISA)	EISA	Micro Channel
LPT1	3BC/IRQ7	3BC/IRQ5 or IRQ7	3BC/IRQ7
LPT2	378/IRQ7	378/IRQ5 or IRQ7	378/IRQ7
LPT3	278/IRQ5	278/IRQ5 or IRQ7	278/IRQ7

Note: On Extended Industry Standard Architecture (EISA) computers, using IRQ5 or IRQ7 depends on the hardware-interrupt level your port supports.

Changing the IRQ Level

To change the IRQ setting on an ISA computer or adapter:

1. Turn off your computer.
2. Remove the parallel-port adapter.
3. Configure the system board or adapter by adjusting the DIP switches or jumpers to set the parallel port to one of the industry standard combinations.

   Ensure that other adapters are not configured to use the same IRQ level. Sound, Musical Instrument Device Interface (MIDI), LAN, and serial adapters might be sharing these same hardware-interrupt levels and creating interference.

For more information, refer to "Setting COM Port Interrupt Request (IRQ) Levels" on page 375 and "Understanding COM Ports" on page 374.

Note: If you have a Sound Blaster adapter installed and have an IRQ conflict, you might be able to use:

  - IRQ10 because it does not conflict with parallel ports (IRQ7 or IRQ5)

    Or
  - IRQ5 if LPT2 is not being used.

PS/2 Direct-Memory-Access Parallel Ports

If you have a Personal System/2* computer that supports direct-memory-access (DMA) parallel ports, OS/2 2.1 can take advantage of it. The current systems with a DMA parallel port include PS/2 models that have been manufactured by IBM within the past few years. If you have one of these systems, ensure that the parallel-port arbitration level is set to SHARED7 (enabled).

Note: PS/2 models 80-A21 and 80-A31 are different. On these models you must set the parallel-port arbitration level to PARALLEL2 (DMA).

OS/2 2.1 will automatically take advantage of DMA parallel ports; no additional OS/2 setup is required. If you are an OS/2 Version 1.3 customer with *Corrective Service Diskette 5150* (or later) installed, and you have disabled the parallel-port arbitration level, you need to re-enable it in order for OS/2 2.1 to take advantage of the feature. Use the Reference Diskette shipped with the computer to view the system configuration, and then set the parallel-port arbitration level to SHARED7.

Selecting OS/2 Printer Drivers for Unsupported Printers

If your printer is not supported by an OS/2 2.1 printer driver, determine if your printer supports a more common printer in emulation mode, then install the corresponding printer driver.

Printer	Substitute Driver	Printer Emulated
Canon** Bubble-Jet** Printer	Use the OS/2 printer driver developed by Canon for optimum support. The Canon BBS number is (714) 438-3325. If you cannot obtain the Canon driver you can choose a different driver and emulate a different printer.	
Bubble-Jet BJ10E	IBM 42xx driver	IBM Proprinter* x24E
Bubble-Jet BJC800	OS/2 Epson** driver	Epson LQ2550
Bubble-Jet LBP8 III+	IBM 42xx driver or OS/2 Epson driver	IBM Proprinter x24E or Epson LQ2550
NEC** P3200	Epson LQ-850 printer driver	
NEC P6200	Epson LG-2550 printer driver	
Star NX-1000	Epson LX-800 printer driver	

HP LaserJet Printer

If you are going to install the OS/2 HP LaserJet printer driver over an existing driver, be sure to delete all the old .FNT files first. Then, delete the printer driver from the OS/2 Workplace Shell printer object, and respond **Yes** when asked if the driver files should be deleted from the hard disk.

HP PaintJet** and PaintJet XL Printers

These printers should use the Micrografx** PaintJet printer driver (SMGXPJET.DRV) shipped with OS/2 2.1 on *Printer Diskette 3*.

Some applications, such as Aldus PageMaker, have problems printing multiple bit maps using this printer driver. If this occurs after the driver is installed:

1. Point to the printer object.
2. Click mouse button 2.
3. Select the arrow to the right of **Open**; then select **Settings**.
4. Select **Printer-specific format** on the Queues page.

Note: The OS/2 PaintJet driver can be used only on OS/2 2.0 and OS/2 2.1.

Okidata Printers

The following table lists printers that some of the specified Okidata printers emulate so that the printer drivers for these printers can be selected from the list of printer drivers when installing Okidata printers.

Table 5 (Page 1 of 2). Okidata Printer Emulation	
Okidata Printer	**Printer Emulated**
Microline 84	IBM 5152
Pacemark 2350	
Pacemark 2410	
Microline 182	
Microline 192	
Microline 193	
Microline 192 Plus	
Microline 193 Plus	
Microline 292	
Microline 293	
Microline 294	
Microline 172	
Microline 182 Plus	
Microline Turbo	
Pacemark 3410	IBM Proprinter
Okimate 20	
Microline 192 Plus	
Microline 193 Plus	
Microline 320	
Microline 321	

Table 5 (Page 2 of 2). Okidata Printer Emulation

Okidata Printer	Printer Emulated
Microline 390 Microline 391 Microline 393B Microline 393B Plus Microline 393C Microline 390 Plus Microline 391 Plus OL800 LED Page Printer OL820 LED Page Printer	IBM Proprinter 24-pin
Pacemark 3410 Okidata 180 Microline 320 Microline 321 Microline 391	Epson FX
Microline 390 Microline 380 Microline 393B Microline 393B Plus Microline 393C Microline 390 Plus Microline 391 Plus	Epson LQ
Laserline 6	HP LaserJet Plus
OL400 LED Page Printer OL800 LED Page Printer OL820 LED Page Printer OL830 LED Page Printer OL840 LED Page Printer	HP LaserJet II
OL830 LED Page Printer OL840 LED Page Printer	Generic Postscript

IBM 4019 and IBM 4029 Printers

For the IBM 4019 and 4029 printers, the Automatic Emulation Switching (AES) utility program is available from the Lexmark** International, Inc. bulletin board service. The file is located in the UTILITIES directory and is called 40X9SU32.EXE.

If you have any problems accessing the Lexmark BBS, call Lexmark at 1-606-232-3000.

OS/2 Version 1.3 Printer Drivers

The OS/2 2.1 operating system contains new graphics capability and some new printer drivers. In this new graphics environment, some of the original OS/2 Version 1.3 printer drivers for IBM printers will not work. However, updates are available for these printer drivers. If you install OS/2 2.1 with these old OS/2 Version 1.3 printer drivers on your system, and then attempt to print, your system will stop and you will have to restart it. Any unsaved data will be lost.

You need to replace each of the following OS/2 version 1.3 printer drivers with the specified printer driver that is included on the OS/2 2.1 installation diskettes.

1.3 Driver	2.1 Driver
IBM4201.DRV	IBM42xx.DRV
IBM4202.DRV	IBM42xx.DRV
IBM4207.DRV	IBM42xx.DRV
IBM4208.DRV	IBM42xx.DRV
IBM5202.DRV	IBM52xx.DRV

Additional OS/2 Version 1.3 printer drivers have been updated for OS/2 2.1. They are not included on the installation diskettes, but are available from other sources, such as electronic bulletin boards and IBM. The OS/2 Version 1.3 printer drivers that have been updated include the following:

Driver	Printer
IBM3852.DRV	IBM Color Inkjet
IBM5152.DRV	IBM Graphics Printer, IBM 3812 Printer
IBM5182.DRV	IBM Color Printer, Model 1
IBM5201.DRV	IBM Quietwriter*, Model 1
IBM5216.DRV	IBM Wheelprinter

The updated OS/2 Version 1.3 printer drivers in the previous lists are available from the following sources:

- CompuServe, Forum OS2SUPPORT, LIB 17
- Bulletin board systems (BBS), such as the OS/2 BBS (call 1-800-547-1283 to register) and the NSC BBS in Atlanta, GA, U.S.A. (1-404-835-6600)

- An IBM support organization, such as the OS/2 Support Line in the United States (1-800-992-4777), or HelpWare*, where available
- Your IBM representative

All OS/2 drivers from these sources are updated periodically with fixes and new features.

WIN-OS/2 Printer Drivers

If your printer has a supported WIN-OS/2 printer driver, but no OS/2 printer driver, do the following:

1. Set up the WIN-OS/2 printer driver using the WIN-OS/2 Control Panel.
2. Create the OS/2 Printer object using the IBMNULL printer driver.
3. Set up the OS/2 Printer object to use the same port that you selected in the WIN-OS/2 Control Panel.

You should be able to print from a WIN-OS/2 session.

Contact your printer manufacturer to obtain an OS/2 2.1 printer driver or to determine what other printers your printer emulates.

Resolving Printing Problems

The following describes the actions you can take to resolve some common printing problems.

Unable to Print

If you encounter printing problems with parallel ports (for example, nothing prints), ensure that you have installed the appropriate printer driver for your model printer (see "Selecting OS/2 Printer Drivers for Unsupported Printers" on page 351). If the printer driver is correct, do the following:

- Check that your parallel ports are configured properly. Refer to "IRQ Settings" on page 349 for configuration settings.
- Verify that your printer cable meets parallel-port specifications. Cable problems can include the following:
  - All interface signals might not be wired. OS/2 2.1 uses all the signals within the parallel port interface, DOS does not; therefore, cables that work in DOS might not work in OS/2 2.1.

- Cables might be improperly shielded or grounded. Improperly shielded or grounded cables can produce electrical interference causing signals that can be incorrectly received and equipment to malfunction.
- Cables that are longer than 6 feet can cause the signal to weaken. This means that your printer might not be able to receive signals from a computer that is too far away.

If you determine that one of the previous problems is preventing you from printing, you might need to purchase a new cable.

- If you still cannot print, and you are convinced it is not a printer-driver problem, interrupt problem, or cable problem, there might be a problem with your I/O adapter. Some older parallel-port adapters fail to generate hardware interrupts; therefore, they will not work with this version of the OS/2 operating system. These adapters usually work correctly under DOS, as DOS does not use hardware interrupts to print. The OS/2 2.1 operating system waits for the printer to send an interrupt when the printer is ready for more data. If your adapter does not generate interrupts, it must be replaced if you want to print under OS/2 2.1. If your printer-buffer light illuminates, or prints one character and then displays an error message (or otherwise behaves erratically), it might be an interrupt problem.

Bit Maps not Printing

Some applications have problems printing multiple bit maps. If this occurs:

1. Point to the printer object.
2. Click mouse button 2.
3. Select the arrow to the right of **Open**; then select **Settings**.
4. Select **Printer-specific format** on the Queues page.

Some complex bit maps might not print completely on some printers. To fix this problem, increase the amount of memory in the printer.

Bit Maps Printing Incorrectly

Some applications have problems printing bit maps. Either they do not appear in the printout or they appear incorrectly. If this occurs:

1. Point to the Printer object
2. Click mouse button 2.
3. Select the arrow to the right of **Open**.
4. Select **Settings**.
5. Select the **Queues** tab.
6. Select **Printer-specific format**
7. Point to the title-bar icon.

8. Double-click.

Print Job Damaged on Retry

If you send a print job to an offline printer, and then retry the operation when the printer is online by responding to the Retry message, your job might be damaged. To fix the problem:

1. Select the job.
2. Click mouse button 2.
3. Select **Start again**.

Printer Stops Printing

If your DOS program sending PostScript output stops printing, do the following:

1. Cancel the print job that caused the printer to stop printing.
2. Point to the printer object.
3. Click mouse button 2.
4. Select the **Queue** tab.
5. Click on the **Print while spooling** check box to deselect the option.
6. Point to the title-bar icon.
7. Double-click.
8. Resend the print job.

Printer Worked under DOS, but Not under OS/2 2.1

If your printer worked under DOS, but does not work under OS/2 2.1, there is probably a problem with your hardware-interrupt level or printer cable. This problem occurs, you will receive the message LPT1 NOT RESPONDING or ABORT, RETRY, IGNORE?. (Refer to "Unable to Print" on page 355.)

Print Job Spooled but Does Not Print

The spooler will not print a job until the program closes the print data stream. Some DOS programs do not immediately close the print data stream. If you see your print job as an icon with an arrow pointing to the document in the Job Icon View window, the job will not print. The arrow must point from the document to the print device. This will not occur until the program closes the data stream.

If the job does not print after 15 seconds, you might need to change a DOS setting. By default, the PRINT_TIMEOUT DOS setting is 15 seconds. If, after 15 seconds, your job does not print, adjust the value. You might need to load the LPTDD.SYS file, wait for the timeout response, or press Ctrl+Alt+Print Screen.

Note: Setting a value of zero (0) disables the PRINT_TIMEOUT DOS setting.

Only Prints in WIN-OS/2 Session

If you are using LPTx but are unable to print from any other session, you must select an LPTx.OS2 port as your printer connection for WIN-OS/2 printing. If you are printing to a redirected port, you must use LPTx.OS2.

Printing Starts Only When DOS Program Ends

If your DOS print job does not begin printing until the program is ended, the program has not closed the data stream. Use the DOS_DEVICE DOS setting to load the C:\OS2\MDOS\LPTDD.SYS device driver. Then, the PRINT_TIMEOUT DOS setting can be used to close the print job without having to exit the program.

Print Job Split into Several Spool Files

If your DOS program print job is split into several spool files, you might need to disable the spooler to correct the problem. Some programs open and close the printer data stream for every character, line, or page. Disabling the spooler (using the Spooler object in the System Setup folder) is one way to correct this problem. Another alternative is to upgrade the program by contacting the manufacturer. If the problem occurs with complex printouts, you might increase the DOS setting PRINT_TIMEOUT value.

Can Print Only from DOS Programs

If you are printing from a DOS program, but are unable to print from another program until you end the DOS program, your DOS program is accessing the parallel-port hardware directly. OS/2 2.1 prevents two or more programs from simultaneously accessing the same parallel-port hardware. The second program must wait for the first program to end, even if the second program is the OS/2 Printer object.

Unable to Print from DOS to Network Printer

If you are unable to print from a DOS session to an LPT port that is redirected to a network printer, you might need to use the LPTDD.SYS device driver (see "Printing Starts Only When DOS Program Ends").

Printer Worked under Windows, but Not under OS/2 2.1

If your printer worked under a Windows operation, but does not work after installing OS/2 2.1, delete the printer driver and reinstall it under WIN-OS/2 using the WIN-OS/2 Control Panel.

If printing from a WIN-OS/2 session is slow, but acceptable everywhere in the system, you might need to set the priority level higher using the Options menu in the WIN-OS/2 Print Manager.

Viewing of the Network Printer Queue is Slow

To improve the performance of viewing the contents of a network printer object, use a long refresh interval or set the interval to 0 (no refresh).

Chapter 29. Hardware Support

 This chapter provides information about hardware device support and audio adapter support for IBM computers and computers from other personal computer manufacturers.

Personal Computer Manufacturer Systems

IBM is currently testing personal computer manufacturer (PCM) systems for compatibility with OS/2 2.1. The compatibility test verifies 18 key functions of OS/2 2.1. Test results are based on selected model configurations provided by the manufacturers. While testing is continuing, current compatibility information about tested systems is available through your dealer or Marketing Representative, as well as through the following online services:

CompuServe G OS2SUP, in Library 17, PCMTAB.TXT. To join CompuServe, call the appropriate phone numbers for your area, or for Membership Service at 1-800-848-8199, and ask for representative 239.

IBM National Support Center Bulletin Board System (NSC BBS).
This service is available 24 hours a day, on a toll-call basis, with no access charge, to anyone in the world who has a modem, asynchronous-communication programs, and a switched telephone line. (The modem should be set for 8 data bits, 1 stop bit, no parity, and the standard transmission speed of 1200 to 9600 baud.)

To access the NSC BBS, call (404) 835-6600.

IBMLink* Eligible customers can obtain installation and usage assistance through IBMLink* Question Support. To obtain information about eligibility, contact your local Branch Office or Marketing Representative.

Note: The compatibility test information is provided for information purposes only. IBM MAKES NO WARRANTY, EXPRESS OR IMPLIED, WITH RESPECT TO THE OPERATION OF THE PERSONAL COMPUTERS LISTED THROUGH THE ABOVE SOURCES.

SCSI Adapters and Device Drivers

Device support for the following adapters is shipped with OS/2 2.1.

When one of the following adapters is installed in a workstation, its presence is normally detected automatically, and the appropriate device support is subsequently installed. If one of these adapters is installed after OS/2 installation, you can install the correct device support using the Selective Install object in the System Setup folder.

SCSI Adapter or Interface	Device Driver	Comments
Adaptec** A/C 6260	AHA152x.ADD	
Adaptec AHA 1510	AHA152x.ADD	
Adaptec AHA 1520/1522	AHA152x.ADD	
Adaptec AHA 1540/1542	AHA154x.ADD	For the Adaptec 1542B SCSI adapter to run properly, set the default data rate to 5.
Adaptec AHA 1640	AHA164x.ADD	
Adaptec AHA 1740/1742/1744		
(Standard mode operation)	AHA154x.ADD	
(Enhanced mode operation)	AHA174x.ADD	
DPT PM-2011/PM-2012	DPT20xx.ADD	
Future Domain TMC-845/850/850IBM /860/875/885	FD8xx.ADD	
Future Domain TMC-1650/1660/1670/1680	FD16-700.ADD	
Future Domain MCS-600/700	FD16-700.ADD	
Future Domain FD7000EX	FD7000EX.ADD	
IBM 16-bit AT Fast SCSI Adapter	FD16-700.ADD	

SCSI Adapter or Interface	Device Driver	Comments
IBM PS/2 SCSI Adapter	IBM2SCSI.ADD	Early versions of the IBM 16-bit SCSI adapters might experience problems and report, erroneously, that the device is not functioning. This can be corrected by replacing the SCSI adapter with an adapter with updated microcode.
IBM PS/2 SCSI Adapter with Cache	IBM2SCSI.ADD	
Other Manufacturers	IBMINT13.I13	Supports a hard disk drive but cannot be used to support a CD-ROM drive. Acquire an OS/2 adapter device driver from the manufacturer of the adapter to support your CD-ROM drive.

SCSI CD-ROM Support

OS/2 2.1 contains a set of device drivers to support the following SCSI attached CD-ROM drives.

Manufacturer	Model	Comments
Hitachi**	CDR-1650S, CDR-1750S, CDR-3650, CDR-3750	
IBM	CD-ROM I, CD-ROM II	
NEC	Intersect** CDR-25, CDR-36, CDR-37, CDR-72, CDR-73, CDR-74, CDR-82, CDR-83, CDR-84 MultiSpin** CDR-38, CDR-74, CDR-84	Many NEC CD-ROM drives are bundled with a Trantor SCSI host adapter. Contact Trantor to obtain an OS/2 adapter device driver (.ADD) for the SCSI adapter.
Panasonic**	CR-501, LK-MC501S, MC501B, MC521	

Manufacturer	Model	Comments
Pioneer**	DRM-600, DRM-604X	Support is for data access only on the DRM-600. Support is for data access only on the DRM-604X, unless it has the SCSI-2 firmware upgrade; then it supports data, audio, and multisession photo CDs.
Sony**	CDU-541, CDU-561, CDU-6111, CDU-6211, CDU-7211	Multisession photo CD is supported on the CDU-561.
Texel	DM-3021, DM-3024, DM-5021, DM-5024	Multisession photo CD is supported on DM-3024 and DM-5024 drives which have the photo CD firmware upgrade.
Toshiba**	XM-3201, XM-3301, XM-3401	Multisession photo CD is supported on the XM-3401.

CD-ROM Drives and SCSI Adapters Combinations

Even though a particular SCSI adapter or CD-ROM drive might be listed in the previous tables as supported, the combination of the SCSI adapter and CD-ROM drive might not be supported. The following table lists those combinations of CD-ROM drives and SCSI adapters that are either not supported or require special setup to work properly.

CD-ROM Model	SCSI Adapter	Comments
Hitachi CDR-1750S	Adaptec AHA-1740/1742/1744:	Synchronous negotiation must be disabled through EISA system setup for the attached CD-ROM drive.
NEC CDR-25, CDR-36, CDR-37, CDR-38	IBM PS/2 SCSI adapter	Not supported.
NEC CDR-25, CDR-36, CDR-37, CDR-38	IBM PS/2 SCSI adapter with cache	Not supported.
NEC CDR-25, CDR-36, CDR-37, CDR-38	Future Domain TMC-7000EX	Not supported.
NEC CDR-25, CDR-36, CDR-37, CDR-38	Adaptec (all adapters except AHA-174X)	Parity must be disabled on card jumper.

CD-ROM Model	SCSI Adapter	Comments
NEC CDR-25, CDR-36, CDR-37, CDR-38	Adaptec AHA-1740/1742/1744	Both parity and synchronous negotiation must be disabled through EISA system setup for the attached CD ROM drive.
NEC CDR-72, CDR-73, CDR-74, CDR-82, CDR-83, CDR-84	Adaptec AHA-1740/1742/1744	Synchronous negotiation must be disabled through EISA system setup for the attached CD-ROM drive.
Panasonic (all models)	IBM PS/2 SCSI adapter	Not supported.
Panasonic (all models)	IBM PS/2 SCSI adapter with cache	The Panasonic drive will identify itself as 8 separate drives during PS/2 system setup. You must disable presence-error reporting of all 8 CD-ROM drives by selecting **Set and View SCSI device configuration** on the PS/2 Reference Diskette.
Pioneer DRM-600, DRM-604X	Adaptec SCSI adapter Future Domain SCSI adapter DPT SCSI adapter	The /ET parameter switch must be added to the BASEDEV= statement for the adapter device driver (.ADD file) in the CONFIG.SYS file. For example: BASEDEV=FD8XX.ADD /ET. **Note:** Set the switch on the back of the Pioneer DRM-604X to SCSI-2 if the drive contains the SCSI-2/PhotoCD firmware upgrade.
Sony CDU-541, CDU-6211, CDU-7211	Future Domain TMC-7000EX	Not supported.
Texel DM-3021, DM-5021	IBM PS/2 SCSI adapter IBM PS/2 SCSI adapter with cache	Not supported.

CD-ROM Model	SCSI Adapter	Comments
Texel DM-3024 and DM-5024 with firmware version 1.09 or lower, see the note following this table.	IBM PS/2 SCSI adapters Future Domain 16-bit SCSI adapters Other SCSI host adapters	IBM SCSI and Future Domain 16-bit SCSI adapters are not supported. For other SCSI host adapters, the synchronous transfer option on the controller must be disabled. In addition, the Texel drive must be the only device attached to the SCSI host adapter.

Note:

> To determine the firmware level of the CD-ROM drive, add a /V switch to the BASEDEV= C:\OS2\OS2CDROM.DMD line in the CONFIG.SYS. When starting OS/2, the product ID and firmware level of the drive will be displayed after the OS/2 logo screen is removed. For example:
>
> ```
> 2 TEXEL   CD-ROM   1.05
> ```
>
> The firmware level is the last set of characters on the line (where 1.05 is the level).

Advanced SCSI Programming Interface

The OS/2 Adaptec SCSI Programming Interface (ASPI) device manager handles host adapter resources and provides the hardware-independent ASPI for SCSI applications and drivers. The ASPI device manager does not need to control all SCSI devices attached to one host adapter.

The OS/2 ASPI support is located in the OS2ASPI.DMD file in the OS2 subdirectory. To enable this support, type the following statement in your CONFIG.SYS file:

```
BASEDEV=OS2ASPI.DMD
```

Note: ASPI support is not available for DOS.

SCSI Removable Media Support

Full-function support is not yet available for SCSI hard disk drives that use removable media. The following table details which drives and functions are supported.

Drive Manufacturer	Adapter	Device Driver	Comments
Bernoulli** 44MB and 89MB	Bernoulli		Does not support. Call the Iomega** Corporation group at 1 800-456-5522 and ask about the update for their adapter.
Bernoulli 44MB and 89MB	• Adaptec • Future Domain • IBM • Other (except Bernoulli)		OS/2 2.1 recognizes the drive as a large diskette. This means that it: • Can be formatted for the FAT file system only. • Cannot be partitioned. (If it is partitioned, it will not be recognized.) • Cannot be used as a startup drive.
SyQuest Technology Drives			OS/2 2.1 recognizes the drive as a large diskette. This means that it: • Can be formatted for the FAT file system only. • Cannot be partitioned. (If it is partitioned, it will not be recognized.) • Cannot be used as a startup drive.
Bernoulli and SyQuest Drives		IBMINT13.I13 driver	Drive is treated as a hard disk. • Cartridge must be in the drive at startup time. Note: To remove the cartridge from the drive, use the Shutdown choice on the desktop pop-up menu.

SCSI Adapter Problems

The following table lists potential compatibility problems with the microcode levels on various adapters and devices.

Adapter	Comment
IBM SCSI	If you experience intermittent data errors with earlier IBM SCSI adapters, you might need to upgrade them. If you have IBM SCSI FRU P/N 15F6561, obtain ECA032. If you have IBM SCSI with cache FRU P/N 64F0124, obtain ECA027. These adapters are standard in 8565 models 061 and 121 and 8580 models 121, 131, A21, and A31.
Adaptec	The Adaptec SCSI Programming Interface (ASPI) is now available for OS/2 device drivers. (ASPI support is not available for DOS) OS/2 ASPI support is located in the OS2ASPI.DMD file in the OS2 subdirectory. To enable this support, type the following statement in your CONFIG.SYS file: `BASEDEV=OS2ASPI.DMD`
Adaptec AHA-154*x*	Drive: IBM 0661 - 320MB SCSI You need to obtain Adapter BIOS level 3.20 or above from Adaptec.
• Future Domain TMC-850/860/875/885 w/BIOS revision level 7.0. • Future Domain TMC-1660/1670/1680 w/BIOS revision level 2.0.	When the Future Domain adapter is controlling the Startup diskette, it will produce the message, Disk read error has occurred when you attempt to start the *Installation Diskette*. Contact Future Domain for a free BIOS upgrade.
Seagate** ST-01, ST-02	Causes contention with MFM and RLL drives. The ST-01 or ST-02 should be the only drive controller installed. This problem is being investigated.
Western Digital WD7000	Newer adapters seem to be supported while earlier ones are not. Western Digital is now owned by Future Domain. Contact Future Domain for assistance.
• AMI** Fast Disk • AMI Fast Disk II SCSI adapters • CEI Cumulus** C5640B SCSI Micro-Channel adapter	These adapters are incorrectly recognized as Adaptec adapters. If you have one of these adapters in your system, do the following: • At the final restart after the installation is completed, delete from the CONFIG.SYS file any line with "BASEDEV=AHA1*xxx*.ADD" (where *x* can be any character). • Ensure the line "BASEDEV=IBMINT13.I13" appears in the CONFIG.SYS file. This line should have been placed there during OS/2 installation.

Adapter	Comment
Always Technology IN-2000 SCSI adapter	If you experience OS/2 problems (such as a TRAP 000D error) either at installation time or after, the BIOS on the adapter might be the problem. If the BIOS revision level is 3.06A or 3.20 (as shown during the system self-test), you should have the BIOS on the adapter upgraded. The current BIOS level is VCN:1-02 and works with OS/2 2.1. If you require this upgrade, you might also need an upgrade to a companion 8-pin serial PROM chip which must have a revision level of 2.5-2.7. Always Technology support can be reached at 818-597-9595.

Additional Device Support Information

The following contains useful information about OS/2 2.1 support for the specified devices.

Device	Comments
Quantum Hard Cards	Access to the Quantum Hard Cards that utilize the driver IBM1S506.ADD can be gained by using the switch settings for a secondary controller. The switches required for the hardcard are the adapter number and the IRQ level. If you have the Quantum XL50 or XL105 Hard Cards, then a BIOS upgrade is required for OS/2. Contact Quantum for assistance with proper Hard Card setup and BIOS upgrades.
HP Scanjet Scanner	If you receive an error message stating that you cannot access your HP scanner, and you are using an ISA (AT-style) bus machine, your adapter switches need to be set to 1010. If you are using a PS/2 computer, you must use the Reference Diskette to set the adapter to ROM addresses C8000 – CBFFF and I/O addresses 268 – 26F.
IBM Tape Drives	If no other device is connected to the SCSI bus on its adapter or the tape adapter, then you might be able to get your drive to work in an external DOS (VMBOOT) session. If the tape drive worked under OS/2 version 1.x and the device is written to ASPI, IBM is currently working on support for your device. IBM does not provide third-party device drivers for peripherals. Refer to your peripheral manufacturer for OS/2-specific support.

Device	Comments
IBM or IRWIN Tape Drives	The tape drives are supported. Two programs that currently work with them are PMTAPE and PS2TAPE. Easy Tape from Maynard** Backup Systems is scheduled for future release. Contact Maynard for information.
Colorado Jumbo Tape Drives	A Colorado Jumbo tape drive connected to a diskette-drive controller, can only run the tape backup program in a DOS Startup session from a diskette image. Refer to the topic "Starting DOS from an image file" in the Master Help Index. The Colorado Jumbo Tape program allows you to specify some hardware and software settings to be used when backing up files. The **Concurrent Disk/Tape operation** option must be set to No. To change the option: 1. Start the program 2. Select the Utilities menu (F3) 3. Select **Software Setups** (F6). 4. Change the option to N. The Colorado company is developing an OS/2-specific version of their program. For more information, contact Colorado.
Mountain Tape Drive	The Mountain company is developing an OS/2-specific version of their program. For more information, contact Mountain at 1-800-458-0300.
Mouse	There have been some intermittent problems using 50 MHz systems with AT-style bus computers with a mouse. The mouse can get out of synchronization. Input will function through the keyboard and the mouse, but to avoid possible problems, shut down the system and restart to resynchronize the mouse.
Logitech 3-Button Mouse	The Logitech 3-button bus mouse is supported as a 2-button mouse. It is treated as a Microsoft 2-button bus mouse. A Logitech serial mouse with 3 buttons behaves as expected in DOS sessions. However, in an OS/2 session, there might be different and more limited functions assigned to the buttons. There are no standards for the functions of a 3-button mouse.

Device	Comments
PS/2 External 5.25-Inch 1.2MB Diskette Drive	If you cannot get the external 5.25-inch 1.2MB diskette drive to work on a PS/2 computer, install the device driver that comes with the drive into the OS2 directory in the startup partition. The device driver is called EXT5DD.SYS. Change your CONFIG.SYS file statement to read OS2\EXT5DD.SYS instead of OS2\EXTDSKDD.SYS.
Screen Reader* Keypad	If you cannot use your Screen Reader keypad, there might be a problem with the statements in your CONFIG.SYS file. Use an editor to look at the file. • If you have a mouse attached to your system, the device driver (DEVICE=) statements might not be in the correct order. Make sure the DEVICE= statement for the mouse driver (MOUSE.SYS) is located before the DEVICE= statement for the keypad driver (KEYPAD.SYS). • If you do not have a mouse attached to your system, you should not have a DEVICE= statement for a mouse. If you have a DEVICE= statement for MOUSE.SYS, remove that statement.
Security Devices	Some security devices (known as *dongles*) attached to a parallel port might not work properly with OS/2 2.1. The DOS program that uses the device can start from one DOS session only. An error message appears when you try to start additional copies of the program. You can press Ctrl+Alt+Print Screen to release access to the parallel-port program prior to starting the second copy of the DOS program or change the port settings to allow multiple applications to access the parallel port hardware at the same time. To change the port settings: 1. Point to the printer object. 2. Click mouse button 2. 3. Select the arrow to the right of **Open**. 4. Select **Settings**. 5. Select the **Output** tab. 6. Point to an LPT port icon. 7. Double-click. 8. Change the port settings in the selection field. 9. Select **OK**. 10. Point to the title-bar icon. 11. Double-click. **Note:** Make sure you are using cables that are properly shielded and wired. (For more information, refer to "Unable to Print" on page 355.)

OEM Diskette Drives

IBM has an *internal development version* of an IBM1FLPY driver that corrects a number of problems with OEM diskette drives parsing command line parameters. This driver is currently not part of the OS/2 product.

Note: Customers are encouraged to discuss OS/2 compatibility problems with their controller supplier because they are best equipped to assist in resolving compatibility problems with IBM.

The IBM1FLPY driver comes with a revised OS2DASD.DMD file. You should retain your copies of these binaries, and then install the driver and .DMD file.

IBM1FLPY normally obtains diskette drive information from the host system BIOS. If the information supplied is incorrect, or if the BIOS does not support a third or fourth party diskette drive, it might be necessary to provide this information on the IBM1FLPY command line.

In addition, command line parameters can be used to support a second installed diskette controller which would not normally have host system BIOS support.

Use the following IBM1FLPY command line parameters in conjunction with the BASEDEV=IBM1FLPY.ADD statement.

/MCA   Load on a Micro Channel computer.

/A: Adapter ID <0 - 1>

/IRQ: Interrupt Request Level <0 - n>. Consult the supplier of the diskette controller for the appropriate setting.

/DMA   DMA Channel Number <0 - n>. Consult the supplier of the diskette controller for the appropriate setting.

/P: Controller I/O Address <hhhh>. Consult the supplier of the diskette controller for the appropriate setting.

/U: Drive Number <0 - 3>

/F: Drive Capacity <360KB - 2.88MB>

/CL: Changeline Type <NONE, AT, PS2>

/SPEC: Controller Specify Bytes <hh, hh>

Examples:

To define a third 1.2MB diskette drive:

```
BASEDEV=IBM1FLPY.ADD /A:0 /U.2
                     /F:1.2MB
```

To override the ChangeLine type for drive B:

```
BASEDEV=IBM1FLPY.ADD /A:0
          /U:1 /CL:NONE
```

To support a 1.2MB OEM drive attached to a Micro Channel system:

```
REM BASEDEV=IBM2FLPY.ADD
BASEDEV=IBM1FLPY.ADD /MCA /A:0
               /U:1 /F:1.2MB
```

Note: The /MCA parameter is required on Micro Channel systems. If it is not specified, the driver will automatically uninstall itself.

To support a second installed diskette controller:

```
BASEDEV=IBM1FLPY.ADD
BASEDEV=IBM1FLPY.ADD /A:0 /DMA:3
              /IRQ:10 /P:370
              /U:0 /F:1.44MB
              /U:1 /F:1.2MB
```

Note: The first drive supported by the second controller will be assigned B: if this drive letter is available.

Specifying /A:1 will cause the second controller to assign drive letters other than A: or B:.

More than two diskette drives can be accessed in systems that use the IBM1FLPY.ADD driver. This driver provides switch settings for support of up to four diskette drives installed in a system. The switch settings for the third and fourth diskette drives might have to be added to the CONFIG.SYS in order to access the drives.

Model-Specific Computer Problems

Model	Comments
IBM PS/2 Model 90 or 95	• If you are experiencing problems with your Model 90 or 95, ensure your system is at the latest engineering change (EC) level. Your IBM service representative can assist you. • If your Model 90 or 95 is a 33 MHz system and you are having intermittent difficulty identifying memory parity errors such as TRAP 0002, forcing you to restart your system, then ECA053 might apply. If your microprocessor card has part number 84F9356, contact your IBM representative to assist you with a replacement. • If your Model 90 is experiencing intermittent memory errors, ECA084 might apply if the part number of your memory riser card is N33F4905 or 84F9356. Again, your IBM representative can assist you with a replacement. • For both Model 90 and 95 computers, you must ensure that you have matched pairs of single in-line memory modules. This means that each pair of single in-line memory modules, as described in your technical reference manual, must be matched in memory size and speed. Mixing these modules can cause some computers to report memory errors. • If your Model 90 or 95 has the Unattended Start Mode option set (through the System Programs), the mouse driver will not load during startup. To correct this situation, disable the Unattended Start Mode.
IBM PS/2 Model 30-286 Upgrades	IBM PS/2 Model 30-286 upgrades to a 386 microprocessor are not supported.
Aox** Systems	If your computer has an Aox add-in microprocessor adapter and you encounter problems either installing or starting up your OS/2 system, you can call the Aox Corporation and ask for the latest "flash-prom" code upgrade.

Understanding COM Ports

On an ISA system, having a shared interrupt-request line can cause problems. ISA systems have what are called *edge triggered* interrupts. Edge triggered interrupts can only be sensed for a very short period.

Micro Channel and EISA systems use *level sensitive* interrupts. If a second interrupt arrives from another adapter while the first interrupt is still being processed, the second interrupt will be lost. In your computer system, losing an interrupt can lead to various difficulties, such as printers that do not seem to print smoothly or reliably, or communications sessions where some characters get lost.

With single-tasking systems such as DOS, the two adapters that are sharing the interrupt might never cause any real problems because they might never be in use at the same time. However, OS/2 2.1 presents a different set of problems. If you have multiple serial communications adapters, there is a greater probability that you might try to use two or more of them at the same time. If some of them have previously been set up using shared interrupts, problems can occur that probably didn't occur in DOS.

OS/2 2.1 can detect that an interrupt line is shared and will not allow simultaneous use. Assume that COM1 and COM3 are sharing Interrupt Request line 4 (IRQ4). If you try to use both COM ports at the same time, the OS/2 operating system will not allow the second one to start. A well-written OS/2 communications program will recognize that the port cannot be opened and an error message will be displayed. However, a DOS program is unprepared to respond to this unfamiliar situation. It will probably suspend, waiting for a port that will not open.

Another potential source of trouble is having multiple hardware adapters that are sharing the same I/O address. The various hardware adapters in your computer must have their own addresses. Consider what might happen, for example, if the commands that were meant for your printer were instead routed to your hard disk.

The solution for all of these problems is to ensure that all your hardware adapters have their own unique I/O addresses and IRQ assignments.

Setting COM Port Interrupt Request (IRQ) Levels

The following information will help you determine what IRQ settings you can use for COM3 or COM4 port adapters to avoid shared interrupts.

On an ISA machine there are a total of 15 IRQ levels available. Many of these are already being used. Most are already in use because they are the standard settings for the more common devices. These standard settings are as follows:

IRQ Level	Device Associated
0	System Timer
1	Keyboard
2	Secondary Interrupt Controller (see note)
3	COM2 (Serial Communications Port 2)
4	COM1 (Serial Communications Port 1)
5	LPT2 (Parallel Port 2)
6	Diskette
7	LPT1 (Parallel Port 1)
8	Real-time Clock
9	open
10	open
11	open
12	Auxiliary Port (Mouse)
13	Math Coprocessor
14	Hard Disk
15	open

Note: On the IBM-AT (ISA bus), the IRQ9 pin is identical with the IRQ2 pin on the original IBM-PC. If you have an earlier, 8-bit adapter whose documentation states that it uses IRQ2, be aware that this will actually be interpreted as IRQ9 when plugged into the 16-bit ISA bus.

The IRQ levels shown as open have no established, standardized use. When setting the IRQ values on your COM3 or COM4 ports, you are likely to find these levels available to use without conflict with some other adapter. Furthermore, if you don't have two parallel ports installed, IRQ5 might be usable for some other purpose, such as COM3 or COM4. Be cautious about doing this because it might cause a problem later if you decide to install a second parallel port. In addition, some other nonstandard device might already be using IRQ5.

When trying to manage the IRQ levels of your various hardware adapters to avoid conflicts, you might find that your 8-bit adapters cause problems. Except for IRQ9, only 16-bit adapters are configurable to use IRQ levels higher than 7. Notice that the IRQ table shows that the low-numbered IRQ lines already have some standard function assigned. It might be that your only alternative for avoiding some IRQ conflicts is to purchase a more versatile 16-bit adapter.

If you have nonstandard 8-bit adapters, be especially careful of interrupt conflicts. For example, the Sound Blaster adapter is configured at the factory to use IRQ7. IRQ7 is the standard assignment for LPT1, the first parallel port. This conflict might not be apparent with DOS because DOS printing typically does not use the interrupt line. However, OS/2 2.1 requires it, and the hidden conflict can become the source of printing problems. It is also fairly common to discover that the interrupt feature on your parallel-port adapter does not work. In DOS, this might not have any effect. In OS/2 2.1, your printer might be very erratic or not work at all.

Enabling COM Ports

The original ISA computer (the IBM Personal Computer AT*) allows for the definition of up to four serial communication ports. However, there has never been any hardware architectural standard that defined the I/O port addresses or IRQ lines associated with communication ports 3 or 4.

Over the years, a convention has developed that places the port addresses for COM3 and COM4 at 03E8 and 02E8 respectively. This is a generally accepted convention, but not a standard. Check the documentation and the settings of the adapters in your system to verify your hardware environment.

After you have checked and set the I/O and IRQ values on your COM ports or internal modems, you must add this information to the communications device-driver (COM.SYS) statement in the CONFIG.SYS file.

You might also need to tell your communications program where the COM ports are. ProComm** software, for example, has a configuration screen that enables you to specify these settings. If the program, operating system, and hardware are not in agreement, then the program will not run.

OS/2 COM ports do not need to be defined in sequence. It is acceptable to have a COM4 without having a COM3. However, DOS might have difficulty if there is a gap in the port definition. To avoid confusion for DOS, you can define COM ports that do not have any physical adapters attached in the COM.SYS statement. These substitute definitions will serve as placeholders. COM1 and COM2 are assumed to have standard values and do not need to be explicitly set up unless you want to set some nonstandard values to accommodate your particular configuration.

The following parameter needs to be specified for COM3 and/or COM4 on ISA/EISA bus systems. Micro-Channel bus systems do not need to specify this parameter unless the system has a COM port with a nonstandard COM port address or non-standard IRQ.

To enable COM3 or COM4, place the following in the CONFIG.SYS file:

`DEVICE=X:\OS2\COM.SYS (n,x,i,s)`

where:

X   The drive where OS/2 is installed.

n   The communication port number (1, 2, 3, 4).

a   The communication port I/O address in hex (for example, 03E8 02E8, 2320).

i   The IRQ level. Valid settings are 1 to 15 (decimal).

s   The spurious interrupt handling switch. Valid settings are D or I. The D setting uninstalls the COM driver if more than 1000 spurious interrupts come in consecutively. The I setting ignores the spurious interrupt. This setting is optional.

For example, to install COM3 at address 03E8 on IRQ5 (assuming that OS/2 is installed on drive C):

        `DEVICE=C:\OS2\COM.SYS (3,03E8,5)`

The I/O address and IRQ level should be noted in the documentation that came with your adapter. Either or both might be fixed values or can be set to a range of values via jumpers or switches. In some cases you might find that the values are fixed or that the range of settings available to you is insufficient to avoid the sharing conflict. In that case, you must purchase a different, more versatile adapter or accept that you cannot use both adapters at the same time.

Resolving COM Port Problems

Most problems with Interrupt Request (IRQ) lines and I/O address settings occur on an AT-bus (ISA) computer as a limitation of the hardware. IRQ lines can be shared on a micro channel computer provided the adapter is Micro Channel computer compatible and is configured with the Reference Diskette.

The following provides some solutions for your communications problems:

- Verify that all IRQ levels and I/O addresses are unique for every adapter card. The normal problem is that communication adapters use COM3 and IRQ4, when IRQ4 is already in use by COM1 (see "IRQ Settings" on page 349). You must change the IRQ on the adapter to one that is not in use. Refer to the documentation that came with the adapter.

- Verify that the correct parameters are being passed to the COM.SYS driver in the CONFIG.SYS file (see "Enabling COM Ports" on page 377).

- Obtain the latest OS/2 2.1 communication drivers.

- During startup, if the message COMx not installed because Interrupt is already in use appears, ensure there is no IRQ conflict with other device drivers or hardware.

- If the system (AT bus or MCA) boots without an error but the communication ports are not working, type the following at an OS/2 command prompt:

      MODE COMx

  Where:

  x is the problem communication port.

  If a message appears indicating the COMx port is not installed, check for IRQ conflicts.

  Note: If the mouse is on a communication port, the message SYS1620 COM port specified is not installed appears.

- To provide a higher priority to all communication programs, edit the following in the CONFIG.SYS file:

      PRIORITY_DISK_IO: NO
      MAXWAIT: 1

- Some DOS programs open all the communication ports. If this occurs, use the COM_SELECT DOS setting in all DOS communication sessions.

- If the program is a DOS communication program, set the DOS settings to the following:

COM_HOLD	On
HW_ROM_TO_RAM	On
HW_TIMER	On
IDLE_SECONDS	60
IDLE_SENSITIVITY	100
COM_DIRECT_ACCESS	On or Off
	Requires the latest device drivers. When the DOS setting COM_DIRECT_ACCESS is set to On, DOS programs use VCOM.SYS to directly access communication ports. COM_DIRECT_ACCESS enables LapLink III, FastLynx, FSDUAT, AS/400* Asynch Router, and MS Word to work in a DOS session. However, because buffers in COM.SYS cannot be used, characters are sometimes lost, and some programs experience difficulties from the lack of buffering. Therefore, on most DOS programs, it is

a good idea to set COM_DIRECT_ACCESS to Off as its default setting.

COM_SELECT   Specified COM*x*

Requires the latest device drivers. COM_SELECT enables a DOS session to select and use one communication port. Communication ports that are not selected are hidden from the DOS session. There are some DOS programs that take over every available communication port, such as LapLink Pro. If LapLink Pro and another program that accesses a communication port are executed at the same time, it is necessary to change COM_SELECT from its default setting.

DOS_DEVICE   X:\OS2\MDOS\COMDD.SYS

The DOS_DEVICE (COMDD.SYS device driver) might require more than one device driver, depending on the program. For example, Intel's SatisFAXtion requires a device driver loaded into each DOS session that uses an adapter. The COMDD.SYS device driver is usually required only for earlier DOS communication programs. Do not use DOS_DEVICE for every DOS communication session; use it only if it resolves the problem.

COM Ports and a Fax Adapter

When certain fax adapters are operating as ordinary modems, they might operate correctly yet fail to work correctly as a fax device in a DOS session. The probable cause of the trouble is the VCOM.SYS device driver. VCOM.SYS might be introducing timing distortions into those hardware commands that are used to control the fax device but are not a part of normal asynchronous communications.

Because there are no standards established for fax controls, it might be that the only solution is to acquire an OS/2-based fax device driver and program. Your fax adapter manufacturer might have information on sources and availability of OS/2-based programs.

Without purchasing new software, you can set the DOS setting COM_DIRECT_ACCESS to On. This might allow your fax adapter to work properly but might have other undesirable side effects. One of the functions of VCOM.SYS is to provide a performance assist. Without VCOM.SYS, you might have to use a reduced baud rate. Also, some programs, such as Prodigy, will not run without it. Therefore, while removing VCOM.SYS is all right in some instances, it might not be the right action for you.

If you have an ISA-bus system, you might consider making changes to the fax adapter so that only part of your system detects it. Then, place all operation into a single DOS session. This is possible on an ISA system if you can set up your fax adapter as COM3 or COM4. Since there are no standards for COM3 or COM4 on an ISA system, OS/2 2.1 will not recognize the adapter unless it is defined for the system in the CONFIG.SYS file (see "Enabling COM Ports" on page 377).

To set up this configuration, set the hardware switches on the fax adapter to indicate either COM3 or COM4. Use a setting that is available and that does not conflict with other adapters. Leave VCOM.SYS in your CONFIG.SYS definition but do not define the fax adapter settings to the COM.SYS device driver. When OS/2 2.1 starts up, it will not recognize the fax adapter, but the normal communications ports will still get the benefit of having VCOM.SYS available.

Next, set up a DOS session so that it loads the DOS programs that you use for faxing and also the DOS device driver used to control the fax adapter if it came with a special driver. Check your documentation to be sure. This single DOS session should now be able to operate your fax adapter normally.

In some cases, this still might not work. If the DOS program treats the adapter as a COM port instead of directly accessing the hardware, then DOS will not recognize the adapter either. The only problem with this configuration is that this single DOS session controls the adapter. Other DOS or OS/2 sessions will not be able to access it at all.

IBM is working on a fix to alleviate this problem, but the best solution is to use OS/2-specific device drivers and programs, especially where performance is critical.

Audio Adapters

The following information pertains to the installation and configuration of audio adapters for use with MMPM/2.

IBM M-Audio Capture and Playback Adapter

You can install as many as four IBM M-Audio Capture and Playback Adapters in your system. However, using all four adapters simultaneously in conjunction with a high data rate (such as the data rates produced by CDs) will affect system performance and possibly cause the temporary loss of playback and record functions.

The M-Audio adapter can be configured to automatically route any audio source attached to its LINE-IN jack to the LINE-OUT jack. This might be necessary if your CD-ROM drive is not attached internally to the audio card outputs. To enable this feature of the M-Audio card, add a **P** to the end of the DEVICE= statement for M-audio in the CONFIG.SYS file, as in the following example. (Note that d in this example represents the drive letter which will already appear in your CONFIG.SYS file.)

```
DEVICE=d:\MMOS2\ACPADD2.SYS A P
```

Note: It is extremely important that your speakers be attached to the LINE-OUT jack (marked "O"). Otherwise, the M-Audio card will generate extremely harsh audio feedback.

Sound Blaster Restrictions

Before you install the Sound Blaster adapter into the MMPM/2 system, you must know the interrupt level, I/O port address, and, for SB PRO, the DMA channels. These values were shown when you installed the adapter into your computer. If you do not know these values, you can do the following:

- On a Micro Channel computer, run the Reference Diskette and look at the system configuration

- On a non-Micro Channel computer, check the Dip switches on your Sound Blaster.

If your computer has a Token Ring Adapter or a SCSI adapter, you might have problems if you set Sound Blaster to use I/O port address 220. Choose a different address if you have either of these adapters installed.

Non-Micro Channel computers use Interrupt level 7 for the printer (LPT) port. If you have this type of computer with a parallel printer, choose a different interrupt.

- This release does not support:

    - MIDI recording
    - Multiple instances or use of the audio adapter by more than one application at a time

- Sound Blaster (non-SB PRO) does not support software volume control. The MMPM/2 Volume Control application will therefore be ineffective for these adapters.

- If you have an older Sound Blaster (non-SB PRO) card, ensure that you upgrade the DSP module to Version 2.0 or higher in order to achieve the full function of MMPM/2.

Pro AudioSpectrum** 16

If you have a Pro-Audio Spectrum 16 adapter and you also have a token ring adapter installed in your computer, do not use the default DMA value of 3. Choose another option.

Some non-Micro Channel computers use Interrupt 12 for the mouse port. If you have this type of computer with a mouse port, you might want to choose a different interrupt level.

Non-Micro Channel computers use Interrupt level 7 for the printer (LPT) port. If you have this type of computer with a parallel printer, choose a different interrupt.

The Pro AudioSpectrum 16 adapter is not compatible with the Sound Blaster adapter. Do not use these two adapters in the same computer.

If you are a previous user of OS/2 Version 1.3 or a previous Microsoft Windows user, the information in Part 6 will help you make the transition to OS/2 2.1.

Chapter 30, "Moving from Previous Versions of OS/2" on page 387, describes the differences between the shell provided with OS/2 Version 1.3 and the Workplace Shell of OS/2 2.1. It describes familiar features in OS.2 Version 1.3 and how to locate them in the Workplace Shell.

Chapter 31, "Moving from Microsoft Windows" on page 395, describes the differences between the shell provided with Microsoft Windows and the Workplace Shell. It describes familiar features in Microsoft Windows and how to locate them in the OS/2 Workplace Shell.

Chapter 30. Moving from Previous Versions of OS/2

The OS/2 2.1 Workplace Shell does not have a Desktop Manager, File Manager, Print Manager, or Control Panel. Everything is on one screen (the desktop) for easy access. This means that you no longer need to switch from one "manager" to another to perform tasks.

Locating OS/2 Version 1.3 Features

The following sections describe familiar features in OS/2 Version 1.3 (or OS/2 Version 1.2), and how to locate them in the Workplace Shell interface. In many instances, these features have been enhanced in OS/2 2.1.

Desktop Manager

You used the Desktop Manager in OS/2 Version 1.3 to manage programs, to start the OS/2 Tutorial, File Manager, Print Manager, System Editor, or command prompt sessions, and to access utility programs. Generally, all of these features are now objects.

You organized your Desktop Manager data into groupings that made sense to you. In this version of the operating system, you do not need to create a group and then add programs to that group. Instead, you create a folder and then drag program objects to that folder.

The following table shows where Desktop Manager features are located in the
Workplace Shell.

Feature	Description	Workplace Shell Location
File Manager	Organizes and manipulates files and directories	The Drives folder
Disk and diskette utility programs	Formats and copies disks; copies and moves files	Pop-up menus on drive objects located in the Drives folder in the OS/2 System folder
Print Manager	Manages the printing of files	Print objects on the desktop
Control Panel	Changes the way your system is set up	System Setup folder
Clipboard	Transfers information from one program to another	Clipboard Viewer in the Productivity folder
Command prompts	Accesses a full-screen or window command prompt	Command Prompts folder
OS/2 System Editor	Edits and creates data files	OS/2 System Editor in the Productivity folder

File Manager

In previous versions of the OS/2 operating system, the File Manager was used to
organize and manipulate your files and directories. You also could use the File
Manager to start your programs.

In the Workplace Shell, your files (objects) and directories (folders) can be organized
and manipulated on the desktop with your mouse. Although common tasks such
as copying, moving, or deleting objects can still be done with menus, the easiest
way to accomplish them is by using your mouse to *drag* and *drop* objects on the
location you want.

In previous versions of the operating system, the File Manager was used to find out
where a file or directory was located, or to rename a file or directory. In the
Workplace Shell, these functions are available from the pop-up menu of an object.

The files and directories you viewed in a tree-structured format in the File Manager can be viewed in the Workplace Shell in the same format.

Print Manager

In OS/2 Version 1.3, you set up your printers through the Control Panel. When you printed from a program, a print file was sent to the Print Manager, which is in Group-Main. From this point on, Print Manager managed the printing of the file.

In the Workplace Shell, you set up print objects that determine how and where your files will be printed.

If you selected a printer during system installation, the print object that represents that printer is on the desktop.

Command Prompts

Command prompts for an OS/2 full-screen or window session or a DOS full-screen session are still available in this version of the operating system. In addition, a DOS window session is now available. This command prompt was added because, in OS/2 2.1, more than one DOS program, like OS/2 programs, can be run at the same time. A WIN-OS/2 full-screen command prompt has also been added because programs that run under Microsoft Windows will now also run in this version of the OS/2 operating system.

Utility Programs

Utility programs that helped you customize the system, work with disks and diskettes, view picture files, and lock up your system are still available. The customization tasks previously available from the Control Panel are now located in the System Setup folder, which is in the OS/2 System folder. In the Workplace Shell, the Control Panel tasks are represented as separate objects in the System Setup folder, as pictured below.

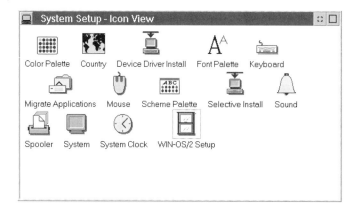

Instead of using menus to access these tasks, you open an object that represents the device or the feature you want to customize, and then change its settings. For example, you might want to customize your screen colors, mouse, or keyboard.

The Picture Utility programs are now located in the Productivity folder, which is located in the OS/2 System folder. The Print Picture, Display Picture, and Convert Picture programs have been combined into one program, Picture Viewer. The Lockup program is now located in the Settings notebook for the Desktop folder (see "Locking Up Your System" on page 40).

System Editor

The System Editor is the default editor for this version of the operating system and is the same System Editor you are already familiar with. The only difference between this System Editor and the System Editor of OS/2 Version 1.3 is its location. The System Editor was listed in the Group-Main window of the Desktop Manager. The System Editor is now an object in the Productivity folder, which is located in the OS/2 System folder.

Other Features

You used the Task List in OS/2 Version 1.3 to switch between or end running programs, to arrange icons, or to tile or cascade open windows. In the OS/2 Workplace Shell, these functions are handled in the Window List.

You used the minimized button in OS/2 Version 1.3 to minimize programs by clicking on the minimize button in the upper-right corner of the window. The programs then became icons located at the bottom of your screen. In the Workplace Shell, these icons are located in the Minimized Window Viewer.

The Minimized Window Viewer is a folder object on the desktop. It contains the icons of the minimized windows of program objects and program-file objects. For more information, see Chapter 13, "Minimized Window Viewer" on page 145.

Shutting Down Your System

You exited from OS/2 Version 1.3 by selecting the **Shutdown** choice from the Desktop menu in the Desktop Manager. You were asked whether you wanted to save the current layout of the Desktop Manager window. If you saved the current layout, all open windows, groups, and icons were saved in their current positions, and appeared in the same positions the next time you started the operating system.

In the Workplace Shell, you can shut down the system and save the current layout by using the desktop pop-up menu.

Making OS/2 2.1 Resemble OS/2 Version 1.3

You can change OS/2 2.1 to have an OS/2 Version 1.3 appearance. The following procedure must be performed after the installation of OS/2 2.1. This procedure should be done only by an experienced user. This is being provided only as a way for existing users of OS/2 Version 1.3 to move over to the Workplace Shell. Remember, this is going to provide only the look of OS/2 Version 1.3, not the functionality, so you might find some inconsistencies.

To make your system look like OS/2 Version 1.3:

1. Place the *Installation Diskette* into drive A.
2. Turn on your computer or press Ctrl+Alt+Del to restart the system.
3. When you see the logo screen, remove the *Installation Diskette* and place *Diskette 1* into drive A.
4. Press Enter.
5. When you see the Welcome screen, press Esc to display the command prompt and then remove the diskette from the drive.
6. Change to the drive where your operating system resides. For example, if the operating system resides on drive C, type:

   ```
   C:
   ```

7. Change to the OS/2 subdirectory by typing:

   ```
   CD\OS2
   ```

   Then press Enter.
8. Modify the existing user INI file by typing:

   ```
   MAKEINI OS2.INI OS2_13.RC
   ```

   Press Enter and then wait for the message of successful completion.
9. Restart your system.

If you decide you want to return to the OS/2 2.1 Workplace Shell appearance, follow steps 1 through 7 and then type:

```
MAKEINI OS2.INI OS2_20.RC
```

Press Enter, and then restart your system.

Chapter 31. Moving from Microsoft Windows

During the installation of OS/2 2.1, if you had Windows programs already installed on your hard disk, you were prompted to migrate these programs. Programs that were migrated during installation can be found on the desktop. During installation, folders were created for you to store these programs. In the Workplace Shell, you can start programs by double-clicking on the appropriate program object on the desktop or from Program Manager in WIN-OS/2.

You can start a program in Microsoft Windows by double-clicking on the appropriate icon in the Program Manager. You also can start a program by double-clicking on a program file (a file with a .COM, .EXE, .PIF, or .BAT file-name extension) in a File Manager directory window.

Locating Microsoft Windows Features

The following sections describe familiar features in Microsoft Windows and how to locate them in the Workplace Shell.

Program Manager

In Microsoft Windows, the Program Manager manages programs, starts the File Manager, Print Manager, or DOS command prompt session, and accesses utility programs. Generally, all of these features are now objects and folders in the OS/2 Workplace Shell.

You organized your Program Manager data into groupings that make sense to you. Similarly, you can organize your data into folders in the Workplace Shell.

For example, Microsoft Windows has a number of games logically located in the Games Group. In the OS/2 Workplace Shell, games are located in the Games folder. The Accessories Group in Microsoft Windows has programs such as word processors, calendars, calculators, and note pads. In the Workplace Shell, these programs are found in the Productivity folder.

The following table shows where Program Manager features are located in the Workplace Shell.

Feature	Description	Workplace Shell Location
File Manager	Organizes and manipulates files and directories	The Desktop folder
Disk and diskette utilities	Format and copies disks; copies and moves files	Pop-up menus on drive objects located in the Drives folder in the OS/2 System folder
Print Manager	Manages the printing of files	Print objects on the desktop
Control Panel	Changes the way your system is set up	System Setup folder
Clipboard	Transfers information from one program to another	Clipboard Viewer in the Productivity folder
Command prompts	Accesses a full-screen or window command prompt	Command Prompts folder
Editors	Edits and creates data files	OS/2 System Editor in the Productivity folder

File Manager

The File Manager in Microsoft Windows helped you organize and manipulate your files and directories. You also could use the File Manager to start your programs.

In the Workplace Shell, your files (objects) and directories (folders) can be organized and manipulated on the desktop with your mouse. Although common tasks such as copying, moving, or deleting objects can still be done with menus, the easiest way to accomplish them is by using your mouse to drag and drop objects on the location you want.

In Windows, the File Manager was used to find out where a file or directory was located, or to rename a file or directory. In the Workplace Shell, these functions are available from the pop-up menu of an object.

The files and directories you viewed in a tree-structured format in the File Manager can be viewed in the Workplace Shell in the same format.

Print Manager

In Microsoft Windows, you set up your printers through the Control Panel. When you printed from a Windows program, a print file was sent to the Print Manager, which is in the Main Group. From this point on, Print Manager managed the printing of the file.

In the Workplace Shell, you set up print objects that determine how and where your files will be printed.

If you selected a printer during system installation, the print object that represents that printer is on the desktop.

Editing Data Files

The Write program in Microsoft Windows is used to create and edit data files.

The System Editor is the default editor for this version of the operating system. The System Editor is an object in the Productivity folder, which is located in the OS/2 System folder. If you open a data-file object that is not associated with any other program object, by default it is associated with the System Editor.

Command Prompts

To run a non-Windows program in Microsoft Windows, you access a full-screen DOS prompt by opening the Main Group in Program Manager, and then double-clicking on **DOS Prompt**.

Command prompts for an OS/2 full-screen or window session, or a DOS full-screen or window session, are available in this version of the operating system. Also available is a WIN-OS/2 window, which allows you to run Microsoft Windows programs.

Control Panel

The Control Panel in Microsoft Windows enables you to change the setup of your system, such as your screen colors, system fonts, keyboard, mouse, and sound rate. You started the Control Panel by opening the Main Group window and double-clicking on **Control Panel**.

In the OS/2 Workplace Shell, the Control Panel tasks are represented as separate objects in the System Setup folder, as pictured below.

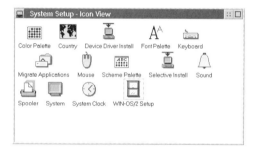

Instead of using menus to access these tasks, you open an object that represents the device or feature you want to customize and then change its settings. For example, you might want to customize your screen colors, mouse, or keyboard.

Other Features

You used the Task List in Microsoft Windows to switch between or end running programs, to arrange icons, or to tile or cascade open windows. In the Workplace Shell, these functions are handled in the Window List.

You used the minimized button in Microsoft Windows to minimize programs by clicking on the minimize button in the upper-right corner of the window. The programs then became icons located at the bottom of your screen. In the Workplace Shell, these icons are located in the Minimized Window Viewer.

The Minimized Window Viewer is a folder object on the desktop. It contains the icons of the minimized windows of program objects and program-file objects. For more information, see Chapter 13, "Minimized Window Viewer" on page 145.

Shutting Down Your System

You exited from Microsoft Windows by selecting **Exit Windows** from the File menu in the Program Manager. You were asked whether you wanted to save the current layout of the Program Manager window. If you saved the current layout, all open windows, groups, and icons were saved in their current position and appeared in the same positions the next time you started the operating system.

In the Workplace Shell, you can shut down the system and save the current layout by using the desktop pop-up menu.

Making OS/2 2.1 Resemble Microsoft Windows

You can change OS/2 2.1 to have a Microsoft Windows appearance. The following procedure must be performed after the installation of OS/2 2.1. This procedure should be done only by an experienced user. It is being provided only as a way for existing Windows users to migrate to the Workplace Shell. Remember, this is going to provide only the appearance of Windows, not the functionality, so you might find some inconsistencies.

To make your system resemble Microsoft Windows:

1. Place the *Installation Diskette* into drive A.
2. Turn on your computer or press Ctrl+Alt+Del to restart the system.
3. When you see the logo screen, remove the *Installation Diskette* and place *Diskette 1* into drive A.
4. Press Enter.
5. When you see the Welcome screen, press Esc to display the command prompt, and then remove the diskette from the drive.
6. Change to the drive where your operating system resides. For example, if the operating system resides on drive C, type:

       C:

7. Change to the OS/2 subdirectory by typing:

       CD\OS2

   Then press Enter.
8. Modify the existing user INI file by typing:

       MAKEINI OS2.INI WIN_30.RC

   Press Enter, and then wait for the message of successful completion.
9. Restart your system.

If you decide you want to return to the OS/2 2.1 Workplace Shell look and WIN-OS/2, follow steps 1 through 7 and then type:

    MAKEINI OS2.INI OS2_20.RC

Press Enter, and then restart your system.

Appendix A. Keyboard and Mouse Use

Keyboard

The following tables list some of the most common tasks you can do, using either the keyboard or a mouse.

The plus (+) sign between key names means to press and hold down the keys in the order shown and release them together.

Mouse

When a column is left blank under the **Mouse** heading, it means that there is no equivalent mouse function. The keyboard must be used.

The following terms are used to describe actions taken with a mouse.

Click   Press and release a mouse button. Instructions explain whether you should click mouse button 1 or 2.

Double-click   Press and release mouse button 1 twice in quick succession.

Drag   Move an object across the computer screen with a mouse.

Open   Point to an item and double-click. Instructions explain which item to point to.

Point   Move the mouse pointer.

Select   Point to an item and click mouse button 1. Instructions explain which item to point to.

Note: For a detailed list of specific key assignments, see the Master Help Index.

System Tasks

Task	Keys	Mouse
Get Help.	F1	Select the word **Help**.
Restart the system.	Ctrl+Alt+Del	
Switch to the next window.	Alt+Tab	Select the window.
Switch to the next window or full-screen session.	Alt+Esc	Press both mouse buttons at the same time; then open the window.

Task	Keys	Mouse
Display the Window List.	Ctrl+Esc	Point to an empty area on the desktop then click both mouse buttons at the same time.

Object Tasks

Task	Keys	Mouse
Move among objects.	↑, ↓, →, or ←	Point to the object.
Select an object.	Use the arrow keys to move among the objects. Press the Spacebar to select an object.	Select the object.
Select more than one object.	Shift+F8 to begin Add mode. Use the arrow keys to move among objects. Press the Spacebar to make each selection. Repeat as needed. Press Shift+F8 again to end Add mode.	Press and hold the Ctrl key. Select an object. Repeat as needed. Release the Ctrl key when done.
Select all objects.	Press Ctrl+/	Press and hold mouse button 1; then drag the pointer over every object.
Deselect all objects.	Press Ctrl+\	Select an empty area on the desktop.
Open an object.	Select it; then press Enter.	Point to the object; then double-click.
Delete an object.	Select it; then press Shift+F10. Select **Delete** from the pop-up menu.	Point to the object; then press and hold down mouse button 2. Drag the object to the Shredder object. Release mouse button 2.
Print an object.	Select it; then press Shift+F10. Select **Print** from the pop-up menu.	Point to the object; then press and hold down mouse button 2. Drag the object to the Printer object. Release mouse button 2.

Task	Keys	Mouse
Move an object.	Select it; then press Shift+F10. Select **Move** from the pop-up menu.	Point to the object; then press and hold down mouse button 2. Drag the object to another folder object. Release mouse button 2.
Copy an object.	Select it; then press Shift+F10. Select **Copy** from the pop-up menu.	Press and hold down the Ctrl key; then point to the object. Press and hold down mouse button 2. Drag the object to where you want a copy to appear. Release mouse button 2; then release the Ctrl key.
Change the name of an object.	Select it; then press Shift+F10. Press →; then press Enter. Select the **General** tab. Select the **Title** field; then edit the name.	Press and hold down the Alt key; select the name (title). Release the Alt key. Edit the name. Select an area away from the name.
Display the pop-up menu for the desktop folder.	Press Alt+Shift+Tab; then press Ctrl+\. Then press Shift+F10.	Point to an empty area of the desktop folder; then click mouse button 2.
Display the pop-up menu for an object.	Select it; then press Shift+F10.	Point to the object; then click mouse button 2.
Select the first choice in a pop-up menu.	Home	Select the choice.
Select the last choice in a pop-up menu.	End	Select the choice.
Select a choice using the underlined letter.	Type the underlined letter.	
Get Help.	Select and object; then press F1.	Point to the object; then click mouse button 2. Select **Help**.
Move between the object and the Help window.	Press Alt+F6.	Select the window or object.

Window Tasks

Task	Keys	Mouse
Get Help.	F1.	Select the word **Help**; then select the type of help you want.
Display the pop-up menu for a window.	Alt+Spacebar	Point to the title-bar icon; then click mouse button 2.
Move a window.	Alt+F7; then use the arrow keys.	Point to the title bar; then press and hold down mouse button 2. Drag the window to the new location. Release mouse button 2.
Size a window.	Alt+F8; then use the arrow keys.	Point to the border; then press and hold down mouse button 2. Drag the border of the window in any direction. Release mouse button 2.
Set a default size for a window.	Press Alt; then press S. Use the up, down, left, or right cursor keys to adjust two of the borders; then press Enter. **Note:** If you press the mnemonic key for Hide, Minimize, or Maximize, instead of the S for Size, the selected choice will become the default size of the window.	Press and hold the Shift key; then point to a corner of the window border. Press and hold mouse button 1; then drag the border to the desired size. Release mouse button 1; then release the Shift key.
Minimize a window.	Alt+F9	Select the Minimize button.
Hide a window.	Alt+F11	Select the Hide button.
Maximize a window.	Alt+F10	Select the Maximize button.
Close a window.	Alt+F4	Double-click on the title bar icon.

Task	Keys	Mouse
Move up through the contents of a window, one page at a time.	Page Up or PgUp.	Select the area above the slider box on the scroll bar.
Move down through the contents of a window, one page at a time.	Page Down or PgDn.	Select the area below the slider box on the scroll bar.
Move to and from the menu bar.	F10	Select the menu bar or the window.

Notebook Tasks

Task	Keys	Mouse
Get Help	F1	Select the **Help** push button.
Move to the next page.	Alt+Page Down	Select a notebook tab.
Move to the previous page.	Alt+Page Up	Select a notebook tab.
Move the cursor from the notebook page to a tab.	Alt+Up Arrow	Select a notebook tab.
Move the cursor from a tab to the notebook page.	Alt+Down Arrow	Select the notebook page.
Move to the next field.	Tab	Select the field.
Move to the next item within a field.	Up, Down, Left, or Right Arrow	
Select an item in a single selection field.	Enter	Select the item.
Select an item in a multiple selection field.	Spacebar	Select the button or box next to the item.

Help Window Tasks

These tasks only work from within a help window.

Task	Keys	Mouse
Switch between a help window and the object or window for which help was displayed.	Alt+F6	Select the window.
Display General help.	F2	Select **Help**; then select **General help**.
Display Keys help.	F9	Select **Help**; then select **Keys help**.
Display Help index.	F11 or Shift+F1	Select **Help**; then select to **Help index**.
Display Using help.	Shift+F10	Select **Help**; then select **Using help**.
Display help for a highlighted word or phrase.	Use Tab to move the cursor to the highlighted word or phrase; then press Enter.	Double-click on the highlighted word or phrase.
Display the previous help window.	Esc	Select the **Previous** push button.
Search for a word or phrase	Ctrl+S	Select **Services**; then select **Search**.

Master Help Index Tasks

Task	Keys	Mouse
Open the Master Help Index.	Enter	Double-click on the Master Help Index.
Move through the topics, one line at a time.	↑ ↓	Select the topic.
Select the area above the slider box on the scroll bar.		
Move down through the topics, one page at a time.	Page Down or PgDn.	Select the area below the slider box on the scroll bar.
Move up through the topics, one page at a time.	Page Up or PgUp.	

Task	Keys	Mouse
Move to the topics beginning with a letter.	Type the letter of the alphabet	Select the letter of the alphabet.
Switch between an entry and the Master Help Index.	Alt+F6	Select the window.
Display related information.	Use Tab to move the cursor to the entry listed under related information; then press Enter.	Double-click on an entry listed under related information.
Return to the previous help window.	Esc	Select the **Previous** push button.

Appendix B. Error Messages

This appendix contains common error messages that might be displayed while you are using OS/2 2.1.

Displaying Help for Error Messages

You can get information to help you understand, correct, and respond to OS/2 messages. The way you request help depends on how and where the message is displayed.

To get help for an error message that appears in a window with a **Help** push button:

Select the **Help** push button.

To get help for a message that appears on a full screen and is enclosed in a box:

1. Use the Up or Down Arrow key to highlight the **Display Help** choice.

2. Press Enter.

To get help for a message that has a message number, preceded by the letters SYS:

At the OS/2 command prompt, type **Help** followed by a space and the message number. (It is not necessary to type the letters SYS or the leading zeros.)

For example, to get help for message:

```
SYS0002:  The system cannot find the file specified.
```

1. Type:

   ```
   HELP 2
   ```

2. Press Enter.

The following help appears:

```
SYS0002:  The system cannot find the file specified.

EXPLANATION:  The file named in the command does
not exist in the current directory or search path
specified.  Or, the file name was entered incorrectly.
ACTION:  Retry the command using the correct file name.
```

Responding to Error Messages

Messages listed in this appendix include the following information:

Number and Message   Identifies the message number and the message text

Explanation   Identifies what caused the problem

Action   Identifies what you need to do to resolve the problem

Some messages listed in this appendix contain %1. When the message is displayed on your system, %1 is replaced by the name of your device.

For example:

"The % device is not ready",

is displayed on your screen as

"The A: device is not ready"

(where A: is the name of your device).

Common Error Messages

If you receive one of the following messages while using OS/2 2.1, take the appropriate corrective action.

SYS0002E The system cannot find the file specified.

Explanation:

The file named in the command does not exist in the current directory or search path specified. Or, the file name was entered incorrectly.

Action:

Retry the command using the correct file name.

SYS0003E The system cannot find the path specified.

Explanation:

The path named in the command does not exist for the drive specified, or the path was entered incorrectly.

Action:

Retry the command using the correct path.

SYS0005E Access is denied.

Explanation:

One of the following has occurred:

1. The file is marked read-only.

2. The resource, such as a file or subdirectory, that you tried to access is in use; or the named pipe, queue, or semaphore is a shared resource in use.

3. You tried to access a resource or to perform an action for which you do not have sufficient privilege. You have LAN Server Version 2.0 or later installed and you tried to access a resource or perform an action for which you do not have sufficient privilege.

4. The filename is incorrect.

5. Extended attributes are lost.

Action:

Do one of the following; then, retry the command:

1. Use the ATTRIB command to change the read-only attribute.

2. Try to access the resource again later.

3. Log on with sufficient privilege. If you do not have sufficient privilege, request it from the administrator who controls access.

4. Correct the filename.

5. Run CHKDSK /F to repair lost extended attributes.

SYS0008E There is not enough storage available to process this command. All available storage is in use.

Explanation:

If segment swapping is active, the swap file may be full, or an input/output (I/O) error may have occurred on the auxiliary storage device that contains the swap file.

Action:

Do one of the following and then retry the command:

- Reduce the number of running programs.
- Reduce the value of the BUFFERS=, TRACEBUF=, DISKCACHE=, THREADS=, RMSIZE=, or DEVICE=VDISK.SYS statement in the CONFIG.SYS file. Then restart the system.
- Remove unwanted files from the swap file disk and restart the system.
- Install additional memory on your system.
- Check the swap file disk for an I/O error.

SYS0015E The system cannot find the drive specified.

Explanation:

One of the following has occurred:

1. The drive specified does not exist.
2. The drive letter is incorrect.
3. You are trying to RESTORE to a redirected drive.
4. You are trying to RESTORE to a read-only drive.

Action:

For situations 1 and 2 above; retry the command using the correct drive letter. For situation 3, you are not allowed to RESTORE to a redirected drive.

SYS0021E The drive is not ready.

Explanation:

One of the following errors occurred:

1. The drive is empty.

2. The drive door is open.

3. The drive is in use.

Action:

Do one of the following:

1. Insert a diskette in the drive and retry the command.

2. Close the drive door and retry the command.

3. Wait until the drive is available and retry the command.

SYS0023E Data error (cyclic redundancy check)

Explanation:

The operating system cannot read or write the data correctly.

Action:

If the error occurred on a hard disk, retry the command. If the error occurs again, the hard disk may have to be reformatted. If the error occurred on a diskette, insert a formatted diskette or the backup diskette, and retry the command.

SYS0026E The specified disk or diskette cannot be accessed.

Explanation:

The disk or diskette is not properly formatted for the operating system.

Action:

Format the disk or diskette for the operating system.

> **SYS0028E The printer is out of paper, or there is not enough space to create a spool file.**

Explanation:

One of the following has occurred:

- There is no paper in the printer.

- There is not enough disk space to create a spool file.

  Note: If printing to a LAN server, the server's disk is full.

Action:

Do one of the following:

- Make sure the printer is loaded properly with paper.

- Make sure the printer is switched on.

- Make sure the printer is installed and connected.

- Delete any unnecessary files from the disk that contains the spool directory; then, retry the command.

> **SYS0029E The system cannot write to the specified device.**

Explanation:

The operating system detected an error while writing to this device.

Action:

Make sure the device is:

- Installed and connected

- Switched on

- Not being used by another process

- In the proper receive mode

- Formatted if the device is a disk.

Retry the command.

SYS0030E The system cannot read from the specified device.

Explanation:

The operating system detected an error while reading from this device.

Action:

Make sure the device is:

1. Installed and connected

2. Switched on

3. Not being used by another process

4. In the proper send mode

5. Formatted if the device is a disk.

Retry the command.

SYS0031E A device attached to the system is not functioning.

Explanation:

An attached device is not working for one of these reasons:

- It is switched off, or connected improperly

- The diskette and drive types are incompatible.

- The diskette is not properly inserted in the drive.

- The drive door is open.

- The diskette is not properly formatted.

Action:

Correct the problem and retry the command.

SYS0043E Drive %1 cannot locate a specific area or track on the disk.

Explanation:

The disk or diskette may be damaged, unformatted, or not compatible with the operating system.

Action:

Do one of the following and retry the command:

- Make sure the diskette is properly inserted.
- Check that the disk or diskette is not damaged.
- Format the disk or diskette for the operating system.

SYS0046E The %1 printer is out of paper.

Explanation:

There is no paper in the printer.

Action:

Make sure the printer is:

- Loaded properly with paper.
- Switched on.
- Installed and connected.

SYS0048E The system cannot read from the %1 device.

Explanation:

The operating system detected an error while reading from this device.

Action:

Make sure the device is:

- Installed, connected, and switched on
- Not being used by another process
- In the proper send mode
- Formatted if the device is a disk.

Retry the command.

SYS0049E The %1 device is not functioning.

Explanation:

An attached device is not working for one of these reasons:

- It is switched off, or connected improperly.
- The diskette and drive types are incompatible.
- The diskette is not properly inserted in the drive.
- The drive door is open.
- The diskette is not properly formatted.

Action:

Correct the problem and retry the command.

SYS0073E The diskette is write protected.

Explanation:

No information can be changed or added to a write-protected diskette.

Action:

Make sure that the proper diskette is being used, or remove the write protection. Retry the command.

SYS0082E The directory or file cannot be created.

Explanation:

One of the following errors occurred:

- The file or directory name already exists.
- The directory path cannot be found.
- The root directory is full or there is not enough space on the disk for the new file or directory.
- The directory name contains unacceptable OS/2 characters or is a reserved file name.
- The disk is not properly formatted.

Action:

Correct the problem and retry the command.

SYS0206E The file name or extension is too long.

Explanation:

The length of the file name or the extension is greater than the maximum length allowed.

Action:

Correct the file name or the extension; then retry the command. For more information about file names, refer Naming Files in the Master Index.

SYS0266E The specified file was not copied.

Explanation:

The specified file was not copied. Either the source and target files are not in the same file system, or the operating system does not support COPY for this file system.

Action:

Check the source and target file names and retry the operation.

SYS0627E Drive %1 was improperly stopped. From the OS/2 command prompt, run CHKDSK with the /F parameter on the specified drive.

Explanation:

A High Performance File System (HPFS) drive returns this message if the system lost power or was turned off before the Shutdown choice in the Desktop was used.

Action:

From the OS/2 command prompt, run CHKDSK with the /F parameter on the specified drive.

Example: CHKDSK D: /F

Note: If you receive this message after your system is started, you need only follow step 5.

1. Insert the Installation diskette in drive A.

2. Press Ctrl+Alt+Del.

3. At the logo screen, press the Esc key to display the OS/2 command prompt

4. Replace the Installation diskette with Diskette 1.

5. Type CHKDSK %1: /F at the command prompt; then, press the Enter key and follow the instructions on the screen.

6. When CHKDSK finishes, remove Diskette 1.

7. Press Ctrl+Alt+Del to restart the system.

To prevent this message from appearing each time you start the system, always use the Shutdown choice in the Desktop before turning off the computer.

SYS0639E The keyboard is not locked. If you want to lock your keyboard and mouse, display the Desktop pop-up menu; then, select Lockup now.

Explanation:

KP.COM and other keyboard-lockup utility programs are not supported in DOS mode in this version of OS/2.

Action:

To set the keyboard and mouse lockup password, display the Desktop pop-up menu; select Lockup now; then, type a password.

SYS1003E The syntax of the command is incorrect.

Explanation:

One of the following occurred:

- An incorrect parameter was specified.
- An incorrect separator was specified.
- A required parameter is missing.
- Too many parameters were entered.
- The parameters were entered in the wrong order.

Action:

Check the syntax of the command. Then retry the command.

SYS1019E The system cannot find the drive specified.

Explanation:

An incorrect disk drive letter was used.

Action:

Retry the command using the correct disk drive letter.

SYS1024E Warning! The directory is full.

Explanation:

The root directory is full and cannot store the files requested.

Action:

Remove some of the files from the root directory of the disk. Then retry the command.

SYS1036E The system cannot accept the date entered.

Explanation:

An incorrect date format was entered.

Action:

Retry the command using a correct date format. For example, mm/dd/yy, mm-dd-yy, or mm.dd.yy.

SYS1044E The system cannot accept the time entered.

Explanation:

An incorrect time format was entered.

Action:

Enter the time using the correct time format.

SYS1057E The file or path name entered is not valid in a DOS session.

Explanation:

The DOS application could not be started because the file or path name is not valid in a DOS session. The file name and all the path names must be limited to the DOS 8.3 file name format (FAT).

Action:

Rename the file or path using DOS file naming conventions (FAT), or move the file to a path whose name is valid in a DOS session.

SYS1061E The system detected a file error.

Explanation:

One of the following errors occurred:

1. The file you tried to write to is read-only.

2. The directory is full.

Action:

Do one of the following:

1. If the file is read-only, you may use the ATTRIB command to change the read-only attribute.

2. If the directory is full, no action can be taken unless files are deleted.

SYS1078E The file cannot be copied onto itself.

Explanation:

You named the target file the same as the source file.

Action:

Ensure that the file name specifications for the target and source files are not the same.

> **SYS1083E A duplicate file name exists, the file cannot be found, or the file is being used.**

Explanation:

The target file name specified with the RENAME or MOVE command already exists, is in use, cannot be created, or the source file cannot be found.

Action:

Check the target and source file names used, or wait until the file is no longer in use; then, retry the command.

> **SYS1102E The system cannot create the directory.**

Explanation:

The JOIN command was unable to create the specified directory.

Action:

Retry the command making sure the directory name is correct.

> **SYS1103E The system cannot find the directory specified.**

Explanation:

The directory specified does not exist on your system.

Action:

Create the directory and retry the command.

> **SYS1184E The system cannot copy the file.**

Explanation:

The source and target files cannot have the same name.

Action:

Retry the command using a different target file name.

> **SYS1234E The source diskette is bad or incompatible with the drive type.**

Explanation:

The diskette and drive type are incompatible with each other or the diskette is unusable.

Action:

Make sure the diskette drives are the same type or that the correct type of diskette is in the drive. For example, high-capacity diskettes (in a high-capacity drive) can only be copied to high-capacity diskettes (in a high-capacity drive).

> **SYS1235E Target diskette is bad or incompatible with the drive type.**

Explanation:

The diskette or drive type are incompatible with each other or the diskette is unusable.

Action:

Make sure the diskette drives are the same type, or that the correct type of diskette is in the drive. For example, high- capacity diskettes (in a high-capacity drive) can only be copied to high-capacity diskettes (in a high-capacity drive).

> **SYS1311E The system files are missing.**

Explanation:

The system transfer option (/S) was used with the FORMAT command, but the system files cannot be found on the default drive.

Action:

Retry the FORMAT command using another disk as the default drive.

> **SYS1601E The MODE parameters are incorrect.**

Explanation:

The MODE command accepts the following parameters:

To set parallel printer modes:

```
MODE LPT# chars,lines,P
MODE PRN  chars,lines,P
```

To set video modes:

```
MODE display,rows
```

To set asynchronous modes for DOS sessions:

```
MODE COM#:baud,parity,databits,stopbits
```

To set asynchronous modes for OS/2 sessions:

```
MODE COM#:baud,parity,databits,stopbits,
TO=ON|OFF,XON=ON|OFF,IDSR=ON|OFF,ODSR=ON|OFF,
OCTS=ON|OFF,DTR=ON|OFF|HS,RTS=ON|OFF|HS|TOG
```

To set diskette verification:

```
MODE DSKT VER=ON|OFF
```

Action: Check the MODE parameters and retry the command.

For more information about MODE, refer to the Command Reference.

SYS1664E The system cannot write to the BACKUP log file. Press Enter to continue, or press Ctrl+Break to cancel.

Explanation:

The /l parameter was specified but there is not enough room to create the log file.

Action:

Press Ctrl+Break to end the BACKUP log file procedure or press Enter to continue without adding more entries to the log file. Delete any unwanted files from the disk and retry the command.

SYS2237E DosKrnl: A NPX instruction was attempted, but no NPX is present.%0

Explanation:

You have an application attempting to use the numeric coprocessor, but no coprocessor is present on this system.

Action:

Install a numeric coprocessor and retry the application.

SYS3171E A program in this session encountered a problem and cannot continue.

Explanation:

The process was terminated without running exception handlers because there was not enough room left on the stack to dispatch the exception. This is typically caused by exceptions occurring in exception handlers.

Action:

If you purchased this program, contact the supplier of the program. If you are the developer of this program, refer to the information in the register.

SYS3176E A program in this session encountered a problem and cannot continue.

Explanation:

An illegal instruction exception was generated when an attempt was made to execute an instruction whose operation was not defined for the host machine architecture. On the Intel 80386 processor, this corresponds to the invalid opcode fault (#6), caused by an invalid instruction.

Action:

If you purchased this program, contact the supplier of the program. If you are the developer of this program, refer to the information in the register.

Appendix C. Backing Up and Restoring Your Desktop

You should make a backup copy of your desktop regularly. This is particularly important if you spent a lot of time customizing the desktop. If something happens to your desktop, the backup copy can be used to restore it.

Important

Do not back up the OS2.INI file before starting OS/2 2.1 for the first time.

Backing Up the Desktop

To backup the desktop:

Note: This procedure requires a blank diskette, the *OS/2 Installation Diskette*, and *Diskette 1*.

1. Insert the *OS/2 Installation Diskette* into drive A.
2. Turn on the computer.

   If it is already on, do a shut down and restart the computer. To shut down the computer:
   a. Point to an empty area on the desktop.
   b. Click mouse button 2.
   c. Select **Shut down**.
   d. Click on **Yes**.
   e. After the computer is shut down, press Ctrl+Alt+Del to restart the computer.
3. When you are prompted to do so, remove the *OS/2 Installation Diskette* and insert *Diskette 1*.
4. Press Enter.
5. When the Welcome screen is displayed, press Esc to display the OS/2 command prompt.
6. Place a blank diskette in drive A.
7. Use the BACKUP command to copy the DESKTOP directory and its subdirectories to the diskette.

   Note: The name of your DESKTOP directory might be slightly different if you use HPFS or you replaced your desktop previously.

   For example: If OS/2 is installed on drive C and your diskette is in drive A, type:

   `BACKUP C:\DESKTOP A: /S`

431

Then, press Enter.

For more information about the BACKUP command, refer to the online *Command Reference*, located in the Information folder.

8. Copy the OS2.INI and OS2SYS.INI files (located in the \OS2 directory) to the diskette. For example, type:

```
COPY C:\OS2\OS2*.INI A:
```

Then, press Enter.

9. Copy the CONFIG.SYS file to the diskette. For example, type:

```
COPY C:\CONFIG.SYS A:
```

Then, press Enter.

10. Remove the diskette from drive A.

Restoring the Desktop

Certain actions might damage your desktop and leave it unusable. (For example, rearranging a hard disk while running a specific version of DOS might damage the .INI files or extended attributes.)

You can recover by:

- Replacing your desktop with a backup copy of the desktop
- Rebuilding your existing desktop
- Reverting back to the original desktop created during installation.

If you decide to return to the original desktop, any modifications made to the desktop and the CONFIG.SYS file are lost and must be re-created.

Replacing the Desktop

You can replace the existing desktop on a computer with a backup copy of the desktop.

Important

If you copy a desktop setup to a computer with a smaller or larger display screen than the original computer, the icons and windows might appear in positions other than those in which they were saved.

To replace the desktop with an backup copy of the desktop:

Note: This procedure requires a diskette containing a backup copy of a desktop, the OS/2 Installation Diskette, and Diskette 1.

1. Insert the *OS/2 Installation Diskette* into drive A.
2. Turn on the computer.

    If it is already on, do a shut down and restart the computer. To shut down the computer:
    a. Point to an empty area on the desktop.
    b. Click mouse button 2.
    c. Select **Shut down**.
    d. Select **Yes**.
    e. After the system is shut down, press Ctrl+Alt+Del to restart the system.
3. When you are prompted to do so, remove the *OS/2 Installation Diskette* and insert *Diskette 1*.
4. Press Enter.
5. When the Welcome screen is displayed, press Esc to display the OS/2 command prompt.
6. Remove *Diskette 1*.
7. Insert the diskette that contains the backup copy of the desktop into drive A. See Appendix C, "Backing Up and Restoring Your Desktop" on page 431 for more information.
8. Copy the OS2.INI and OS2SYS.INI files into the \OS2 directory on the computer.

    For example, if the diskette is in drive A and OS/2 is installed on drive C, type:

    ```
    COPY A:\OS2*.INI C:\OS2
    ```

    Then, press Enter.
9. Copy the CONFIG.SYS file to drive C. For example, type:

    ```
    COPY A:\CONFIG.SYS C:\
    ```

10. Use the RESTORE command to copy the DESKTOP directory and its subdirectories from the diskette to the computer.

    ```
    RESTORE A: C: /S
    ```

11. Remove the diskette from drive A.
12. Press Ctrl+Alt+Del to restart the computer.

Rebuilding the Desktop

Tip

Use the "Rebuilding the Desktop" procedure instead of the "Reversing to the Original Desktop" procedure if you do not want to replace both the CONFIG.SYS file and the desktop.

To rebuild the existing desktop:

1. Restart your computer using the *OS/2 Installation Diskette* then insert *Diskette 1*.
2. Press Esc to display the OS/2 command prompt.
3. Insert *Diskette 2*.
4. Type:

   ```
   CHKDSK C: /F (where C: is your OS/2 drive)
   ```

   Make sure the CHKDSK reports no errors.
5. Change to the OS/2 directory on your hard disk. Type:

   ```
   C:    (and press Enter)
   CD\OS2   (and press Enter)
   ```

6. Type:

   ```
   MAKEINI OS2.INI INI.RC   (and press Enter)

   MAKEINI OS2SYS.INI INISYS.RC   (and press Enter)
   ```

7. Delete the hidden file WP?ROOT.?SF in the startable partition. Type:

   ```
   ATTRIB -h -s -r \WP?ROOT.?SF   (and press Enter)

   DEL \WP?ROOT.?SF (and press Enter)
   ```

Reverting to the Original Desktop

Use this procedure to change your desktop back to the way it looked when OS/2 was first installed. During this procedure, your CONFIG.SYS file is also replaced.

Tip

Use the "Rebuilding the Desktop" procedure instead of the "Reversing to the Original Desktop" procedure if you do not want to replace both the CONFIG.SYS file and the desktop.

To revert back to the original desktop:

1. Turn on the computer, or press Ctrl+Alt+Del if the computer is already on.
2. As soon as you hear the single beep, press the Alt+F1 keys.

Notes:

a. If the power-on password prompt appears, enter your password then immediately press the Alt+F1 keys.

b. If the Boot Manager menu appears, press Enter then immediately press Alt+F1.

3. The OS/2 logo screen appears on the screen for a short amount of time, then the following messages are displayed:

```
The \CONFIG.SYS file was renamed to \CONFIG.001
The \OS2\OS2.INI file was renamed to \OS2\OS2.001
The \OS2\OS2SYS.INI file was renamed to \OS2\OS2SYS.001
```

4. Check the contents of the CONFIG.SYS file against the contents of the CONFIG.001 file. Transfer program and device information into the CONFIG.SYS file. (If you make any changes, you must restart the computer to activate the changes.)

Re-creating the .INI Files

If reverting to the original desktop does not fix the damaged desktop, do the following to re-create the .INI files and the desktop:

1. Restart your system using the *OS/2 Installation Diskette*; then insert *Diskette 1*.
2. Press Esc to display the OS/2 command prompt; then change to the OS2 directory, on your hard drive.
3. Delete the current .INI files. Type:

```
DEL OS2.INI (and press Enter)

DEL OS2SYS.INI (and press Enter)
```

4. Re-create both files using the MAKEINI command. Type:

```
MAKEINI OS2.INI INI.RC (and press Enter)

MAKEINI OS2SYS.INI INISYS.RC (and press Enter)
```

5. Change to the DESKTOP directory.
6. Delete all subfolders (subdirectories) in this directory.
7. Change to the root directory.

8. Delete the hidden file WP?ROOT.?SF in the startable partition. Type:

```
\OS2\ATTRIB -h -s -r WP?ROOT.?SF  (and press Enter)
```

Type:

```
DEL WP?ROOT.?SF  (and press Enter)
```

9. Press Ctrl+Alt+Del. The desktop is reinstalled to its initial installation setup.
10. Shut down the system using the **Shut down** choice on the desktop pop-up menu.

Appendix D. The OS/2 File Systems

A file system is that part of an operating system that provides access to files and programs on a disk. The OS/2 operating system has two file systems: the file allocation table (FAT) file system and the high performance file system (HPFS).

Both file systems support:

Extended attributes   Provide additional information about a file or object. OS/2 2.1 stores these attributes in a separate file and uses them to identify the file or object.

Lazy write to disk   Writes information to the disk when the disk is not being used. This improves the speed of the computer by allowing an application to run uninterrupted during the write.

Disk caching   Places frequently accessed data in a high-speed buffer called a *cache*. This improves the speed of the computer by reducing the amount of time needed to retrieve data.

Read ahead   Detects sequential read requests and then reads ahead and places the data in a cache. This improves the speed of the computer by reducing the amount of time needed to retrieve data.

The following table lists the differences of the file systems.

FAT	HPFS
Places the root directory at either the beginning or end of the partition. This directory is used by the operating system to locate information on the disk.	Places the root directory at the seek center of the partition. This improves the access time on very large partitions. This directory is used by the operating system to locate information on the disk.
Searches files sequentially.	Uses a B-tree to improve the speed of file searches.
Fragments files.	Allocates contiguous space for files.
Does not require extra system memory to run.	Requires 500K of system memory. If your computer has less than 6MB of memory, performance will be adversely affected.
Does not recognize drives formatted as HPFS.	Can recognize drives formatted with FAT and HPFS.

FAT	HPFS
Supports all versions of DOS and all versions of the OS/2 operating system. They can be installed on disks that use the FAT file system.	Does not support versions of DOS and versions 1.0 and 1.1 of the OS/2 operating system. They cannot be installed on disks that use HPFS.
Supports conventional file names. File names can have up to 12 characters, with a maximum of 8 characters, a period, and a maximum of a 3-character extension. The period and extension are optional. Blanks and some characters are not supported. Example: `MYNEW.SCR MYFILE` are both valid file names.	Supports conventional file names and long file names. File names can have up to 254 characters, composed of characters and blanks. For example: `PROGRESS.REPORT`, `MY NEW FILE` and `MYNEW.SCR` are all valid file names. **Notes:** 1. Files whose names violate the 12 character convention used by the FAT file system will not be visible from DOS sessions. 2. File names that contain blanks must include double quotation marks around the name whenever a command is specified. For example: `ERASE "THIS IS MY FILE"` 3. Files with long file names or blank spaces can be copied only to a diskette or a disk formatted with FAT using the direct-manipulation method. (All diskettes are formatted with FAT regardless of the file system on the computer.) 4. The system shortens the long file name when the file is copied to a diskette or a disk formatted with FAT. The long file name is saved as an extended attribute until the file is copied back to an HPFS disk using the direct-manipulation method and the Workplace Shell.

Appendix E. File Locations

Special directories are created to hold all the files copied to your system during installation the installation of OS/2 and MMPM/2. The installation program also sets up empty directories to hold the information created as a result of using OS/2 and MMPM/2.

This appendix shows where files are placed on your system during the OS/2 2.1 and MMPM/2 installations. It assumes that you installed both OS/2 2.1 and MMPM/2 on drive C of your computer. If you did not, then the files are placed in the same directories but on the drive you selected. This appendix also lists file names for programs and features so that you can delete them and save hard disk space.

The directory names and file names in this appendix use the HPFS file naming conventions. If you use the FAT file system, your directory and file names will be similar but not exactly like those listed.

Note: The files and directories in this appendix might differ slightly from those on your system. The actual directories and files are dependant upon the type of computer, the devices attached to the computer, and the options selected during the installation of OS/2 2.1 and MMPM/2.

439

OS/2 Directories

The OS/2 2.1 operating system created the following directories on your system at installation time. For information about what files are in the directories, refer to the tables on the next few pages. Directories that do not refer you to a table, are empty.

- C:\ (See Table 6 on page 441 for a list of files.)
- C:\Desktop
  - C:\Desktop\Information
  - C:\Desktop\Minimized^Window Viewer
  - C:\Desktop\OS!2 System
    - C:\Desktop\OS!2 System\Command Prompts
    - C:\Desktop\OS!2 System\Drives
    - C:\Desktop\OS!2 System\Games
    - C:\Desktop\OS!2 System\Startup
    - C:\Desktop\OS!2 System\System Startup
  - C:\Desktop\Productivity
  - C:\Desktop\Templates (See Table 6 on page 441 for a list of files.)
    - C:\Desktop\Templates\Folder
  - C:\Desktop\WIN-OS!2 Groups
    - C:\Desktop\WIN-OS!2 Groups\WIN-OS!2 Accessories
    - C:\Desktop\WIN-OS!2 Groups\WIN-OS!2 Main
  - C:\Desktop\Windows Programs
- C:\Nowhere
- C:\OS2 (See Table 7 on page 442 for a list of files.)
  - C:\OS2\APPS (See Table 8 on page 443 for a list of files.)
    - C:\OS2\APPS\DLL (See Table 8 on page 443 for a list of files.)
  - C:\OS2\BOOK (See Table 9 on page 444 for a list of files.)
  - C:\OS2\DLL (See Table 9 on page 444 for a list of files.)
    - C:\OS2\DLL\IBMNULL (See Table 10 on page 445 for a list of files.)
  - C:\OS2\DRIVERS (See Table 10 on page 445 for a list of files.)

- C:\OS2\HELP (See Table 10 on page 445 for a list of files.)

    - C:\OS2\HELP\GLOSS (See Table 10 on page 445 for a list of files.)

    - C:\OS2\HELP\TUTORIAL (See Table 10 on page 445 for a list of files.)

- C:\OS2\INSTALL (See Table 11 on page 446 for a list of files.)

- C:\OS2\MDOS (See Table 11 on page 446 for a list of files.)

    - C:\OS2\MDOS\WINOS2 (See Table 12 on page 447 for a list of files.)

        • C:\OS2\MDOS\WINOS2\SYSTEM (See Table 13 on page 448 for a list of files.)

- C:\OS2\SYSTEM (See Table 14 on page 449 for a list of files.)

- C:\PSFONTS

- C:\SPOOL

    - C:\SPOOL\IBM4019L (Actual directory name depends on the printer attached to your system)

The OS2 directory and its subdirectories contain the majority of all files in the OS/2 2.1 operating system.

Directory and File List

Table 6. OS/2 Directories and Files		
Directory name: C:\		
AUTOEXEC.BAT	README	OS2
CONFIG.SYS	Desktop	PSFONTS
OS2VER	Nowhere	SPOOL
Directory name: C:\Desktop\Templates		
BITMAP.BMP	ICON.ICO	PIF FILE.PIF
DATA FILE	METAFILE.MET	POINTER.PTR
FOLDER		

Table 7. *OS/2 Directories and Files*

Directory name: C:\OS2

000000.BIO	ICONEDIT.EXE	RCPP.EXE
ABIOS.SYS	INI.RC	RECOVER.COM
ANSI.EXE	INISYS.RC	REINSTAL.INI
APPS	INSTALL	REPLACE.EXE
APSYMBOL.APS	IPFC.EXE	RESTORE.EXE
ATTRIB.EXE	KBD02.SYS	REXXTRY.CMD
BACKUP.EXE	KEYB.COM	RXQUEUE.EXE
BITMAP	KEYBOARD.DCP	RXSUBCOM.EXE
BMTAG.TAG	LABEL.COM	SAMPLE.SEP
BOOK	LINK.EXE	SCREEN02.SYS
BOOT.COM	LINK386.EXE	SETBOOT.EXE
CACHE.EXE	LOCK.RC	SETVGA.CMD
CDFS.IFS	LOG.SYS	SORT.EXE
CDROM.SYS	MAKEINI.EXE	SPOOL.EXE
CHKDSK.COM	MDOS	STHR.EXE
CLIPOS2.EXE	MODE.COM	SVGA.EXE
CLOCK02.SYS	MORE.COM	SYSLEVEL.EXE
CMD.EXE	MOUSE.SYS	SYSLOG.EXE
COM.SYS	OS2.INI	SYSLOGPM.EXE
COMP.COM	OS2ASPI.DMD	SYSTEM
CREATEDD.EXE	OS2CDROM.DMD	TESTCFG.SYS
DISKCOMP.COM	OS2DASD.DMD	TRACE.EXE
DISKCOPY.COM	OS2SCSI.DMD	TRACEFMT.EXE
DLL	OS2SYS.INI	TREE.COM
DOS.SYS	OS2_13.RC	TUTORIAL.EXE
DOSCALLS.LIB	OS2_20.RC	UNDELETE.COM
DRIVERS	PATCH.EXE	UNPACK.EXE
E.EXE	PCLOGIC.SYS	UPINI.RC
EAUTIL.EXE	PCMCIA.SYS	VDISK.SYS
EPM.INI	PMCHKDSK.EXE	VIEW.EXE
EXTDSKDD.SYS	PMCONTRL.INF	VIEWDOC.EXE
FDISK.COM	PMDD.SYS	VIOTBL.DCP
FDISKPM.EXE	PMDIARY.INI	W020100.BIO
FIND.EXE	PMFORMAT.EXE	W020101.BIO
FORMAT.COM	PMREXX.EXE	W050000.BIO
HELP	PMSHELL.EXE	W050100.BIO
HELP.CMD	POINTDD.SYS	W050101.BIO
HELPMSG.EXE	PRINT.COM	W060100.BIO
HPFS.IFS	PRINT02.SYS	W0F0000.BIO
IBM2ADSK.ADD	PSCRIPT.SEP	WIN_30.RC
IBM2FLPY.ADD	PSTAT.EXE	XCOPY.EXE
IBM2SCSI.ADD	RC.EXE	XGA.SYS
IBMINT13.I13	RCPP.ERR	XGARING0.SYS

Table 8. OS/2 Directories and Files

Directory name: C:\OS2\APPS

ACLASS2.RCV	GREEN.GRF	PMDMONTH.EXE
ACLASS2.SND	HELP.EX	PMDNOTE.EXE
ACSACDI.DAT	INVEST.DAT	PMDTARC.EXE
BOX.EX	INVEST.GRF	PMDTODO.EXE
CARDSYM.FON	JIGSAW.EXE	PMDTUNE.EXE
CTLSACDI.EXE	KLONDIKE.EXE	PMMBASE.EXE
CUSTOM.MDB	MATHLIB.EX	PMSEEK.EXE
DLL	NEKO.EXE	PMSPREAD.EXE
DRAW.EX	OS2CHESS.BIN	PMSTICKY.EXE
E3EMUL.EX	OS2CHESS.EXE	PULSE.EXE
EPM.EX	PICVIEW.EXE	PUT.EX
EPM.EXE	PMCHART.EXE	REVERSI.EXE
EPMHELP.QHL	PMDALARM.EXE	SASYNCDB.SYS
EPMLEX.EX	PMDCALC.EXE	SCRAMBLE.EXE
EXTRA.EX	PMDCALEN.EXE	SIMUL.RCV
FASHION.DAT	PMDDARC.EXE	SIMUL.SND
FASHION.GRF	PMDDIARY.EXE	SOFTERM.EXE
GET.EX	PMDIARY.$$A	
GREEN.DAT	PMLIST.EXE	

Directory name: C:\OS2\APPS\DLL

ACLASS2.DLL	ODBM.DLL	OTTY.DLL
CHESSAI.DLL	OFMTC.DLL	OVIO.DLL
CTLSACDI.DLL	OIBM1X.DLL	OVM.DLL
ETKE551.DLL	OIBM2X.DLL	OVT.DLL
ETKR551.DLL	OKB.DLL	OXMODEM.DLL
ETKTHNK.DLL	OKBC.DLL	OXRM.DLL
KLONBGA.DLL	OKERMIT.DLL	PICVIEW.DLL
MGXLIB.DLL	OLPTIO.DLL	PMDIARY.DLL
MGXVBM.DLL	OMCT.DLL	PMDIARYF.DLL
NEKO.DLL	OMRKCPY.DLL	PMFID.DLL
OACDISIO.DLL	OPCF.DLL	PMSEEK.DLL
OANSI.DLL	OPM.DLL	PMSTICKD.DLL
OANSI364.DLL	OPROFILE.DLL	SACDI.DLL
OCHAR.DLL	ORSHELL.DLL	SAREXEC.DLL
OCM.DLL	OSCH.DLL	SCRAMBLE.DLL
OCOLOR.DLL	OSIO.DLL	SCRCATS.DLL
OCSHELL.DLL	OSOFT.DLL	SCRLOGO.DLL
ODBM.DLL	OTEK.DLL	SIMUL.DLL

Table 9. OS/2 Directories and Files		
Directory name: C:\OS2\BOOK		
CMDREF.INF REXX.INF		
Directory name: C:\OS2\DLL		
ANMT.DLL	MONCALLS.DLL	PMWP.DLL
ANSICALL.DLL	MOUCALLS.DLL	PMWPMRI.DLL
BDCALLS.DLL	MSG.DLL	QUECALLS.DLL
BKSCALLS.DLL	NAMPIPES.DLL	REXX.DLL
BMSCALLS.DLL	NLS.DLL	REXXAPI.DLL
BUTTON.DLL	NPXEMLTR.DLL	REXXINIT.DLL
BVHINIT.DLL	NWIAPI.DLL	REXXUTIL.DLL
BVHMPA.DLL	OASIS.DLL	SELECT.DLL
BVHVGA.DLL	OS2CHAR.DLL	SERIAL.PDR
BVHWNDW.DLL	OS2SM.DLL	SESMGR.DLL
BVHXGA.DLL	PARALLEL.PDR	SHPIINST.DLL
BVSCALLS.DLL	PICV.DLL	SOM.DLL
COURIER.FON	PMATM.DLL	SPL1B.DLL
CPISPFPC.DLL	PMBIND.DLL	SPOOLCP.DLL
DISPLAY.DLL	PMCHKDSK.DLL	STARTLW.DLL
DLL	PMCLIP.DLL	STARTMRI.DLL
DMQSPROF.DLL	PMCTLS.DLL	STXTDMPC.DLL
DOSCALL1.DLL	PMDCTLS.DLL	SVGAINST.DLL
DOSRFICO.DLL	PMDDE.DLL	SYSFONT.DLL
DRAG.DLL	PMDRAG.DLL	SYSLOG.DLL
DSPRES.DLL	PMFORMAT.DLL	SYSMONO.FON
DTM.DLL	PMGPI.DLL	TIMES.FON
EHXDLMRI.DLL	PMGRE.DLL	TRACEFMT.DLL
FDISKPM.DLL	PMMLE.DLL	TUT.DLL
FKA.DLL	PMPIC.DLL	TUTDLL.DLL
HELPMGR.DLL	PMPRINT.QPR	TUTMRI.DLL
HELV.FON	PMREXX.DLL	UCDFS.DLL
HPMGRMRI.DLL	PMSDMRI.DLL	UHPFS.DLL
IBMNULL	PMSHAPI.DLL	VIOCALLS.DLL
IBMXGA32.DLL	PMSHAPIM.DLL	WCFGMRI.DLL
IMP.DLL	PMSHELL.DLL	WINCFG.DLL
INACALL.DLL	PMSHLTKT.DLL	WINPRF.DLL
KBDCALLS.DLL	PMSPL.DLL	WPCONFIG.DLL
MINXMRI.DLL	PMTKT.DLL	WPCONMRI.DLL
MINXOBJ.DLL	PMVDMP.DLL	WPPRINT.DLL
MIRRORS.DLL	PMVIOP.DLL	WPPRTMRI.DLL
MISC.FON	PMWIN.DLL	WPPWNDRV.DLL

Table 10. OS/2 Directories and Files		
Directory name: C:\OS2\DLL\IBMNULL		
IBMNULL.DRV		
Directory name: C:\OS2\DRIVERS		
152XPRES.EXE	DPTPRES.EXE	FD8XX.EXE
154XPRES.EXE	FD16-700.EXE	IBM2SCPR.EXE
164XPRES.EXE	FD7000EX.EXE	
174XPRES.EXE	FD850IBM.EXE	
Directory name: C:\OS2\HELP		
ACDISIO.HLP	IBMSIO.HLP	REVERSI.HLP
ANIMAT.AMT	ICONEDIT.HLP	SCRAMBLE.HLP
ANSI364.HLP	INSTALL.HLP	SOFTERM.HLP
ANSIIBM.HLP	JIGSAW.HLP	START.HLP
CLIPVIEW.HLP	KLONDIKE.HLP	SYSLOGH.HLP
DDINSTAL.HLP	MIGRATE.HLP	TRACEFMT.HLP
DSPINSTL.HLP	NEKO.HLP	TTY.HLP
EHXHP.HLP	OS2CHESS.HLP	TUTORIAL
EPM.HLP	PICVIEW.HLP	VIEWH.HLP
FDISKPMH.HLP	PMCHART.HLP	VTTERM.HLP
GLOSS	PMDIARY.HLP	WPHELP.HLP
HMHELP.HLP	PMREXX.HLP	WPINDEX.HLP
IBM31011.HLP	PMSEEK.HLP	WPMSG.HLP
IBM31012.HLP	PULSE.HLP	XRM.HLP
Directory name: C:\OS2\HELP\GLOSS		
WPGLOSS.HLP		
Directory name: C:\OS2\HELP\TUTORIAL		
TUTORIAL.HLP		

Table 11. OS/2 Directories and Files

Directory name: C:\OS2\INSTALL

BLISTLAY.OUT	INSTALL.LOG	PSSVGA32.DSC
CDROM.TBL	INSTSHEL.EXE	PSTRID.DSC
CLEANUP.EXE	ISPD.MSG	PSTSENG.DSC
CONFIG.SYS	ISPM.MSG	PSVGA32.DSC
DATABASE.DAT	MIGRATE.EXE	PSWD.DSC
DATABASE.TXT	OS2.INI	PSXGA32.DSC
DBTAGS.DAT	OS2SYS.INI	REINSTAL.INI
DDINSTAL.EXE	PARSEDB.EXE	RSPDDI.EXE
DMPC.EXE	PRDESC.LST	RSPDSPI.EXE
DSPINSTL.EXE	PRDRV.LST	RSPINST.EXE
DSPINSTL.LOG	PSATI.DSC	RSPMIG.EXE
ESSTART.CMD	PSBGA16.DSC	SAMPLE.RSP
INSTAID.CNF	PSCGA16.DSC	SCSI.TBL
INSTAID.EXE	PSCL.DSC	SYSLEVEL.GRE
INSTAID.LIB	PSEGA16.DSC	SYSLEVEL.OS2
INSTAID.PRO	PSHEAD.DSC	USER.RSP
INSTAIDE.EXE	PSMONO.DSC	
INSTALL.EXE	PSSPDW.DSC	

Directory name: C:\OS2\MDOS

ANSI.SYS	JOIN.EXE	VEGA.SYS
APPEND.EXE	LPTDD.SYS	VEMM.SYS
ASSIGN.COM	MEM.EXE	VESA.EXE
BASIC.COM	MORTGAGE.BAS	VFLPY.SYS
BASICA.COM	MOUSE.COM	VKBD.SYS
COMDD.SYS	QBASIC.EXE	VLPT.SYS
COMMAND.COM	QBASIC.HLP	VMDISK.EXE
DEBUG.EXE	SETCOM40.EXE	VMONO.SYS
DOSKEY.COM	SQ4FIX.COM	VMOUSE.SYS
DOSKRNL	SUBST.EXE	VNPX.SYS
EDLIN.COM	V8514A.SYS	VPCMCIA.SYS
EGA.SYS	VAPM.SYS	VPIC.SYS
EMM386.SYS	VBIOS.SYS	VSVGA.SYS
EXIT_VDM.COM	VCDROM.SYS	VTIMER.SYS
FFIX.EXE	VCGA.SYS	VTOUCH.COM
FSACCESS.EXE	VCMOS.SYS	VVGA.SYS
FSFILTER.SYS	VCOM.SYS	VWIN.SYS
GRAFTABL.COM	VDMA.SYS	VXGA.SYS
HELP.BAT	VDPMI.SYS	VXMS.SYS
HIMEM.SYS	VDPX.SYS	WINOS2
ISWINDOW.COM	VDSK.SYS	

Table 12. OS/2 Directories and Files		
Directory name:	C:\OS2\MDOS\WINOS2	

APPS.HLP	MPLAYER.INI	SSMARQUE.SCR
ATM.INI	MSD.EXE	SSMYST.SCR
ATMCNTRL.EXE	MSD.INI	SSSTARS.SCR
CALC.EXE	NETWORKS.WRI	STARTUP.GRP
CALC.HLP	NOTEPAD.EXE	SYSINI.WRI
CALENDAR.EXE	NOTEPAD.HLP	SYSTEM
CALENDAR.HLP	PACKAGER.EXE	SYSTEM.INI
CANYON.MID	PACKAGER.HLP	TADA.WAV
CARDFILE.EXE	PBRUSH.DLL	TASKMAN.EXE
CARDFILE.HLP	PBRUSH.EXE	TEMP
CHARMAP.EXE	PBRUSH.HLP	WIN.COM
CHARMAP.HLP	PRINTERS.WRI	WIN.INI
CHIMES.WAV	PRINTMAN.EXE	WINFILE.EXE
CHORD.WAV	PRINTMAN.HLP	WINFILE.HLP
CLIPBRD.EXE	PROGMAN.EXE	WINFILE.INI
CLIPBRD.HLP	PROGMAN.HLP	WINHELP.EXE
CLOCK.EXE	PROGMAN.INI	WINHELP.HLP
CONTROL.EXE	README.ATM	WININI.WRI
CONTROL.HLP	REG.DAT	WINOS2.COM
CONTROL.INI	REGEDIT.EXE	WINOS2.ICO
DING.WAV	REGEDIT.HLP	WINSHELD.EXE
DRWATSON.EXE	REGEDITV.HLP	WINVER.EXE
EXPAND.EXE	SCRNSAVE.SCR	WOS2ACCE.GRP
GLOSSARY.HLP	SETUP.EXE	WOS2MAIN.GRP
MORICONS.DLL	SETUP.HLP	WRITE.EXE
MOUSE.INI	SOUNDREC.EXE	WRITE.HLP
MPLAYER.EXE	SOUNDREC.HLP	
MPLAYER.HLP	SSFLYWIN.SCR	

Directory name:	C:\OS2\MDOS\WINOS2\SYSTEM	

COUNTRY.SYS	OSO001H.MSG	SPLH.MSG
DEV002.MSG	REX.MSG	SWAPPER.DAT
HARDERR.EXE	REXH.MSG	TRACE
LOGDAEM.EXE	SACDI.MSG	UCDFS.MSG
OSO001.MSG	SPL.MSG	

Table 13. OS/2 Directories and Files		
Directory name:	C:\OS2\MDOS\WINOS2\SYSTEM	
APPS.INF	MIDIMAP.CFG	TIMES.FOT
ARIAL.FOT	MIDIMAP.DRV	TIMES.TTF
ARIAL.TTF	MMSOUND.DRV	TIMESB.FON
ARIALB.FON	MMSYSTEM.DLL	TIMESBD.FOT
ARIALBD.FOT	MMTASK.TSK	TIMESBD.TTF
ARIALBD.TTF	MODERN.FON	TIMESBI.FOT
ARIALBI.FOT	MOUSE.DRV	TIMESBI.TTF
ARIALBI.TTF	MPU401.DRV	TIMESI.FOT
ARIALI.FOT	MSADLIB.DRV	TIMESI.TTF
ARIALI.TTF	NOMOUSE.DRV	TOOLHELP.DLL
ATM16.DLL	OLECLI.DLL	UNIDRV.DLL
ATM32.DLL	OLESVR.DLL	UNIDRV.HLP
ATMSYS.DRV	OS2K386.EXE	VER.DLL
COMM.DRV	OS2USER.EXE	VGA850.FON
COMMDLG.DLL	ROMAN.FON	VGA860.FON
CONTROL.INF	SCRIPT.FON	VGA861.FON
COUR.FOT	SERIFE.FON	VGA863.FON
COUR.TTF	SERIFG.FON	VGA865.FON
COURBD.FOT	SETUP.INF	VGAFIX.FON
COURBD.TTF	SETUP.INI	VGAOEM.FON
COURBI.FOT	SETUP.REG	VGASYS.FON
COURBI.TTF	SETUP.SHH	WIN87EM.DLL
COURE.FON	SHELL.DLL	WINGDING.FOT
COURG.FON	SMALLE.FON	WINGDING.TTF
COURI.FOT	SMALLG.FON	WINOA386.MOD
COURI.TTF	SND.CPL	WINOLDAP.MOD
DDEML.DLL	SNDBLST.DRV	WINSCLIP.DLL
DMCOLOR.DLL	SNDBLST2.DRV	WINSDDE.DLL
DRIVERS.CPL	SOUND.DRV	WINSMSG.DLL
DRVMAP.INF	SSERIFE.FON	XGA.DRV
FINSTALL.DLL	SSERIFG.FON	XGAFIX.FON
FINSTALL.HLP	SXGA.DRV	XGAOEM.FON
GDI.EXE	SYMBOL.FOT	XGASYS.FON
KEYBOARD.DRV	SYMBOL.TTF	XLAT850.BIN
LZEXPAND.DLL	SYMBOLE.FON	XLAT860.BIN
MAIN.CPL	SYMBOLG.FON	XLAT861.BIN
MCICDA.DRV	SYSEDIT.EXE	XLAT863.BIN
MCISEQ.DRV	SYSTEM.DRV	XLAT865.BIN
MCIWAVE.DRV	TIMER.DRV	

Table 14. OS/2 Directories and Files

Directory name:	C:\OS2\SYSTEM	
COUNTRY.SYS	OSO001H.MSG	SPLH.MSG
DEV002.MSG	REX.MSG	SWAPPER.DAT
HARDERR.EXE	REXH.MSG	TRACE
LOGDAEM.EXE	SACDI.MSG	UCDFS.MSG
OSO001.MSG	SPL.MSG	

MMPM/2 Directories

MMPM/2 created the following directories on your system during installation. For information about what files are in the directories, refer to the tables on the next few pages. Directories that do not refer you to a table, are empty.

- C:\MMOS2 (See Table 15 for a list of files.)

    - C:\MMOS2\DLL (See Table 16 on page 451 for a list of files.)

    - C:\MMOS2\DSP (See Table 16 on page 451 for a list of files.)

    - C:\MMOS2\HELP (See Table 16 on page 451 for a list of files.)

    - C:\MMOS2\INSTALL (See Table 17 on page 452 for a list of files.)

    - C:\MMOS2\MACROS (See Table 17 on page 452 for a list of files.)

    - C:\MMOS2\MOVIES

    - C:\MMOS2\SOUNDS (See Table 17 on page 452 for a list of files.)

MMPM/2 Directory and File List

Table 15. OS/2 Directories and Files		
Directory name: C:\MMOS2		
32BITGRE.LUT	MIDITYPE.INI	RECORD.CMD
ACPADD2.SYS	MINSTALL.EXE	SB16D2.SYS
ADSHDD.SYS	MME.MSG	SBD2.SYS
AMPM.EXE	MMPM.INI	SBP2D2.SYS
AUDIODD.MSG	MMPM2.INI	SBPD2.SYS
AUDIOVDD.SYS	MMPMCD.INI	SMVDD.SYS
CDPM.EXE	MMPMMMIO.INI	SOUNDS
DLL	MOVIES	SPI.INI
DSP	MPMCDIMG.CMD	SSMDD.SYS
FFC.EXE	MPPM.EXE	STPM.EXE
HELP	MVPRODD.SYS	VAUDIO.SYS
INSTALL	PLAY.CMD	WEPM.EXE
MACROS	README	

Table 16. OS/2 Directories and Files		
Directory name: C:\MMOS2\DLL		
AMPMMRI.DLL	MIPM.DLL	SND.DLL
AMPMXMCD.DLL	MISH.DLL	SNDBLAST.DLL
AUDIOIF.DLL	MMIO.DLL	SSM.DLL
AUDIOMCD.DLL	MMMRI.DLL	SSMINI.DLL
AVCAPROC.DLL	MMOTPROC.DLL	SSMRES.DLL
AVCIIOPR.DLL	MMPMCRTS.DLL	SSSH.DLL
AVIO.DLL	MMSND.DLL	STDL.DLL
CDAUDIO.DLL	MMSNDMRI.DLL	STDLMRI.DLL
CDDASH.DLL	MPPM.DLL	STPMMRI.DLL
CDPMMRI.DLL	MPPMMRI.DLL	SVMC.DLL
CDTBL.DLL	MTSH.DLL	SVMCH.HLP
FFCMRI.DLL	NULLSH.DLL	SVMCMRI.DLL
FSSH.DLL	OS13PROC.DLL	SVSH.DLL
GENCDVSD.DLL	OS20PROC.DLL	SW.DLL
HHP.DLL	QRYAD.DLL	ULBDC16.DLL
IBMCDXA.DLL	QRYADMRI.DLL	ULBDC4.DLL
IOPRNLS.DLL	QRYCD.DLL	ULBDC8.DLL
ITERM.DLL	QRYCDMRI.DLL	ULDC16.DLL
MCIAPI.DLL	QRYMV.DLL	ULDC8.DLL
MCIERR.DLL	QRYMVMRI.DLL	ULIO.DLL
MCIMRI.DLL	QRYSB.DLL	WAVEPROC.DLL
MDM.DLL	QRYSBMRI.DLL	WEPMMRI.DLL
MEMSH.DLL	QRYUM.DLL	WEPMPINT.DLL
MIDIIO.DLL	QRYUMMRI.DLL	WEPMPLUS.DLL
MIDIMCD.DLL	RDIBPROC.DLL	WI30PROC.DLL
Directory name: C:\MMOS2\DSP		
IBMAUDF.DSP	IBMPCMP.DSP	WI0007.ASP
IBMAUDG.DSP	IBMPCMR.DSP	WI0200.ASP
IBMAUDP.DSP	IBMPCMR8.DSP	WO0006.ASP
IBMAUDR.DSP	IBMPMM48.DSP	WO0007.ASP
IBMAUDS.DSP	IBMXA.DSP	WO0200.ASP
IBMMPC.DSP	WI0006.ASP	
Directory name: C:\MMOS2\HELP		
AMPMH.HLP	MMINSTH.HLP	QRYSBH.HLP
CDPMH.HLP	MMSNDH.HLP	STDLH.HLP
FFC.HLP	MPPMH.HLP	STPMH.HLP
MCIREC.HLP	QRYADH.HLP	WEPMH.HLP
MMEINDEX.HLP	QRYMVH.HLP	WEPMPLUS.HLP

Table 17. OS/2 Directories and Files		
Directory name: C:\MMOS2\INSTALL		
AUDFILE.ICO	INSTSND.CMD	SBBASE.SCR
AUDPLAY.ICO	LSI.MSG	SMVCONF.CH
AUDREC.ICO	LSIH.MSG	SMVINI.SCR
AVSFILM.ICO	MIDIFILE.ICO	SOUNDS.EAS
BASE.SCR	MIDIICO.EAS	SOUNDS.ICO
BASE1.SCR	MIDIPLAY.ICO	SYSLEVEL.MPM
BASECONF.CH	MINSTALL.EAS	VDSCPLAY.ICO
CDPLAYER.ICO	MINSTALL.LOG	VIDICON.EAS
CDPM.EAS	MMPMDATA.ICO	VIDPLAY.ICO
COMPLIST.INI	MMPMFLDR.ICO	VOLCTRL.ICO
DATACONV.ICO	MMPMINST.ICO	WAVEFILE.EAS
DINSTSND.CMD	MMSETUP.ICO	WAVEICO.EAS
IBMLANLK.EXE	MPPM.EAS	WEPM.EAS
IBMLANLK.SYS	PASBASE.SCR	
Directory name: C:\MMOS2\MACROS		
AUDIO.WG2	AUDIO.XLM	
Directory name: C:\MMOS2\SOUNDS		
APPLAUSE.WAV	CHARGE.WAV	LASER.WAV
BACH.MID	CUCKOO.WAV	POP.WAV
BALLGAME.MID	DOINK.WAV	RATATTAT.WAV
BBEE.MID	DOORCLS.WAV	SHRED.WAV
BEEOONG.WAV	DRUMROLL.WAV	TAKEMY.WAV
BELLS.WAV	DRWCLOSE.WAV	TONK.WAV
BLUEJAM.MID	DRWROPEN.WAV	TWIP.WAV
BOING.WAV	EEEOOOP.WAV	WM_TELL.WAV
BOO.WAV	EEERRUPP.WAV	WOOEEP.WAV
BWAAANG.WAV	HOLIDAY.MID	ZIPPER.WAV
BWEEEP.WAV	IBMRALLY.MID	

Appendix F. Removing Programs

You might want to remove programs that were previously installed on your hard disk to increase hard disk capacity. The following is a listing of programs that can be deleted from your hard disk.

- Advanced Power Management (APM)

  Used on systems that contain required hardware, usually notebook type systems.

  > \OS2\APM.SYS

- Bit Maps

  These are extra bit maps provided for background display.

  - \OS2\BITMAP\SWAN.BGA

  - \OS2\BITMAP\LIGHTHOU.VGA

- CID

  These files are used for LAN installation of OS/2.

  - \OS2\INSTALL\SEDISK.EXE

  - \OS2\INSTALL\SEINST.EXE

  - \OS2\INSTALL\SEIMAGE.EXE

  - \OS2\INSTALL\SEMAINT.EXE

- Command Reference

  This file is the system command reference (on-line help).

  > \OS2\BOOK\CMDREF.INF

- High Performance File System

  These files are associated with HPFS.

  - \OS2\CACHE.EXE

  - \OS2\DLL\STARTLW.DLL

  - \OS2\HPFS.IFS

  - \OS2\DLL\UHPFS.DLL

- Linker

  The linker files are used by application developers to link compiled/assembled files into programs. Users not developing applications might wish to delete these files.

  - \OS2\RCPP.ERR
  - \OS2\RC.EXE
  - \OS2\LINK.EXE
  - \OS2\RCPP.EXE
  - \OS2\LINK386.EXE

- PCMCIA Support

  PCMCIA support might not be needed on your system. You can remove this file.

  \OS2\PCMCIA.SYS

- REXX

  Users that do not need REXX support can delete these files.

  Note: REXX support is required for IBM Communication Manager Support.

  - \OS2\REXXTRY.CMD
  - \OS2\DLL\PMREXX.DLL
  - \OS2\PMREXX.EXE
  - \OS2\DLL\REXX.DLL
  - \OS2\RXQUEUE.EXE
  - \OS2\DLL\REXXAPI.DLL
  - \OS2\RXSUBCOM.EXE
  - \OS2\DLL\REXXINIT.DLL
  - \OS2\REX.MSG
  - \OS2\DLL\REXXUTIL.DLL
  - \OS2\REXH.MSG
  - \OS2\HELP\PMREXX.HLP
  - \OS2\BOOK\REXX.INF

- RIPL

    These files are used for remote IPL.

    - \OS2\HELP\RIPLINST.HLP
    - \OS2\INSTALL\RIPLINST.EXE

- Tutorial

    These files are used by the tutorial. If you have completed the tutorial and would like to delete it, you can remove these files.

    - \OS2\TUTORIAL.EXE
    - \OS2\HELP\TUTORIAL.HLP
    - \OS2\DLL\TUTDLL.DLL

- Chess

    These are the files for the Chess program.

    - \OS2\APPS\OS2CHESS.BIN
    - \OS2\APPS\DLL\CHESSAI.DLL
    - \OS2\APPS\OS2CHESS.EXE
    - \OS2\HELP\OS2CHESS.HLP

- EPM

    These are the files for the Enhanced Editor program.

    - \OS2\APPS\BOX.EX
    - \OS2\APPS\MATHLIB.EX
    - \OS2\APPS\DRAW.EX
    - \OS2\APPS\PUT.EX
    - \OS2\APPS\E3EMUL.EX
    - \OS2\APPS\EPM.EXE
    - \OS2\APPS\EPM.EX
    - \OS2\APPS\DLL\ETKE551.DLL
    - \OS2\APPS\EPMLEX.EX
    - \OS2\APPS\DLL\ETKR551.DLL
    - \OS2\APPS\EXTRA.EX
    - \OS2\APPS\DLL\ETKTHNK.DLL

- \OS2\APPS\GET.EX

- \OS2\HELP\EPM.HLP

- \OS2\APPS\HELP.EX

- \OS2\HELP\EPMHELP.QHL

- Jigsaw

  These are the files for the Jigsaw program.

  - \OS2\APPS\JIGSAW.EXE

  - \OS2\HELP\JIGSAW.HLP

- Klondike

  These are the files for klondike (solitaire).

  - \OS2\APPS\CARDSYM.FON

  - \OS2\DLL\KLONBGA.DLL

  - \OS2\APPS\KLONDIKE.EXE

  - \OS2\HELP\KLONDIKE.HLP

- NEKO

  These are the files for neko (the cat).

  - \OS2\APPS\NEKO.EXE

  - \OS2\HELP\NEKO.HLP

  - \OS2\DLL\NEKO.DLL

- PICVIEW

  These are the files for picview.

  - \OS2\APPS\PICVIEW.EXE

  - \OS2\HELP\PICVIEW.HLP

  - \OS2\APPS\DLL\PICVIEW.DLL

- PMChart

  These are the files for the PM Chart productivity aid.

  - \OS2\APPS\FASHION.DAT

  - \OS2\APPS\INVEST.GRF

  - \OS2\APPS\GREEN.DAT

- \OS2\APPS\DLL\MGXLIB.DLL

- \OS2\APPS\INVEST.DAT

- \OS2\APPS\DLL\MGXVBM.DLL

- \OS2\APPS\PMCHART.EXE

- \OS2\APPS\DLL\PMFID.DLL

- \OS2\APPS\FASHION.GRF

- \OS2\HELP\PMCHART.HLP

- \OS2\APPS\GREEN.GRF

- PM Diary

  These are the files for the PM Diary productivity aid.

  - \OS2\APPS\PMDALARM.EXE

  - \OS2\APPS\PMDTODO.EXE

  - \OS2\APPS\PMDCALC.EXE

  - \OS2\APPS\PMDTUNE.EXE

  - \OS2\APPS\PMDCALEN.EXE

  - \OS2\APPS\PMMBASE.EXE

  - \OS2\APPS\PMDDARC.EXE

  - \OS2\APPS\PMSPREAD.EXE

  - \OS2\APPS\PMDDIARY.EXE

  - \OS2\APPS\PMSTICKY.EXE

  - \OS2\APPS\PMDLIST.EXE

  - \OS2\APPS\DLL\PMDIARY.DLL

  - \OS2\APPS\PMDMONTH.EXE

  - \OS2\APPS\DLL\PMDIARYF.DLL

  - \OS2\APPS\PMDNOTE.EXE

  - \OS2\APPS\DLL\PMSTICKD.DLL

  - \OS2\APPS\PMDTARC.EXE

  - \OS2\HELP\PMDIARY.HLP

- PM Seek

  These are the files for the PM Seek productivity aid.

  - \OS2\APPS\PMSEEK.EXE
  - \OS2\HELP\PMSEEK.HLP
  - \OS2\DLL\PMSEEK.DLL

- Pulse

  These are the files for the Pulse (CPU meter) program.

  - \OS2\APPS\PULSE.EXE
  - \OS2\HELP\PULSE.HLP

- Reversi

  These are the files for the Reversi program.

  - \OS2\APPS\REVERSI.EXE
  - \OS2\HELP\REVERSI.HLP

- Scramble

  These are the files for the Scramble program.

  - \OS2\APPS\SCRAMBLE.EXE
  - \OS2\DLL\SCRLOGO.DLL
  - \OS2\DLL\SCRAMBLE.DLL
  - \OS2\HELP\SCRAMBLE.HLP
  - \OS2\DLL\SCRCATS.DLL

- SoftTerm

  These are the files for SoftTerm (the terminal emulator).

  - \OS2\APPS\ACSACDI.DAT
  - \OS2\DLL\OPROFILE.DLL
  - \OS2\APPS\CTLSACDI.EXE
  - \OS2\DLL\ORSHELL.DLL
  - \OS2\APPS\SOFTERM.EXE
  - \OS2\DLL\OSCH.DLL
  - \OS2\APPS\CUSTOM.MDB
  - \OS2\DLL\OSIO.DLL

- \OS2\APPS\SASYNCDA.SYS
- \OS2\DLL\OSOFT.DLL
- \OS2\APPS\SASYNCDB.SYS
- \OS2\DLL\OTEK.DLL
- \OS2\DLL\CTLSACDI.DLL
- \OS2\DLL\OTTY.DLL
- \OS2\DLL\OACDISIO.DLL
- \OS2\DLL\OVIO.DLL
- \OS2\DLL\OANSI.DLL
- \OS2\DLL\OVM.DLL
- \OS2\DLL\OANSI364.DLL
- \OS2\DLL\OVT.DLL
- \OS2\DLL\OCHAR.DLL
- \OS2\DLL\OXMODEM.DLL
- \OS2\DLL\OCM.DLL
- \OS2\DLL\OXRM.DLL
- \OS2\DLL\OCOLOR.DLL
- \OS2\DLL\SACDI.DLL
- \OS2\DLL\OCSHELL.DLL
- \OS2\DLL\SAREXEC.DLL
- \OS2\DLL\ODBM.DLL
- \OS2\DLL\SACDI.MSG
- \OS2\DLL\OFMTC.DLL
- \OS2\HELP\ACDISIO.HLP
- \OS2\DLL\OIBM1X.DLL
- \OS2\HELP\ANSI364.HLP
- \OS2\DLL\OIBM2X.DLL
- \OS2\HELP\ANSIIBM.HLP
- \OS2\DLL\OKB.DLL
- \OS2\HELP\IBM31011.HLP

- – \OS2\DLL\OKBC.DLL
- – \OS2\HELP\IBM31012.HLP
- – \OS2\DLL\OKERMIT.DLL
- – \OS2\HELP\IBMSIO.HLP
- – \OS2\DLL\OLPTIO.DLL
- – \OS2\HELP\SOFTERM.HLP
- – \OS2\DLL\OMCT.DLL
- – \OS2\HELP\TTY.HLP
- – \OS2\DLL\OMRKCPY.DLL
- – \OS2\HELP\VTTERM.HLP
- – \OS2\DLL\OPCF.DLL
- – \OS2\HELP\XRM.HLP
- – \OS2\DLL\OPM.DLL

- Touch

  These are the files for Touch.

  - – \OS2\TOUCO21D.BIN
  - – \OS2\DLL\TCP.DLL
  - – \OS2\TOUMOU.BIO
  - – \OS2\DLL\TOUCALLS.DLL
  - – \OS2\CALIBRAT.DAT
  - – \OS2\HELP\TCP.HLP
  - – \OS2\CALIBRAT.EXE
  - – \OS2\MDOS\VTOUCH.COM
  - – \OS2\TOUCH.INI
  - – \OS2\MDOS\VTOUCH.SYS
  - – \OS2\PDITOU01.SYS
  - – \OS2\MDOS\WIN
  - – OS2\SYSTEM\TOUCH.DRV
  - – \OS2\PDITOU02.SYS
  - – \OS2\SYSTEM\TDD.MSG

- – \OS2\TOUCH.SYS
- – \OS2\SYSTEM\TDDH.MSG
- – \OS2\CALIBRAT.TXT
- – \OS2\SYSTEM\TDI.MSG
- – \OS2\DLL\FSGRAPH.DLL
- – \OS2\SYSTEM\TDIH.MSG

Appendix G. Recording Information about Your Computer

Having the following information might be useful when you need technical assistance, depending on your problem. Therefore, you might want to record as much information as you can, for future reference. Also, space is provided to record BBS and CompuServe information, if you use these services.

Some information, such as manufacturer, model number, and size of a diskette drive, might be printed on the hardware. Other details, such as the size of a cache or the resolution of a monitor, might be provided in the documentation that came with the hardware.

If you have a problem you could not resolve using the tables in Chapter 24, "Solving Problems" on page 265, one of the tables might have directed you to include the manufacturer and date of the BIOS in your computer. Some computers display the BIOS information on the screen when you start the computer. If you need this information before you call for technical support, and the BIOS information is not displayed on the screen, contact the manufacturer of your computer.

When you describe a problem, include information such as:

- The frequency of the problem
- Whether you can re-create the problem
- The text of any message that was displayed on the screen
- Which hardware and programs you were using when the problem occurred
- Other sessions and programs you had open at the time of the problem
- What, if anything, was running in the background
- Anything you tried to do to resolve the problem

General Information

Support Phone Numbers:_____

BBS ID:_____CompuServe ID:_____

My Fax Number with Area Code:_____

OS/2 Warranty Registration Number:_____
    (On inside front cover)

OS/2 Base Version:_____
    (Type **VER** at a command prompt to get this information.)

Current CSD level of OS/2 Base Operating System:_____
    (Type **SYSLEVEL** at a command prompt to get this information.)

Computer Manufacturer, Model, and Microprocessor:_____

_____

Type of bus architecture your computer has:

  ___ EISA   ___ ISA (IBM-AT)
  ___ MicroChannel

BIOS:_____
    (Manufacturer, Version, and Date)

System Board Cache Manufacturer:_____

Cache Size:

  ___ 64KB   ___ 256KB
  ___ 128KB   ___ Other:_____

Amount of Memory (RAM):_____MB

Indicate the size of each hard disk drive to the left of its manufacturer.

___	Conner	___	NEC
___	CMS Enhancements	___	Plus Development
___	Core Technology	___	Quantum
___	Fujitsu	___	Rodime
___	Hewlett Packard	___	Seagate
___	Hard Drives Int.	___	Storeage Dimension
___	Hitachi	___	Toshiba
___	IBM	___	Western Digital
___	Maxtor	___	Other:_____
___	Micropolis		

Hard Disks:_____
    (Manufacturer and Size)

Hard Disk Controllers:

    Manufacturer:

___	Adaptec	___	IBM
___	Future Domain	___	Other:_____
___	Iomega		

    Type:

___	ESDI	___	MFM/RLL
___	SCSI	___	Other:_____
___	IDE		

Partition Information:
(Type **FDISKPM** at an OS/2 command prompt to get this information.)

Status: Access: File System Type:

_____   _____   _____

_____   _____   _____

_____   _____   _____

Amount of Free Space Remaining on OS/2 Partition:_____
(Refer to CHKDSK procedure in "Checking a Disk" on page 103.)

Diskette Drives:_____
(Manufacturer, Size, and Type)

Displays (Monitors):_____
(Manufacturer and Model)

Display Adapters (Manufacturer):_____

Model:

____ ATI WonderXL   ____ IBM EGA
____ ATI Vantage SVGA   ____ IBM Image Adapter
____ ATI 8514 Ultra   ____ IBM Monochrome
____ ATI Graphics Ultra   ____ IBM VGA
____ ATI Graphics Ultra Pro   ____ IBM XGA
____ ATI Local Bus   ____ IBM XGA-2
____ Diamond Speedstar   ____ IBM 8514
____ Diamond Speedstar 24   ____ Orchid Prodesigner II, IIs
____ Diamond Speedstar 24X   ____ Orchid Fahrenheit
____ Diamond Stealth   ____ Paradise EGA
____ Genoa 7000, 8000   ____ Paradise VGA, VGA 1024
____ Headland Video 7   ____ QVISION (Compaq)
____ Hercules EGA   ____ STB Powergraph
____ Hercules Monochrome   ____ Other:_____
____ IBM CGA

Mode:

___ CGA   ___ XGA
___ EGA   ___ XGA-2
___ Monochrome   ___ Image Adapter
___ VGA   ___ Other:_____
___ SVGA

Memory—Video RAM (VRAM):

___ 256KB   ___ 2MB
___ 512KB   ___ 3MB
___ 1MB   ___ Other:_____

Mouse:_____
     (Manufacturer, Model, Type, Number of Buttons, Emulation Mode)

Printers and Plotters:_____
     (Manufacturer, Model, and Printer Adapter)

     Emulation Mode:_____

Other Devices, Adapters, or Coprocessors, for example, CD-ROM, Tape Drive,
or Optical Disc.

Hardware   Manufacturer   Model

_____   _____   _____
_____   _____   _____
_____   _____   _____
_____

Installation Information

How did you install or attempt to install OS/2 2.1?

___ OS/2 only   ___ Boot Manager
___ Dual boot   ___ Local Area Network (LAN)

What chip set or BIOS is on the display adapter?

___ TSENG ET3000   ___ S3
___ TSENG ET4000   ___ Trident (TVGA)
___ Headland Video 7   ___ Western Digital
___ IBM   ___ Other:_____

If you have an external hard disk drive, who manufactured it?

___ Bernoulli   ___ IBM
___ Cumulus   ___ Other:_____

Printing Information

Which type of printing devices do you have? List each device
(printers and plotters).

_____

_____

What type of adapter do you have?

___ Parallel   ___ Serial

What port is the adapter attached to?

___ COM1   ___ COM3   ___ LPT1   ___ LPT3
___ COM2   ___ COM4   ___ LPT2   ___ LPT4

What is the IRQ level for the port?_____
   (Refer to "Understanding COM Ports" on page 374.)

What type of printer driver is installed?_____
   (Name, version, and manufacturer)

_____

Is your computer attached to a network?

___ Yes   ___ No

If yes, do you print from the network?

___ Yes   ___ No

On the appropriate line below, write the manufacturer, name, and
version of the program you were running when you tried to print.

DOS program:_____

Windows program:_____

OS/2 program:_____

If you were using a DOS program, did you start the program from a DOS command prompt?   ___ Yes   ___ No

If you were using a DOS or Windows program, what are the COM port settings for the DOS or Windows session? (For example: 9600,NONE,8,1)

Type MODE COMx at an OS/2 command prompt. ("x" stands for the COM port that is involved.) Then record the information exactly as it is displayed on the screen.

BAUD=_____   PARITY=_____

DATABITS=_____   STOPBITS=_____

TO=_____   XON=_____

IDSR=_____   ODSR=_____

OCTS=_____   DTR=_____

RTS=_____   BUFFER=_____

Did you see a **TRAP** message on the screen? If so, complete form "TRAP Messages" on page 478.

DOS Session Information

What is the name and version number of the DOS program in question?

Name:_____Version:_____

Who is the program manufacturer?_____

Did you contact the manufacturer for assistance?   ___ Yes   ___ No

Is there an upgrade available for this program?   ___ Yes   ___ No

How was the DOS program installed on the desktop?

   ___ Migrated   ___ Did not migrate it
   ___ I created a program object for it

What type of session is defined for the DOS program?

   ___ DOS Full Screen
   ___ DOS Window
   ___ Virtual Machine Boot (VMB)

Can you start any full screen DOS session?   ___ Yes   ___ No

Does the DOS program run under a specific version of DOS?
If yes, which version?_____

Are any Terminate-and-Stay-Resident (TSR) programs running?
If yes, are they running in the same DOS session or separate
DOS sessions?

___ Same DOS Session   ___ Different DOS Sessions

Have any of the DOS settings been customized for this DOS session?
If yes, list the changes:

Setting Changed: New Values:

_____   _____

_____   _____

_____   _____

_____   _____

Is the application being run locally or from a Local Area Network
(LAN) server?

           ___ Locally   ___ LAN Server

WIN-OS/2 Session Information

How did you set up the WIN-OS/2 program?

___ Migrated   ___ Did not migrate it
___ I created a program object for it

Can you start a WIN-OS/2 full-screen session?

___ Yes   ___ No

What is the name and version number of the Windows program running
when the problem occurred?

Name:_____Version:_____

Who is the program manufacturer?_____

Did you contact the manufacturer for assistance?   ___ Yes   ___ No

In what type of session were you running the program?

___ WIN-OS/2 full-screen session   ___ WIN-OS/2 window session
___ WIN-OS/2 window separate session

What were you trying to do when the problem occurred?

___ Install a program   ___ Use a modem, fax, or scanner
___ Start or run a program   ___ Use a CD-ROM
___ Select a printer or font   ___ Use an adapter card for sound,
___ Use a printer   video, or communications

___ Other:_____

Have any of the WIN-OS/2 settings been customized for this session?
If yes, list the changes:

Setting Changed: New Values:

_____   _____

_____   _____

_____   _____

_____   _____

Which Windows printer driver is installed?

Are Adobe Type Manager (ATM) fonts installed?

___ Yes   ___ No

Is your computer attached to a network? If so, what is the type
of your network requestor or server?

___ No network attachment   ___ DOS LAN Server
___ DOS Netware Requestor   ___ OS/2 LAN Server
___ OS/2 Netware Requestor (NETX)

OS/2 Program Information

How did you set up the OS/2 program?

   ___ Migrated it   ___ Installed it
   ___ Did not migrate it   ___ Restored it

What is the name and version number of the Windows program running when the problem occurred?

Name:_____Version:_____

Who is the program manufacturer?_____

Did you contact the manufacturer for assistance?   ___ Yes   ___ No

If this program ran correctly in a previous version of OS/2, which version?

   ___ OS/2 1.3   ___ OS/2 2.0 with Service PAK
   ___ OS/2 2.0

Is OS/2 2.1 set up for DOS Dual Boot or Boot Manager?   ___ Yes   ___ No

If so, does the program use some of the same files as a DOS program?

If you ran CHKDSK, did you get any errors?

Mouse Information

What type of mouse are you using?

    ___ Trackball   ___ 3-Button Mouse
    ___ 2-Button Mouse   ___ Laptop Rail

How is your mouse attached?

    ___ Bus   ___ Serial
    ___ In-port   ___ Cordless

What is the IRQ level for the port?_____
    (Refer to "Understanding COM Ports" on page 374.)

What mouse driver is installed?_____
    (Refer to the DEVICE= statements in your CONFIG.SYS file.)

When does the problem occur?

    ___ In DOS Session   ___ On OS/2 Desktop
    ___ In WIN-OS/2 Session   ___ While starting the system

Did you install Dual Boot on your computer?   ___ Yes   ___ No

Which communications port is involved?

___ COM1   ___ COM3
___ COM2   ___ COM4

What is the IRQ level for the port?_____
   (Refer to "Understanding COM Ports" on page 374.)

When does the problem occur?

___ In a DOS Program   ___ In an OS/2 Program
___ In a WIN-OS/2 Program   ___ While starting the system

Indicate the size in KB of each file to the left of its name.
The C indicates the drive on which OS/2 2.1 is installed.

_____KB C:\OS2\COM.SYS

_____KB C:\OS2\MDOS\VCOM.SYS

_____KB C:\OS2\MDOS\WINOS2\SYSTEM\COMM.DRV

Type MODE COMx at an OS/2 command prompt. ("x" stands for the
COM port that is involved.) Then record the information
exactly as it is displayed on the screen.

BAUD=_____   PARITY=_____

DATABITS=_____   STOPBITS=_____

TO=_____   XON=_____

IDSR=_____   ODSR=_____

OCTS=_____   DTR=_____

RTS=_____   BUFFER=_____

TRAP Messages

When the message on the screen starts with TRAP, complete the following form to record the information *exactly* as it is displayed on the screen.

```
TRAP _____     ERRCD= _____     ERACC= _____     ERLIM= _____

EAX= _____     EBX= _____       ECX= _____       EDX= _____

ESI= _____     EDI= _____       EBP= _____       FLG= _____

CS:EIP= ____ : _____     CSACC= _____     CSLIM= _____

SS:ESP= ____ : _____     SSACC= _____     SSLIM= _____

DS= ____     DSACC= _____     DSLIM= _____     CR0= _____

ES= ____     ESACC= _____     ESLIM= _____     CR2= _____

FS= ____     FSACC= _____     FSLIM= _____

GS= ____     GSACC= _____     GSLIM= _____

THE SYSTEM DETECTED AN INTERNAL PROCESSING ERROR AT

LOCATION ## ____ : _____ - ____ : _____

_____ , ___

_____

INTERNAL REVISION _ . ___     DATE: __/__/__
```

After you have recorded the information from the screen, place a check mark next to the type of session you were using when the system stopped.

___ OS/2   ___ DOS   ___ WIN-OS/2

INTERNAL PROCESSING ERROR Messages

When the screen displays INTERNAL PROCESSING ERROR at the top of a message, complete the following form to record the information *exactly* as it is displayed on the screen.

```
THE SYSTEM DETECTED AN INTERNAL PROCESSING
   ERROR AT LOCATION ##  ____ : _____ - ____ : _____
   ____ , ____
   _____

   INTERNAL REVISION  _ . ___ DATE: __ / __ / __
```

Hard Error Messages

When the error message is displayed in a box with text followed by two choices, use the following to record the information on the screen.

First, use the lines below to record the message text *exactly* as it is displayed on the screen.

_____

_____

_____

Then, select **Display register information** and use the fields below to record the information *exactly* as it is displayed on the screen.

P1= _____ P2= _____ P3= _____ P4= _____

EAX= _____ EBX= _____ ECX= _____ EDX= _____

ESI= _____ EDI= _____

DS= _____ DSACC= _____ DSLIM= _____

ES= _____ ESACC= _____ ESLIM= _____

FS= _____ FSACC= _____ FSLIM= _____

GS= _____ GSACC= _____ GSLIM= _____

CS:EIP= ____ : _____ CSACC= ____ CSLIM= _____

SS:EIP= ____ : _____ SSACC= ____ SSLIM= _____

EBP= _____ FLG= _____

Appendix H. Warranty and Service Information for Mini-Applications and Productivity Aids

This appendix contains two lists that define the warranty and service for the mini-applications and productivity aids that are provided with OS/2 2.1.

Mini-Applications and Productivity Aids That Are Serviceable and Warranted

Following is a list that identifies the mini-applications and productivity aids that are warranted for three months, and for which the IBM Technical Support Team will provide technical assistance:

- Productivity folder

    - Clipboard Viewer
    - Enhanced Editor
    - Icon Editor
    - OS/2 System Editor
    - Picture Viewer

- MMPM/2

    - Compact Disc
    - Volume Control
    - Digital Audio
    - Digital Video
    - MIDI
    - Multimedia Data Converter
    - Multimedia Setup
    - Multimedia Install
    - Sound effect files (.MID and .WAV)

Mini-Applications That Are Provided As Is

Following is a list that identifies the mini-applications that are provided **as is,** without warranty or service:

- Productivity folder

    - Activities List
    - Alarms
    - Calculator
    - Calendar

- – Daily Planner
- – Database
- – Monthly Planner
- – Notepad
- – Planner Archive
- – PM Chart
- – PM Terminal
- – Pulse
- – Seek and Scan Files
- – Spreadsheet
- – Sticky Pad
- – To-Do List
- – To-Do List Archive
- – Tune Editor

- • Games folder

  - – Cat and Mouse
  - – Jigsaw
  - – OS/2 Chess
  - – Reversi
  - – Scramble
  - – Solitaire-Klondike

- • Mahjongg

- • WIN-OS/2 Accessories folder

  - – Calculator
  - – Calendar
  - – Cardfile
  - – Character Map
  - – Clock
  - – Media Player
  - – Notepad
  - – Object Packager
  - – Paintbrush
  - – Sound Recorder
  - – Write

The multimedia and bit map files also are provided **as-is**.

Appendix I. The OS/2 2.1 Memory Dump Process

A memory dump is the process a computer system uses to record its state at the time of a failure. A memory dump is performed when a problem is difficult to reproduce, or other methods of problem determination do not identify the problem. In the OS/2 2.1 operating system, the CREATEDD utility program prepares a diskette for an OS/2 memory dump. The diskettes containing the memory dump information are sent to the IBM OS/2 Technical Support Team for analysis and problem determination.

There are two types of memory dumps:

- An automatic memory dump (used only for application programs or Ring 3 traps)
- A manual memory dump (used for hangs, and traps that cause the system to stop)

Different situations determine which type of memory dump is needed. The IBM OS/2 Technical Support Team will help you determine which process is correct for your situation.

Using TRACE in CONFIG.SYS File

Before you create the memory dump diskette, you must use the OS/2 Event Tracing Service to capture a sequence of system events. To enable system event-tracing, edit your CONFIG.SYS file as follows:

```
TRACE=ON
TRACEBUF=63
TRACE=OFF 4,24,47,50,97,98
```

The default for TRACE=ON is to trace all static system events. The TRACE=OFF statement in the CONFIG.SYS file turns off major codes 4, 24, 47, 50, 97, and 98.

Restart your system to activate trace.

Also turn on two dynamic trace points as follows:

1. Open **OS/2 System**.
2. Open **Command Prompts**.
3. Open **OS/2 Full Screen** or **OS/2 Window**.
4. Type the following at the command prompt:

```
trace on kernel (press Enter)
trace on doscall1 (press Enter)
```

Creating the Memory Dump Diskettes

To prepare for the memory dump to diskettes, create the *memory dump diskettes*. These diskettes must be created on a working machine prior to system failure. The diskettes are then saved until needed. Diskette sizes must be the same. In other words, they must all be 1.44MB 3.5-inch or 2.88MB 3.5-inch diskettes.

To create the diskettes for the memory dump procedure, do the following:

1. Open **OS/2 System**.
2. Open **Command Prompts**.
3. Open **OS/2 Full Screen** or **OS/2 Window**.
4. Type the following:

   ```
   CREATEDD A:  (press Enter)
   ```

   The following message will be displayed:

   ```
   Insert a new diskette in drive A and press Enter when you are ready.
   ```

5. Insert the diskette in Drive A and press Enter. The following message is displayed if you have a 1.44MB diskette drive:

   ```
   Are you using a 1.44 megabyte diskette in drive A: (Y/N)?
   ```

   (You will not get this message if you inserted a 2.88MB diskette.)

6. Select **Y** for yes or **N** for no (selecting No causes the diskette to be formatted as 720KB) and press Enter. CREATEDD displays the following message:

   ```
   The operating system dump diskette is being created.
   ```

7. After the command prompt reappears, use the FORMAT command to format any remaining diskettes. This number will vary with the amount of random access memory (RAM) in your system. Generally, one 1.44MB diskette is used for each 2MB of RAM. For example, if you have a 16MB system, you will probably use eight 1.44MB formatted diskettes.

8. Label the diskette that you created with the CREATEDD command as Dump Diskette 1. The diskettes that you create using the FORMAT command should be labeled as Dump Diskette 2, Dump Diskette 3, and so forth.

Running the Memory Dump

To run a memory dump:

1. Start the Memory Dump facility. This facility can be started by (a) the manual or (b) the automatic method (use this method only for ring 3 traps) as follows:

a. Press and hold down the Ctrl and Alt keys, and then press the Num Lock key twice. After a few seconds, the screen clears; then, after a minute the system beeps and the following message is displayed:

```
Insert the dump diskette created by the CREATEDD utility into drive A
and press any key to continue.
```

b. Type the following statement in your CONFIG.SYS file:

```
TRAPDUMP=ON
```

Restart your system.

TRAPDUMP will now automatically initiate a memory dump when a trap (for example, a General Protection Fault – 000D) occurs that would normally force the application program to end. When dumping is initiated, the screen clears and the following message is displayed:

```
Insert the dump diskette created by the CREATEDD utility into drive A
and press any key to continue.
```

Warning: Enabling TRAPDUMP automatically allows your system to initiate a memory dump every time an error occurs in the application code. Do not enable TRAPDUMP unless you need to troubleshoot your operating system and have been instructed to do so by your technical coordinator.

2. When prompted, insert the diskette labeled *Dump Diskette 1* and press any key to start the dump process. The following message will be displayed:

```
The memory dump is being performed...
```

3. When the memory dump has completed or the current dump diskette is full, the following messages are displayed:

```
The diskette is full.  Insert another formatted diskette in drive A.



The storage address ranges on this diskette are:

DUMPDATA.xxx            yyy - zzz

Press any key to continue.
```

where *xxx* is the dump diskette number, *yyy* is the beginning memory address, and *zzz* is the ending memory address on the disk.

Note: If you press Enter without changing the diskette, the system will prompt you once more before the dump process overwrites the contents of the current diskette in the drive.

4. Insert the next dump diskette into drive A and press any key. This action continues the dump process and displays the following message:

```
The memory dump is being performed...
```

Warning: Any data on the dump diskettes will be overwritten by the Memory Dump facility.

5. Repeat steps 3 and 4 until the dumping is completed and the following message is displayed:

```
Insert memory dump diskette number 1 to complete dump.


The storage address ranges on this diskette are:

DUMPDATA.xxx              yyy – zzz

Press any key to continue.
```

You must reinsert *Dump Diskette 1* at this point to properly terminate the dump process. The control program will write the dump summary record to *Dump Diskette 1* and end the process. After the process has ended, the following messages are displayed:

```
The memory dump has completed.  Remove the dump diskette and restart
the system.
```

Mailing the Dump Diskettes to IBM

Do not send dump diskettes unless instructed by the IBM OS/2 Technical Support Team. Diskettes must be clearly labeled with the identification number (provided by the IBM OS/2 Technical Support Team member) and your name. Also, be sure to number the diskettes.

Send the dump diskettes to:

IBM Corporation
Att: HNGTR Team (OS/2 Defect Support)
Problem Identification Number _____
Internal Zip 1024
1000 NW 51st Street
Boca Raton, FL 33431

Or, if you have IBM Network access, you can create disk images using OS2IMAGE.EXE, or another disk image utility program, and send the image files to APARCTL at BCRVMPC1. The dump formatter requires disk images (as opposed to just the contents of each diskette). Please notify the IBM OS/2 Technical Support Team member assisting you that you have forwarded the disk images.

Appendix J. Notices

References in this publication to IBM products, programs, or services do not imply that IBM intends to make these available in all countries in which IBM operates. Any reference to an IBM product, program or service is not intended to state or imply that only IBM's product, program, or service may be used. Any functionally equivalent product, program, or service that does not infringe any of IBM's intellectual property rights or other legally protectable rights may be used instead of the IBM product, program, or service. Evaluation and verification of operation in conjunction with other products, programs, or services, except those expressly designated by IBM, are the user's responsibility.

IBM may have patents or pending patent applications covering subject matter in this document. The furnishing of this document does not give you any license to these patents. You can send license inquiries, in writing, to the IBM Director of Commercial Relations, IBM Corporation, Purchase, NY 10577.

Trademarks and Service Marks

The following terms, denoted by an asterisk (*) in this publication, are trademarks or service marks of the IBM Corporation in the United States or other countries:

AT	IBM
IBMLink	Micro Channel
Operating System/2	OS/2
PC/XT	Personal System/2
Presentation Manager	Proprinter
PS/2	Screen Reader
WIN-OS/2	Workplace Shell
XGA	XT

The following terms, denoted by a double asterisk (**) in this publication, are trademarks of other companies as follows:

Trademark	Owner
Adobe	Adobe Systems Incorporated
Adobe Type Manager	Adobe Systems Incorporated
Aox	Aox Corporation
APM	Astek International
AutoCAD	AutoDesk, Inc.
Borland C++	Borland International, Inc.
Bubble-Jet	Canon, Inc.
Canon	Canon Kabushiki Kaisha

Central Point Backup	Central Point Software, Inc.
CodeView	Microsoft Corporation
Commute	Central Point Software
CompuServe	CompuServe Incorporated
Control Room	Ashton-Tate Corporation
Corel	Corel Systems Corporation
Crosstalk	Digital Communications Associates, Inc.
dBASE	Borland International
Distinct	Distinct Corporation
DynaComm	Future Soft Engineering, Inc.
Epson	Seiko Epson Kabushiki Kaisha
Everex	Everex Systems, Inc.
Excel	Microsoft Corporation

Trademark	Owner
Fastback Plus	Fifth Generation Systems, Inc.
FastLynx	Rupp Corporation
FotoMan	Logitech International
Framework III	Aston-Tate Corporation
Freelance Graphics	Lotus Development Corporation
Harvard Graphics	Software Publishing Corporation
Helvetica	LinoType Company
Hewlett-Packard	Hewlett-Packard Company
HP	Hewlett-Packard Company
Intel	Intel Corporation
Iomega	Iomega Corporation
LANtastic	Artisoft, Inc.
LapLink	Traveling Software, Inc.
LaserJet	Hewlett-Packard Company
Lexmark	Lexmark International, Inc.
Logitech	Logitech, Inc.
Lotus	Lotus Development Corporation
MAGICorp	MAGICorp Ltd.
Mathcad	MathSoft, Inc.
Micrografx	Micrografx Incorporated
Microsoft	Microsoft Corporation
Mirrors	Micrografx Incorporated
More Windows	Aristosoft, Inc.
MS	Microsoft Corporation
MS Bookshelf	Microsoft Corporation
MS Excel	Microsoft Corporation
MS Flight Simulator	Microsoft Corporation
MS Money	Microsoft Corporation
MusicPrinter Plus	Temporal Acuity Products, Inc.
National Geographic	National Geographic Society
NEC	NEC Corporation
Norton Backup	Peter Norton Computing, Inc.
Norton Utilities	Peter Norton Computing, Inc.
Omnipage Professional	Caere Corporation
Orchid	Orchid Technology Inc.

Trademark	Owner
PageMaker	Aldus Corporation
Paradox	Borland International, Inc.
Peachtree	Peachtree Software, Inc.
Peachtree Complete	Peachtree Software, Inc.
Persuasion	Aldus Corporation
PFS	Software Publishing Corporation
PFS First Choice	Software Publishing Corporation
Phar Lap	Phar Lap Software, Inc.
PostScript	Adobe Systems Incorporated
PowerGraph	STB Systems, Inc.
Prodigy	Prodigy Services Company
Publishers PowerPak	Atech Software
QMS	QMS, Inc.
Quattro Pro	Borland International, Inc.
Quicken	Intuit Company
Quicken for Windows	Intuit Company
Realizer	Within Technologies, Inc.
SideKick	Borland International, Inc.
Smartfax	American Data Technology, Inc.
Stacker	Stac Electronics
TI	Texas Instruments Incorporated
Times New Roman	Monotype Corporation, Ltd.
Tseng	Tseng Laboratories Inc.
Turbo C++	Borland International, Inc.
Turbo Pascal	Borland International, Inc.
VGAWONDER XL	ATI Technologies Inc.
Windows	Microsoft Corporation
Winfax Pro	Delrina Technology Systems, Inc.
Wing Commander	Origins Systems, Inc.
WordPerfect	WordPerfect Corporation
8514/ULTRA	ATI Technologies, Inc.

Defect Report Form

When you finish problem determination and still suspect an OS/2 2.1 defect is causing the problem, complete the form below and mail to IBM.

(   )

Name   Phone

System Unit and Model

Hardware Options Installed

Hard Disk Size   Memory Size

Problem Report

Error Code and Message

Problem Description

Did the operation work correctly before?   ____Yes ___No

If YES, what has changed? _____

How can this problem be reproduced? _____

--------------------------------Fold Here--

_____

_____

_____

IBM Corporation
Att: OS/2 Service Delivery
Internal Zip 1020
1000 NW 51st Street
Boca Raton, FL 33431

OS/2 2.1

PROOF of LICENSE

Version 2.1

IBM

Programming Family

Glossary

A

archive. (1) A flag of files and directories that OS/2 2.1 uses to determine which files are new or modified. Files with this flag are included when a backup copy is made or when all the files are restored on a hard disk. (2) A copy of one or more files or a copy of a database that is saved for future reference or for recovery purposes in case the original data is damaged or lost.

attribute. A characteristic or property of a file, directory, or object; for example, its size, last modification date, or flag. See also setting.

audio. Pertaining to the portion of recorded information that can be heard.

AUTOEXEC.BAT. A batch file whose main purpose is to process commands that set up the operating system for DOS sessions.

audio. Pertaining to the portion of recorded information that can be heard.

audio processing. In multimedia applications, manipulating digital audio; for example, by editing or creating special effects.

audio segment. A contiguous set of recorded data from an audio track. An audio segment might or might not be associated with a video segment.

audio track. (1) The audio portion of a program. (2) The physical location where the audio is placed beside the image. (A system with two audio tracks can have either stereo sound or two independent audio tracks.) (3) Synonymous with *sound track*.

AudioVisual Connection (AVC). An IBM product that enables a user to develop and deliver professional-quality audio-visual shows on a PS/2 computer.

authoring. A structured approach to combining all the media elements in an interactive production, assisted by computer software designed for this purpose.

authoring system. The software tools necessary to integrate computers and peripherals, such as *CD-ROMs* and laser videodiscs.

B

background. In multiprogramming, the conditions under which low-priority programs run when high-priority programs are not using the system resources. A background session runs one program step at a time. It does not run interactively with the user; processing continues on other sessions in the foreground.

back up. To copy information onto a diskette or hard disk for record keeping or recovery purposes.

497

batch file. A file that contains a series of commands to be processed sequentially. A batch file can have either a CMD or a BAT extension.

baud rate. A number representing the speed at which information travels over a communication line. The higher the number, the faster communication occurs.

bit map. A representation of an image by an array of bits.

bookmark. A menu choice in online books that is used to save your place in the document that you are viewing, by marking the topic that is displayed.

border. A visual indicator of a window's boundaries.

button. A mechanism on a pointing device, such as a mouse, or an area on the computer screen, used to request or initiate an action. See also maximize button, hide button, push button, radio button, and restore button.

byte. A group of eight adjacent binary digits that are treated as a unit, and that often represent a character.

C

cache. A storage buffer that contains frequently accessed instructions and data; it is used to reduce hard disk access time.

cascade. A choice in a menu that arranges the secondary windows so that each window is offset on two sides from the window it overlaps. The windows appear to be stacked, one behind the other.

cascading choice. A menu choice that has an arrow to the right of it. If this arrow is selected, a cascaded menu appears. A three-dimensional arrow indicates that a cascaded choice is preselected and is the default action when you select the main choice. A one-dimensional arrow indicates that additional choices are available; however, there is no default action. See also cascaded menu.

cascaded menu. A menu that appears when the arrow to the right of a cascading choice is selected. It contains a set of choices that are related to the cascading choice. Cascaded menus are used to reduce the length of a menu.

case-sensitive. A condition in which entries for an entry field must conform to a specific lowercase, uppercase, or mixed-case format in order to be valid.

CD-ROM. High capacity, read-only memory in the form of an optically read compact disc. See also compact disc.

character. A letter, digit, or other symbol that is used as part of the organization, control, or representation of data.

check box. A square box with associated text that represents one choice in a set of multiple choices. When you select a choice, a check mark appears in the check box to indicate that the choice is in effect. You can clear the check box by selecting the choice again. Contrast with radio button.

check mark. A symbol that shows that a choice is currently active. This symbol is used in menus and check boxes. See also checkbox.

chip set. An integrated circuit or a set of integrated circuits which provide hardware support for a related set of functions, such as generation of video.

choice. Any item that you can select. A choice can appear in a selection field, in a menu, or in text (a list of selectable choices), or it might be represented by an icon.

circular slider control. A knob-like control that performs like a control on a TV or stereo.

click. To press and release the select button on a pointing device without moving the pointer off the choice. See also double-click.

clip. A section of recorded, filmed, or videotaped material.

clipboard. An area of memory that temporarily holds data being passed from one program to another. Data is placed on the clipboard by selecting from a menu.

close. A choice in Window List and in those programs that have a system menu. This is also a cascading choice from the Windows choice on a pop-up menu. This

choice ends highlighted programs and objects and their associated windows.

command prompt. A displayed symbol that indicates where you enter commands.

compact disc. A disc, usually 4.75 inches in diameter, from which data is read optically by means of a laser.

CONFIG.SYS. A file that the operating system adds to the root directory during installation. This file contains statements that set up the system configuration each time you restart the operating system.

configuration. (1) The manner in which hardware and software of an information processing system are organized and interconnected. (2) The arrangement and relationship of the components in a system or network.

configure. To describe to a system the devices, optional features, and programs installed on the system.

container. An object that holds other objects. A folder is an example of a container object.

copy. (1) A reproduction of an original. (2) To make a reproduction of an object in a new location. After the copy action, the original object remains in the original location and a duplicate exists in the new location. A menu choice that places onto the clipboard a copy of what you have selected. This choice is also used to make copies of objects from a pop-up menu.

cut. A choice in a menu of a program that removes a selected object, or a part of an object, to the clipboard, usually compressing the space it occupied in a window. Removes a selected object or a part of an object to the clipboard, usually compressing the space it occupied in a window.

D

data. The coded representation of information for use in a computer. Data has certain attributes such as type and length.

database. A collection of data with a given structure for accepting, storing, and providing, on demand, data for multiple users.

data-file object. An object that represents a file in the file system. The primary purpose is to convey information, such as text, graphics, audio, or video. A letter or spreadsheet is an example of data-file objects.

default. A value, attribute, or option that is assumed when another is not explicitly specified.

default action. An action that is performed when you press Enter while pointing at an object, double-click the selection button on an object, or perform a direct-manipulation operation. The default action is intended to be the action that you would most likely want in the given situation.

default choice. A selected choice that a program provides for the initial appearance of a group of selection choices.

deselect. The process of removing selection highlighting from one or more choices. Contrast with select.

desktop. A folder that fills the entire screen and holds all of the objects that enable you to interact with and perform operations on the system.

device driver. A program that contains the code needed to attach and use a device, such as a display, plotter, printer, or mouse. The driver might also include data such as help information.

device font. A font particular to, and loaded in the memory of a device such as a video display or printer. Some device fonts have size and language-support restrictions.

device object. An object that provides a means of communication between a computer and another piece of equipment, such as a printer or disk drive. See also printer object.

digital. Pertaining to data in the form of numeric characters.

digital audio. Audible information that has been converted to and stored in digital form.

digital video. Visual material that has been converted to digital form.

direct manipulation. The action of using a mouse or another pointing device to work with objects, rather than through menus. For example, changing the size of a window by dragging one of its edges is direct manipulation. Moving or printing an object by dragging it to the printer is another example. See also drag.

directory. (1) A list of the files that are stored on a disk or diskette. A directory also contains information about the file such as size and date of last change. (2) A named grouping of files in a file system. See also folder.

directory tree. An outline of all the directories and subdirectories on the current drive.

disk. A round, flat, data medium that is rotated in order to read or write data. See also compact disc, hard disk, and diskette.

diskette. A removable magnetic disk enclosed in a protective cover used to store information. See also diskette drive.

diskette drive. A mechanism used to seek, read, and write data on diskettes.

DOS command prompt. A displayed symbol that indicates where you enter commands. The DOS command prompt is displayed in a DOS window or DOS full screen. Contrast with OS/2 command prompt.

DOS session. A session created by the OS/2 operating system that supports the independent execution of a DOS program. The DOS program appears to run independent of any other programs in the system.

double-click. To press and release the select button on a pointing device twice in rapid succession while the pointer is over the intended target of the operation. See also click.

downloaded font. A soft font copied (downloaded) to the memory of a printer.

drag. To use a mouse or another pointing device to move an object. The following are examples: (1) pointing to an object; then pressing and holding mouse button 2 while moving to a new location, or (2) pointing to a window border; then holding down mouse button 1 or 2 while moving the border to change the size of the window. Dragging ends when the mouse button is released.

dynamic data exchange. The exchange of data between programs or between a program and a data-file object. Any change you make to information in one program or session is applied to the identical data created by the other program. For example, with the dynamic data exchange (DDE) feature enabled, you can select the duplicate of a spreadsheet that is embedded in a report. Then, if you make changes to the spreadsheet copy in the report, the same changes are made to the original spreadsheet file.

E

enable. (1) To make functional. (2) The state of a processing unit that allows the occurrence of certain types of interruptions. (3) To initiate the operation of a circuit or device.

environment variables. A series of commands placed in the AUTOEXEC.BAT and CONFIG.SYS files that dictate the way the operating system is going to run and what external devices it is going to recognize. These commands also can be specified as settings of DOS programs.

extended attributes. Additional information that the system or a program associates with a file. An extended attribute can be any format, for example text, a bit map, or binary data.

F

field. An identifiable area in a window used to contain data. Examples of fields are: an entry field, into which you can type text; and a field of radio buttons, from which you can select one choice.

file. A collection of related data that is stored and retrieved by an assigned name. For example, a file can include information that starts a program, program-file object, can contain text or graphics data-file object, or can process a series of commands such as a batch file.

file allocation table (FAT). A table used by DOS to allocate disk space for a file. It also locates and chains together parts of the file that may be scattered on different sectors so that the file can be used in a random or sequential manner. Contrast with High Performance File System (HPFS).

file name. (1) The name used by a program to identify a file. (2) When referring to the file allocation table (FAT) file system, the file name is the portion of the identifying name that precedes the extension. When referring to the high performance file system (HPFS), the file name includes an extension (if there is one).

If you are using the HPFS, the file name can be up to 254 characters and can include any number of periods. The following is an example of a path and file name in the HPFS file system where C: is the drive, the first \ is the root, INCOME is the directory, and SALES.FIGURES.SEPTEMBER is the file name:

C:\INCOME\SALES.FIGURES.SEPTEMBER

If you are using the FAT file system, the file name can be up to eight characters and can be followed by an optional three-character extension. The following is an example of a path and file name in the FAT file system where C: is the drive, the first \ is the root, INCOME is the directory, TAX is a subdirectory, and SALES.TXT is the file name and extension:

C:\INCOME\TAX\SALES.TXT

flag. A characteristic of a file or directory that enables it to be used in certain ways. See also archive, hidden, read-only, and system.

folder. A container used to organize objects, programs, documents, other folders, or any combination of these. The folders on the desktop represent the directories in the file system. For example, a folder can have other folders within it. This is similar to a subdirectory within a directory.

font. A particular style (shape), size, slant, and weight, defined for an entire character set; for example, 9-point Helvetica italic bold. When applied to outline or scalable character sets, which can be scaled to any size, font refers to style, slant, and weight, but not to size.

foreground. In multiprogramming, the environment in which interactive high-priority programs run. These programs run interactively with the user.

format. To check a hard disk or diskette for defects and prepare it to hold information.

Format 0 MIDI file. All MIDI data is stored on a single track.

Format 1 MIDI file. All MIDI data is stored on multiple tracks.

H

hard disk. A rigid disk in a hard disk drive that you cannot remove. The hard disk can be partitioned into storage areas of variable sizes that are subdivided into directories and subdirectories. See also partition.

Help. A choice on a pop-up menu that gives you assistance and information; for example, general help about the purpose of the object. (This information is the same as highlighting the choice and pressing F1.) If you select the arrow to the right of **Help**, a cascaded menu appears from which you can request further help.

The **Help** choice also can appear in those programs that have a menu bar.

Help Index. A choice in the **Help** cascaded menu that presents an alphabetic listing of help topics for an object.

The **Help index** choice also can appear in those programs that have **Help** on a menu bar.

Help push button. A push button that, when selected, provides information about the item the cursor is on or about the entire window.

hidden. A flag that indicates that a file or directory should not be displayed in the directory tree or the directory window.

hide. To remove a window from the desktop. Hidden windows are displayed in the Window List.

hide button. A small button located in the right-hand corner of the title bar of a window that, when selected, removes all of the windows associated with that window from the screen and are displayed in the Window List.

highlighting. Emphasizing a display element or segment by modifying its visual attributes. For more information about highlighting, refer to the *OS/2 Tutorial*.

high performance file system (HPFS). An installable file system that uses high-speed buffer storage, known as a cache, to provide fast access to large disk volumes. The file system also supports the coexistence of multiple, active file systems on a single personal computer, with the capability of multiple and different storage devices.

File names used with HPFS can have as many as 254 characters.

I

icon. A graphical representation of an object, consisting of an image, image background, and a label.

image file. A file that is created from a DOS startup diskette. The image file is a copy of the information on the startup diskette. Just as a DOS session can be started from a DOS startup diskette, a DOS session can be started from an image file of that same diskette.

inactive window. A window you are not currently interacting with. This window cannot receive input from the mouse or keyboard. Contrast with active window.

install. (1) To physically copy the files from the shipped diskettes of an operating system or program to specified areas (directories) of a hard disk. (2) Installing a printer driver, queue driver, or port means adding the driver to the INI file (and copying to the hard disk only if required). Deleting a printer driver, queue driver, or port removes the entry from the INI file, but leaves the program file on your hard disk.

J

job. A data file sent to a printer to be printed.

K

kernel. (1) The part of an operating system that performs basic functions such as allocating hardware resources. (2) A part of a program that must be in main storage in order to load other parts of the program.

keys help. A choice in the **Help** cascaded menu that presents a listing of all the key assignments for an object or a product. This choice also can appear in those programs that have **Help** on a menu bar.

kilobyte (KB). A term meaning 1024 bytes.

L

LAN. Local Area Network. (1) Two or more computing units connected for local resource sharing. (2) A network in which communications are limited to a moderate-sized geographic area, such as a single office building, warehouse, or campus, and that do not extend across public rights-of-way.

list box. A vertical, scrollable list of objects or settings choices that you can select.

log in. (1) To begin a session with a remote resource (2) The act of identifying yourself as authorized to use the resource. Often, the system requires a user ID and password to check your authorization to use the resource.

log out. (1) To end a session or request that a session be ended. (2) The act of removing access to a remote resource from a workstation. Contrast with log in.

M

M-Audio Capture and Playback Adapter (M-ACPA). An adapter card (for use with the IBM PS/2 product line) that provides the ability to record and play back high quality sound. The adapter converts the audio input (analog) signals to a digital format that is compressed and stored for later use.

mark. A menu choice of a program that you select to highlight text or graphics that you want to perform clipboard operations on. The clipboard operations are cut, copy, paste, clear, and delete.

Master Help Index. An object on the desktop that, when selected, presents an alphabetic listing of operating system tasks and topics.

maximize. A menu choice available from the Windows choice on a pop-up menu. Select this choice to enlarge the window to its largest possible size.

maximize button. A large, square button located in the rightmost corner of the title bar of a window that, when selected, enlarges the window to its largest possible size. Contrast with hide button. See also restore button.

megabyte (MB). A term meaning approximately 1 000 000 bytes.

memory. (1) The storage on electronic chips; for example, random access memory, where your programs and data are held while you use them, or read-only memory where information is stored that your system can refer to but not change. (2) Program-addressable storage; the locations by which the operating system and your programs can locate information that is temporarily held in memory. With the OS/2 operating system, program-addressable memory might be larger than the electronic chip memory in your computer.

menu. A displayed list of available items from which you can make a selection. See also popup menu.

menu bar. The area near the top of the window, below the title bar and above the rest of the window, that contains choices that provide access to other menus.

MIDI. Musical Instrument Digital Interface.

MIDI Mapper. Provides the ability to translate and redirect MIDI messages to achieve device-independent playback of MIDI sequences.

migrate. (1) To move to a changed operating environment, usually to a new release or version of a system. (2) To move data from one hierarchy of storage to another.

minimize. To remove a window (using the minimize button) to one of the following:

- Minimized Window Viewer
- Window List
- Desktop Folder.

See also hide.

minimize button. A button, located next to the rightmost button in a title bar, that when selected, reduces the window to its smallest possible size and removes all of the windows associated with that window from the screen. Contrast with maximize button and hide button.

Minimized Window Viewer. A folder that contains icons of minimized windows. See also minimize button and minimize.

mix. The combining of audio or video sources during postproduction.

mixer. A device used to simultaneously combine and blend several inputs into one or two outputs.

modem. A device that converts digital data from a computer to an analog signal that can be transmitted on a telecommunications line and that converts the received signal to data for the computer.

mouse. A pointing device that you move on a flat surface to position a pointer on the screen. It allows you to select a choice or function to be performed or to perform operations on the screen, such as dragging or drawing lines from one position to another.

mouse button. A mechanism on a mouse that you press to select choices or initiate actions.

move. To change the location of an object. After the move action, the original exists in its new location and no longer exists in its original location. Contrast with copy.

Move. A choice on the pop-up menu of objects that you select to move the objects to other containers. Select to position a window on the screen.

multimedia. (1) The combination of different elements of media (for example, text, graphics, audio, and still images) for display and control from a personal computer. (2) Material presented in a combination of text, graphics, video, image, animation, and sound.

multimedia system. A system capable of presenting multiple types and formats of material in their entirety.

multiple DOS sessions. A system service that coordinates the concurrent operation of separate DOS sessions.

multiple virtual DOS machines. See multiple DOS sessions.

multitasking. A mode of operation that provides for concurrent performance, or interleaved execution of two or more tasks

Musical Instrument Digital Interface (MIDI). A protocol that enables a synthesizer to send signals to another synthesizer or to a computer, or enables a computer to send signals to a musical instrument or to another computer.

N

network. A configuration of data-processing devices and software connected for the purpose of sharing resources and for information interchange. See also LAN.

network administrator. The person responsible for the installation, management, and control of a network. The network administrator gives authorization to you for accessing shared resources and determines the type of access those users can have.

network group. A folder representing a Local Area Network or a group of objects that you have permission to access.

notebook. A graphical representation that resembles a bound notebook that contains pages separated into sections by tabbed divider-pages. It contains a mechanism that you can use to turn the pages. For example, you can select a tab to turn the page to the section identified by the tab label.

O

object. Something that you work with to perform a task. Text and graphics are examples of objects. See also data-file object, folder, program object and device object.

open. To create a file or make an existing file available for processing or use.

operating system. Software that controls the processing of programs and that may provide services such as resource allocation, scheduling, input/output control, and data management. Although operating systems are predominantly software, partial hardware implementations are possible.

OS/2 command prompt. A displayed symbol that indicates where you enter commands. The OS/2 command prompt is displayed in an OS/2 window or OS/2 full screen. Contrast with DOS command prompt.

P

parallel. Pertaining to the simultaneous transmission of individual parts of a whole. When a printer is connected to a parallel port, it receives an entire byte (character) at a time. See also serial.

parameter. A variable used in conjunction with a command to affect its result.

parity check. A mathematical operation on the numerical representation of the information communicated between two pieces. For example, if parity is odd, any character represented by an even number has a bit added to it, making it odd, and an information receiver checks that each unit of information has an odd value.

PARSEDB.   A utility program that creates a similar database to the Migrate Applications default database (DATABASE.DAT). The Migrate Applications program uses information in this database when migrating programs. The database you create with PARSEDB contains similar information to the default database, but for different programs.

partition.   A fixed-size division of storage. On a personal computer hard disk, one of four possible storage areas of variable size; one might be accessed by DOS, and each of the others might be assigned to another operating system.

password.   A string of characters that you, a program, or a computer operator must specify to meet security requirements before gaining access to a system and to the information stored within it.

paste.   (1) A choice in the menu of a program that, when selected, moves the contents of the clipboard into a preselected location that you can select in a window. (2)Move the contents of the clipboard into a preselected location that you can select in a window.

path.   A statement that indicates where a file is stored on a particular drive. The path consists of all the directories that must be opened to get to a particular file. The directory names are separated by the

backslash (\). The first backslash represents the root directory. For example, a file named *things* that is located in the EDIT directory of drive C has a path of:

        c:\edit\things

A path is sometimes followed by a file name and a file name extension (if there is one). It is sometimes preceded by a drive letter and a colon (:).

path and file name.   The path and file name make up a statement that indicates where a file is stored in a particular drive. It consists of all the directories that must be opened to get to a particular file. The backslash (\) separates directory names and the file name; the first \ indicates the root.

File names in the HPFS file system can be up to 254 characters and can include any number of periods. The following is an example:

\INCOME\SALES.FIGURES.FOR.SEPTEMBER

File names in the FAT file system can be up to eight characters and can be followed by an optional three-character extension. The following is an example:

\INCOME\TAX\SALES.TXT

plotter.   An output device that uses multiple pens to draw on paper or transparencies.

pointer.   The symbol displayed on the screen that you move with a pointing device, such as a mouse.

pop-up menu.   A menu that, when requested, is displayed next to the object it is associated with. It contains choices appropriate for a given object or set of objects in their current context. The menu is displayed by clicking mouse button 2 on an object or on the desktop.

pop-up window. A movable window, fixed in size, in which you provide information required by an application so that the application can continue to process your request.

port. A connector on a computer to which cables for devices, such as display stations and printers, or communications lines are attached. Ports can be parallel or serial.

port designation. A 4-character identifier (such as LPT1 or COM1) assigned to a printer, plotter, or communications device so that the system has a unique way to refer to the resource.

printer driver. A file that describes the physical characteristics of a printer, plotter, or other peripheral device, and is used to convert graphics into device-specific data at the time of printing or plotting. A Presentation Manager printer driver allows you to print or plot from an application program that creates printer-independent files.

printer-independent file. A file in a format that is independent of a particular printer type. For example, with a Presentation Manager spooler, a file in the metafile format is printer-independent. See also printer-specific file.

printer object. An object representing a physical printer or plotter, its printer driver, queue, and other settings. See also device object.

printer-specific file. A file that can be printed on only one type of printer. See also printer-independent file.

private. When the **WIN_CLIPBOARD** setting is set to **Off**, this disables (makes private) the sharing of clipboard information among DOS, OS/2 and Windows programs.

When the **WIN_DDE** (dynamic data exchange) setting is set to **Off**, this disables (makes private) the sharing of data among OS/2 and Windows programs.

program. A sequence of instructions that a computer can interpret and process.

program-file object. An object that starts a program. Program files commonly have extensions of .EXE, .COM, .CMD, or .BAT. Contrast with data-file object.

program object. An object representing the file that starts a program. You can change the settings for this object to specify how you want the program to start or where the files related to the program are stored. For example, you can specify that an editor always starts with the NOTABS option.

See also program-file object.

program title. A name that you type for a selected program. It is displayed with the icon. It can be any name you want to use to refer to the program. For example, My Favorite Editor could be used as the program title for an editor whose actual title is ABC.

program type. See session.

property. (1) Synonym for setting. (2) Like a setting, but used by the OS/2 operating system to refer to printer, plotter, or print job set up.

public. When the **WIN_CLIPBOARD** setting is set to **On**, this enables (makes public) the sharing of clipboard information among DOS, OS/2, and Windows programs.

When the **WIN_DDE** (dynamic data exchange) setting set to **On**, this enables (makes public) the sharing of data among OS/2 and Windows programs.

push button. A rounded-corner rectangular control containing text or graphics, or both. Push buttons are used in windows for actions that occur immediately when the push button is selected.

Q

queue. A line or list formed by items waiting to be processed; for example, a list of print jobs waiting to be printed. See also spooling and spooler.

queue driver. A software processor that takes a print job from a queue, and sends it to the appropriate printer driver to prepare it for printing.

R

radio button. A round button on the screen with text beside it. Radio buttons are combined to show you a fixed set of choices from which only one can be selected. The circle is partially filled when

a choice is selected. Contrast with check box.

read-only. A flag that prevents a file from being modified. The file with this flag set can be viewed, copied, or printed.

refresh. An action that updates changed information to its current status.

remote. Pertaining to a system, program, or device that is accessed through a telecommunication line.

resolution. (1) Density or sharpness of an image. For bit-map material, resolution is expressed in dots-per-inch, with higher quality output having more dots-per-inch. Resolution can be adjusted for some printers. Low-resolution images are printed faster, but appear coarser than high-resolution images. A printer's memory size can limit the resolution you can choose. (2) The number of lines in an image that an imaging system (for example, a telescope, the human eye, or a camera) can resolve. Higher resolution makes text and graphics appear clearer.

resource. Any facility of a computing system or operating system needed to perform required operations; includes disk storage, input devices, output devices (such as printers), a processing unit, data files, and programs.

restore button. A button that appears in the rightmost corner of the title bar after a window has been maximized. When the restore button is selected, the window returns to the size it was before it was maximized. See also maximize button and hide button.

root directory. The first directory on a drive in which all other files and subdirectories exist, such as C:\.

S

scroll. To move a display image vertically or horizontally to view data that is not otherwise visible in a display screen or window.

scroll bar. A part of a window, associated with a scrollable area, that you interact with to see information that is not currently visible. Scroll bars can be displayed vertically and horizontally. The scroll bar can be selected only with a mouse.

select. To use the selection button to highlight or choose an item such as an object or a menu choice. When you make a selection, there is a subsequent action that will apply. Contrast with deselect.

serial. Pertaining to the sequential transmission of one element at a time. Serial ports pass one bit at a time. If a port has word length 7, it must pass seven separate elements before the receiver can assemble those elements into a single recognizable whole unit (character). See also parallel.

server. (1) On a local area network (LAN), a workstation that provides facilities to other workstations. (2) A computer that shares its resources with other computers on a network. An example of a server is a file server, a print server, or a mail server.

session. (1) A logical connection between two machines on a network. (2) One instance of a started program or command prompt. Each session is separate from all other sessions that might be running on the computer. The operating system is responsible for coordinating the resources that each session uses, such as computer memory, allocation of processor time, and windows on the screen. The session types are OS/2 window, OS/2 full screen, DOS window, DOS full screen, WIN-OS/2 full screen, WIN-OS/2 window, and WIN-OS/2 window separate session.

setting. A unique characteristic of an object that can be changed or modified. The setting of an object describes the object. The name of the object is an example of a setting.

Settings. A choice that defines characteristics of objects or displays identifying characteristics of objects.

shadow. A link between duplicate objects. The objects can be located in different folders. If you make a change in either the duplicate or the original, the change takes effect in the other as well. Or, suppose you have a program on a drive other than drive C and want to use it from the desktop. You can make a shadow of the program for the desktop. The program is not physically moved or copied, which means you save space on your hard disk, but you can use it from the desktop.

shutdown. The process of selecting the **Shut down** choice before the computer is powered off so that data and configuration information is not lost.

slider. A control that represents a quantity and its relationship to the range of possible values for that quantity. In some cases, you can change the value of the quantity.

soft font. Optional fonts shipped as files. Soft fonts must be installed onto the hard disk before they can be selected from programs. See also downloaded font.

source diskette. In a diskette-copying procedure, the diskette from which information is read. Contrast with target diskette.

source drive. The drive from which information is read. Contrast with target drive.

specific DOS. An actual DOS program product that is purchased independently of the OS/2 operating system. Examples include IBM DOS Version 3.x, Microsoft DOS Version 3.x, Digital Research** Version 5.0. Some programs are dependent on the internals of a specific DOS version. You can run these programs with the OS/2 operating system by starting a DOS session with a specific DOS version. Contrast with DOS session.

spooler. A program that intercepts data going to a device driver and writes it to disk. The data is later printed or plotted when the required device is available. A spooler prevents output from different sources from being intermixed.

spooling. The process of temporarily storing print jobs while waiting for an available printer or port. Spooling jobs frees system resources from waiting for a

relatively slow device to provide output, and keeps the contents of each print job separated from the contents of every other print job.

sticky keys. An input method that enables you to press and release a series of keys sequentially (for example, Ctrl+Alt+Del), yet have the keys behave as if they were pressed and released at the same time. This method can be used for those who require special-needs settings to make the keyboard easier to use.

system. A flag that indicates that a file or directory is part of the operating system.

system font. One of the fonts available for screen display and printing. You can specify any size for this font, and it supports any language. Contrast with device font.

T

tab. (1) An action, achieved by pressing the Tab key that moves the cursor to the next field. (2) A graphical representation of a book-like tab on a notebook that, when selected, turns the notebook page.

target diskette. In a diskette or storage copying procedure, the diskette onto which information is written. Contrast with source diskette.

target drive. The drive to which information is written. Contrast with source drive.

template. An object that you can use as a model to create additional objects. When you drag a template you create another of the original object, as though you were peeling one of the objects off a stack.

tile. A choice in a menu that modifies the size of each window and arranges them so that they appear side-by-side and top-to-bottom.

title bar. The area at the top of each window that can contain the window title and a title-bar icon. When appropriate, it also contains the hide, maximize, and restore buttons.

title-bar icon. The mini-icon in the upper-left corner of the title bar that represents the object that is open in the window. You can use the object to display the pop-up menu or close a window.

U

user interface. The hardware, software, or both that allows you to interact with and perform operations on a computer.

Using Help. A cascaded choice on the Help menu that gives you information about how the help function works. This choice is also available on those programs that have **Help** as a choice on a menu bar.

V

value. A quantity assigned to a constant, a variable, or a parameter.

videodisc. A disc on which programs are recorded for playback on a computer (or a television set); a recording on a videodisc.

view. The appearance of the contents of an open object (for example, a folder can be displayed in icon view, tree view, settings view or details view.

virtual device driver. A type of device driver used by DOS programs running in a DOS virtual machine, in order to access devices such as the screen or mouse which must be shared with other processes in the system. The virtual device driver maps DOS device commands to the normal (physical) device driver under OS/2 Version 2.1.

virtual DOS machine. See DOS session.

W

waveform. (1) A graphic representation of the shape of a wave that indicates the wave's characteristics, such as frequency and amplitude. (2) A digital method of storing and manipulating audio data within a computer. (3) A series of digital samples of the audio input stream taken at regular intervals over the duration of the audio event.

wildcard character. Either a question mark (?) or an asterisk (*) used as a variable in a file name or file name extension when referring to a particular file or group of files.

WIN-OS/2*. WIN-OS/2 is a feature of OS/2 2.1 that enables OS/2 2.1 to run supported Windows programs. See supported Windows programs.

WIN-OS/2 session. A WIN-OS/2 session created by the OS/2 2.1 operating system that supports the independent processing of a Windows program. The Windows program can run in a WIN-OS/2 full-screen, WIN-OS/2 window, or WIN-OS/2 window separate session.

window. An area of the screen with visible boundaries within which information is displayed. A window can be smaller than or the same size as the screen. Windows can appear to overlap on the screen.

Window List. A menu choice that displays a list of all of the open windows in a product. Use the **Window List** choice to switch to an active program, to tile or cascade open program windows, to surface hidden windows, or to close a program.

Windows program. A program written for the Microsoft Windows application programming interface.

workarea. A folder setting that enables you to organize your desktop by grouping together objects for a specific task. For example, you could group a plotter object with data-file objects that contain charts and documents.

working directory. A specified directory that becomes the current directory when a program is started. The current directory is the first directory in which the operating system looks for programs and files and stores temporary files and output. Some programs require a working directory.

Workplace shell. A graphical user interface that makes working with your computer easier. The Workplace shell lets you manage your work without having to learn the complexities of the operating system.

Index

Numerics